HARBINGER
WARS

JOSHUA DYSART | DUANE SWIERCZYNSKI | CLAYTON HENRY | PERE PÉREZ

CONTENTS

Harbinger Wars 1
7.15 18

Collection Cover Art: Clayton Crain

9 781939 346094

VALIANT

Peter Cuneo
Chairman

Dinesh Shamdasani
CEO and Chief Creative Officer

Gavin Cuneo
CFO and Head of Strategic Development

Fred Pierce
Publisher

Warren Simons
VP Executive Editor

Walter Black
VP Operations

Hunter Gorinson
Director of Marketing, Communications and Digital Media

Atom! Freeman
Sales Manager

Travis Escarfullery
Production and Design Manager

Alejandro Arbona
Associate Editor

Josh Johns
Assistant Editor

Peter Stern
Operations Coordinator

Ivan Cohen
Collection Editor

Steve Blackwell
Collection Designer

Rian Hughes/Device
Trade Dress and Book Design

Russell Brown
President, Consumer Products, Promotions and Ad Sales

Jason Kothari
Vice Chairman

Harbinger Wars®: Harbinger Wars.
Published by Valiant Entertainment, LLC. Office of Publication: 424 West 33rd Street, New York, NY 10001. Printed in the U.S.A. First Printing.
ISBN: 9781939346094.

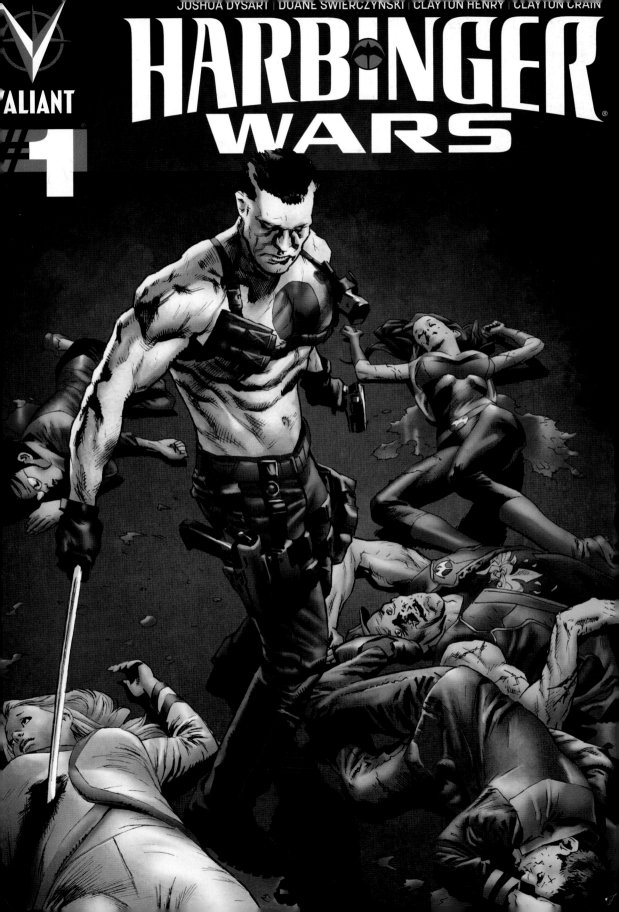

JOSHUA DYSART | DUANE SWIERCZYNSKI | CLAYTON HENRY | CLAYTON CRAIN

HARBINGER WARS

VALIANT

#1

HARBINGER WARS

PSIOT CHILDREN

During a violent confrontation with Project Rising Spirit, Bloodshot freed a group of super-powered adolescents from a maximum-security research facility where they were experimented on and used as weapons of war. Now they are out in the open and are being hunted by the most powerful forces in the Valiant Universe, including Toyo Harada and Peter Stanchek and his Renegades.

PETER STANCHEK and the RENEGADES

Peter Stanchek was once Toyo Harada's prize pupil before he abandoned his would-be mentor and formed his own team of psiot Renegades. Together they have set out on their own, looking for others like themselves to oppose Harada and his Eggbreakers. Peter and the Renegades will do everything in their power to prevent the P.R.S. psiot children from winding up in the hands of Toyo Harada.

On the run from the authorities for most of his life, Peter has used his abilities recklessly and often self-medicated to drown out the voices in his head

Possesses immense telepathic and telekinetic abilities

PETER'S TEAM:
- **Torque**, a.k.a. John Torkelson – *Incredible strength and durability*
- **Flamingo**, a.k.a. Charlene Dupre – *Pyrotelekinetic ability to create and direct fire*
- **Kris Hathaway** – *A non-psiot, brilliant and resourceful*
- **Zephyr**, a.k.a. Faith Herbert – *Flight*

TOYO HARADA

A survivor of the bombing of Hiroshima, Toyo Harada has used his extraordinary telepathic abilities to build the incredibly powerful Harada Global Conglomerates. With HGC as a front, Harada has created the Harbinger Foundation, where he can train and build his own private army of psiots that will help him carry out his vision for a better world. However, Harada will stop at nothing to see his dream come to pass. Harada wants the escaped P.R.S. psiot children to join his ranks.

Possesses immense telepathic and telekinetic abilities

Perhaps the most powerful man on the planet

THE HARBINGER FOUNDATION
- The elite of these psiots form Harada's personal guard and are known as "Eggbreakers"
- One in four latent psiots are killed in the surgical attempt to activate them

Project: BLOODSHOT is a super-weapon created by Project Rising Spirit programmed to undertake incredibly dangerous missions, including capturing psiot children. Once Bloodshot freed himself from his programming, he went rogue and liberated the children from the facility. Bloodshot feels he must protect the children from forces that would control them since he is largely, if indirectly, responsible for capturing them in the first place.

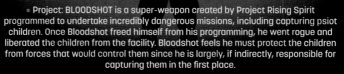

BLOODSHOT

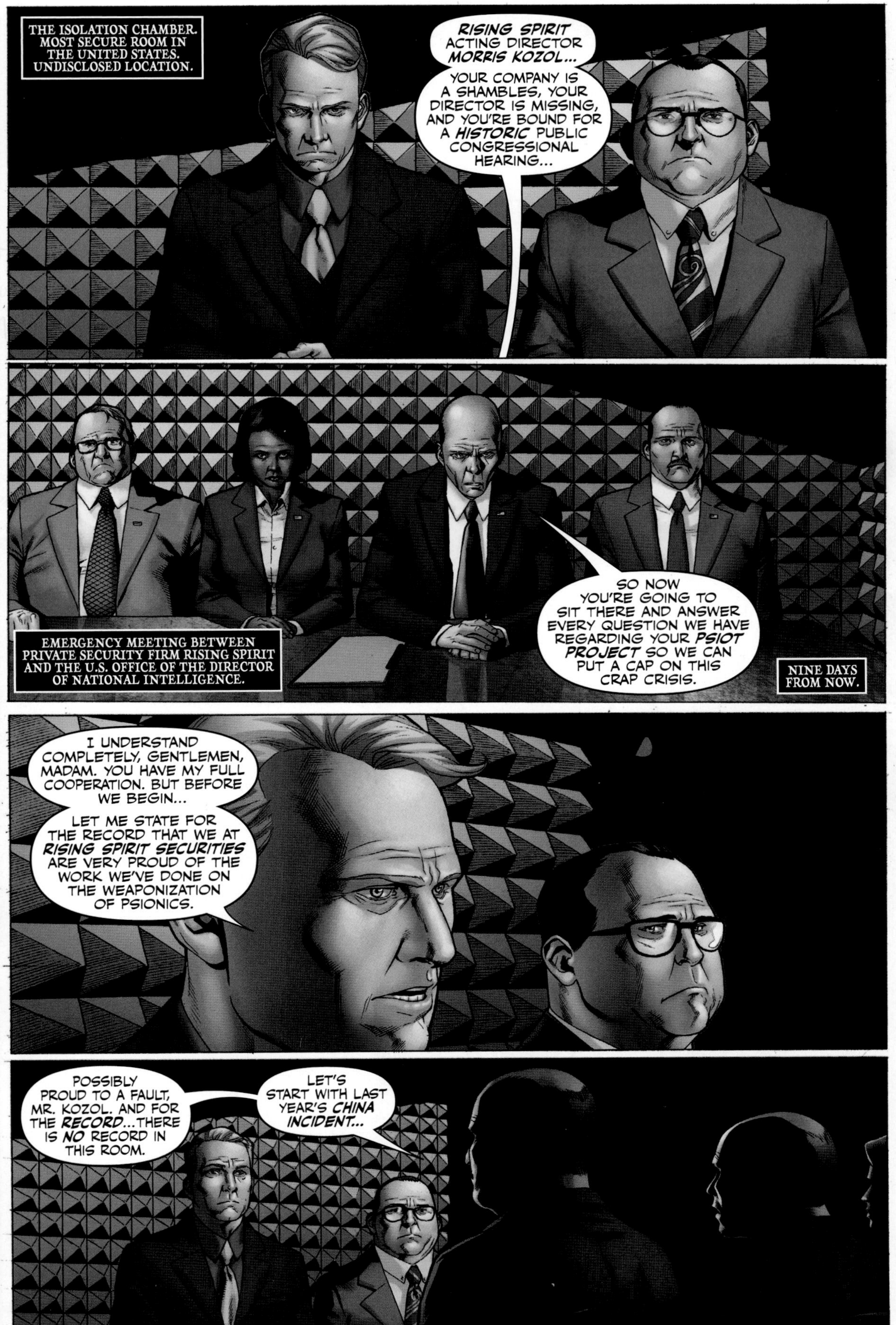
THE ISOLATION CHAMBER. MOST SECURE ROOM IN THE UNITED STATES. UNDISCLOSED LOCATION.
RISING SPIRIT ACTING DIRECTOR MORRIS KOZOL...
YOUR COMPANY IS A SHAMBLES, YOUR DIRECTOR IS MISSING, AND YOU'RE BOUND FOR A HISTORIC PUBLIC CONGRESSIONAL HEARING...
EMERGENCY MEETING BETWEEN PRIVATE SECURITY FIRM RISING SPIRIT AND THE U.S. OFFICE OF THE DIRECTOR OF NATIONAL INTELLIGENCE.
SO NOW YOU'RE GOING TO SIT THERE AND ANSWER EVERY QUESTION WE HAVE REGARDING YOUR PSIOT PROJECT SO WE CAN PUT A CAP ON THIS CRAP CRISIS.
NINE DAYS FROM NOW.
I UNDERSTAND COMPLETELY, GENTLEMEN, MADAM. YOU HAVE MY FULL COOPERATION. BUT BEFORE WE BEGIN...
LET ME STATE FOR THE RECORD THAT WE AT RISING SPIRIT SECURITIES ARE VERY PROUD OF THE WORK WE'VE DONE ON THE WEAPONIZATION OF PSIONICS.
POSSIBLY PROUD TO A FAULT, MR. KOZOL. AND FOR THE RECORD...THERE IS NO RECORD IN THIS ROOM.
LET'S START WITH LAST YEAR'S CHINA INCIDENT...

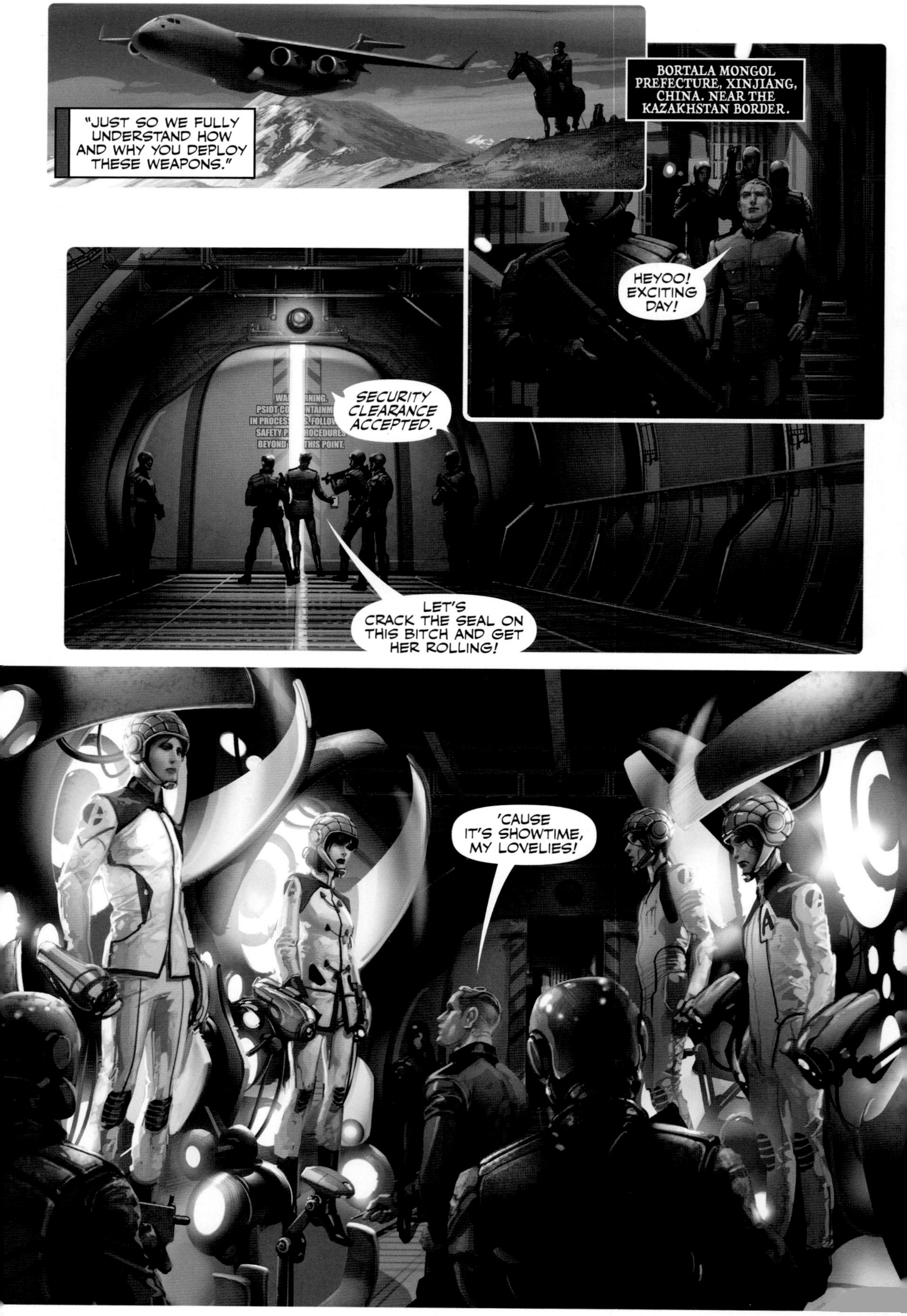
"JUST SO WE FULLY UNDERSTAND HOW AND WHY YOU DEPLOY THESE WEAPONS."
BORTALA MONGOL PREFECTURE, XINJIANG, CHINA. NEAR THE KAZAKHSTAN BORDER.
HEYOO! EXCITING DAY!
SECURITY CLEARANCE ACCEPTED.
LET'S CRACK THE SEAL ON THIS BITCH AND GET HER ROLLING!
'CAUSE IT'S SHOWTIME, MY LOVELIES!

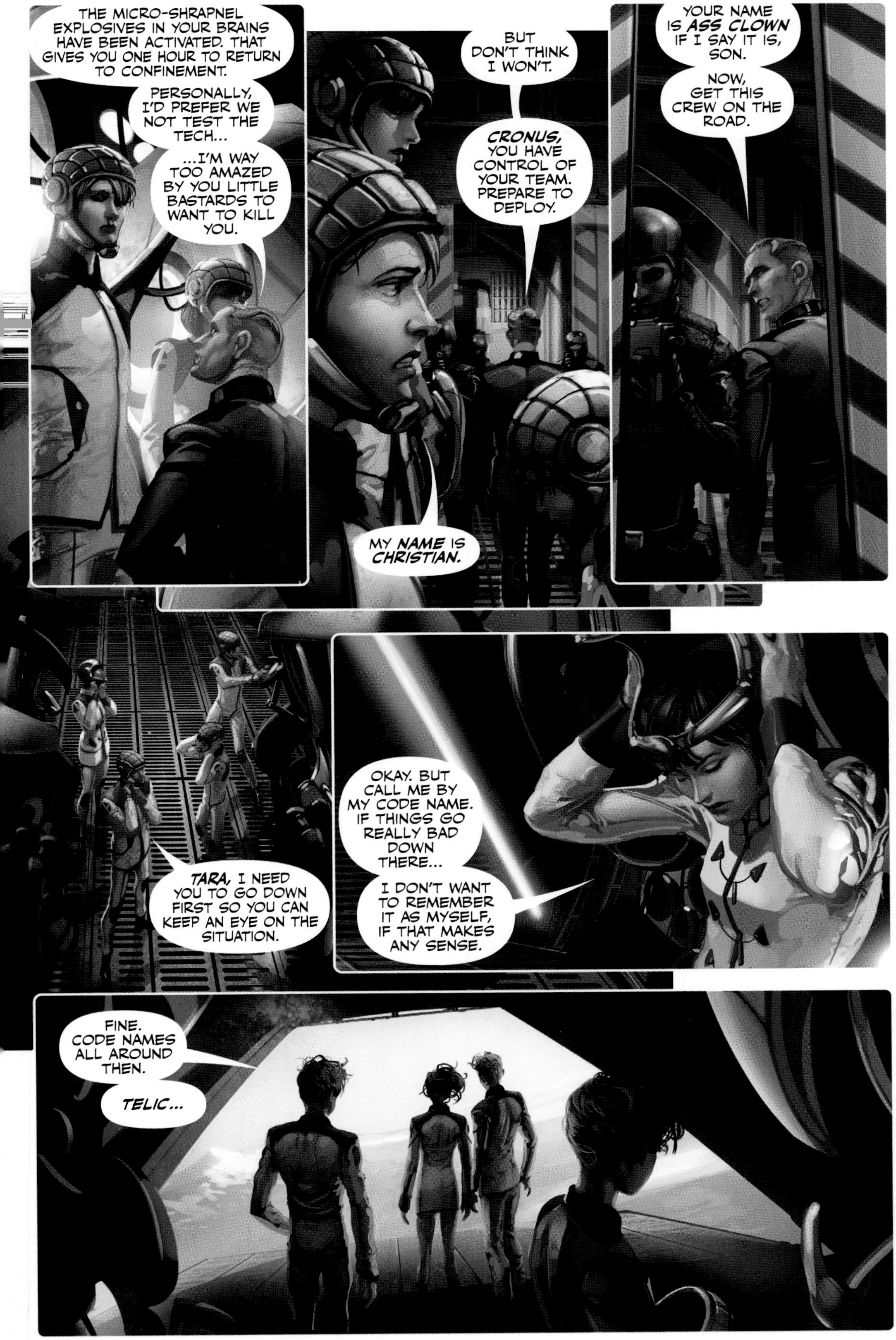
THE MICRO-SHRAPNEL EXPLOSIVES IN YOUR BRAINS HAVE BEEN ACTIVATED. THAT GIVES YOU ONE HOUR TO RETURN TO CONFINEMENT.
PERSONALLY, I'D PREFER WE NOT TEST THE TECH...
...I'M WAY TOO AMAZED BY YOU LITTLE BASTARDS TO WANT TO KILL YOU.
BUT DON'T THINK I WON'T.
CRONUS, YOU HAVE CONTROL OF YOUR TEAM. PREPARE TO DEPLOY.
MY NAME IS CHRISTIAN.
YOUR NAME IS ASS CLOWN IF I SAY IT IS, SON.
NOW, GET THIS CREW ON THE ROAD.
TARA, I NEED YOU TO GO DOWN FIRST SO YOU CAN KEEP AN EYE ON THE SITUATION.
OKAY. BUT CALL ME BY MY CODE NAME. IF THINGS GO REALLY BAD DOWN THERE...
I DON'T WANT TO REMEMBER IT AS MYSELF, IF THAT MAKES ANY SENSE.
FINE. CODE NAMES ALL AROUND THEN.
TELIC...

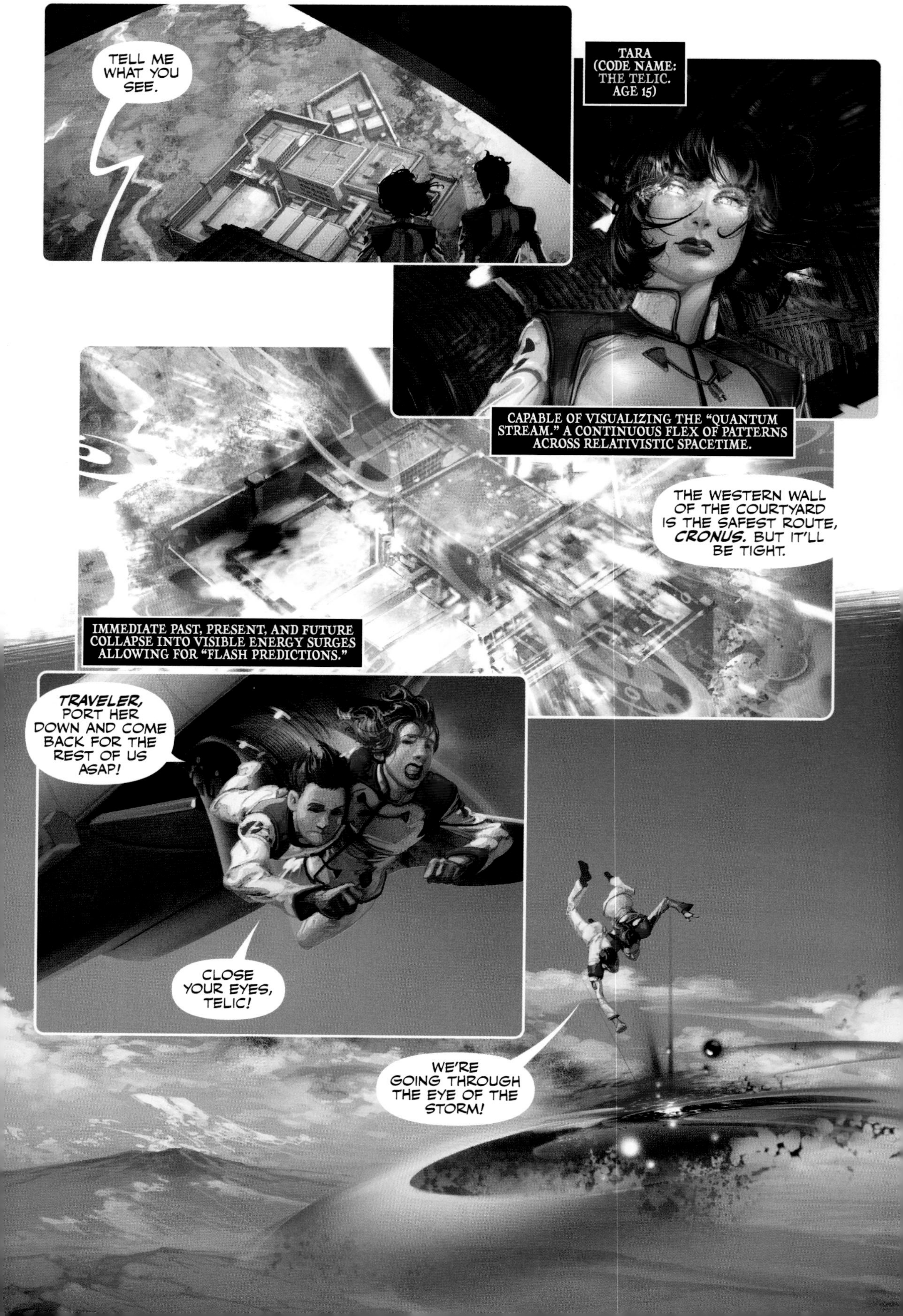
TELL ME WHAT YOU SEE.
TARA (CODE NAME: THE TELIC. AGE 15)
CAPABLE OF VISUALIZING THE "QUANTUM STREAM." A CONTINUOUS FLEX OF PATTERNS ACROSS RELATIVISTIC SPACETIME.
THE WESTERN WALL OF THE COURTYARD IS THE SAFEST ROUTE, *CRONUS.* BUT IT'LL BE TIGHT.
IMMEDIATE PAST, PRESENT, AND FUTURE COLLAPSE INTO VISIBLE ENERGY SURGES ALLOWING FOR "FLASH PREDICTIONS."
TRAVELER, PORT HER DOWN AND COME BACK FOR THE REST OF US ASAP!
CLOSE YOUR EYES, TELIC!
WE'RE GOING THROUGH THE EYE OF THE STORM!

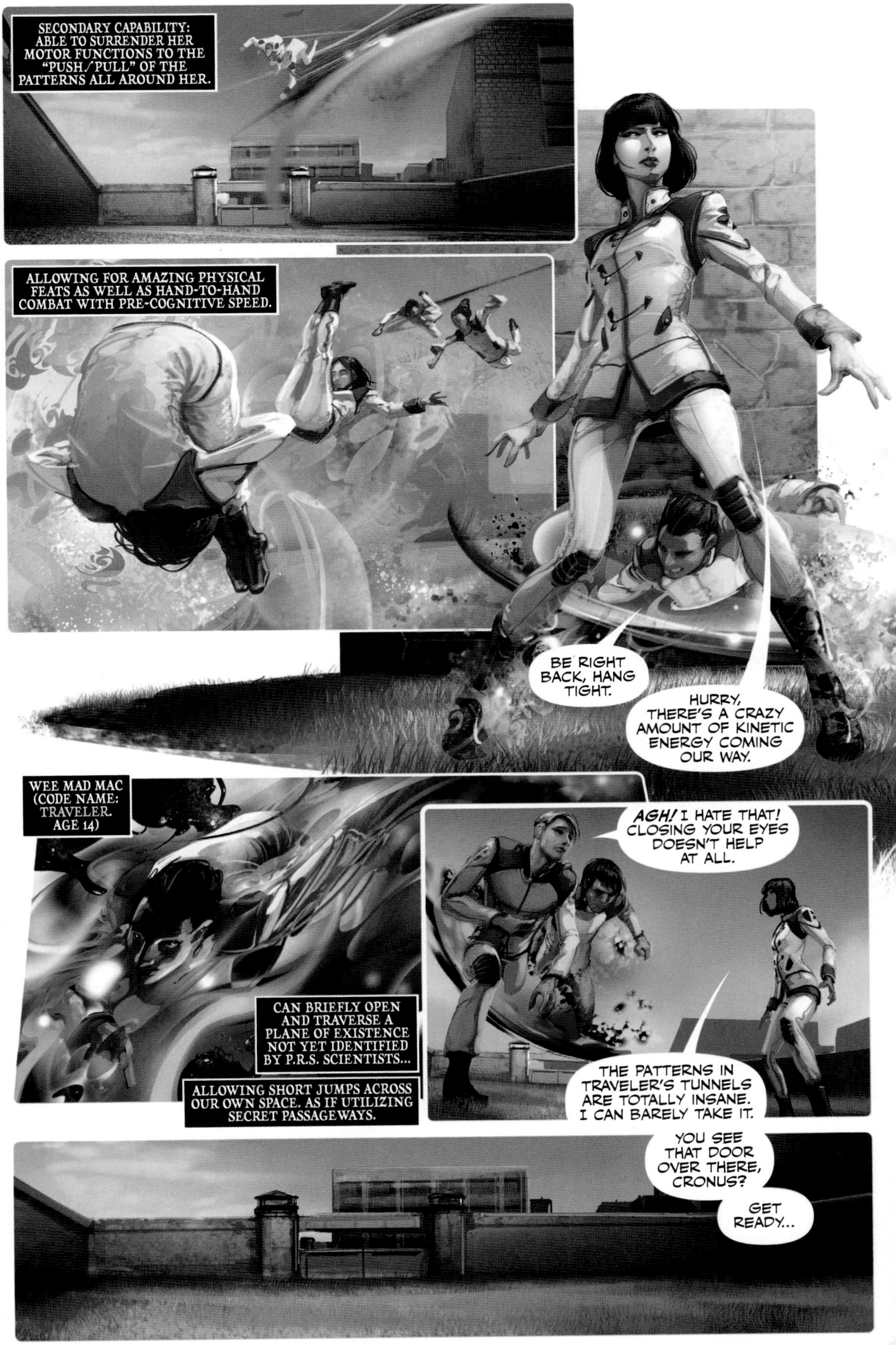
SECONDARY CAPABILITY: ABLE TO SURRENDER HER MOTOR FUNCTIONS TO THE "PUSH./PULL" OF THE PATTERNS ALL AROUND HER.
ALLOWING FOR AMAZING PHYSICAL FEATS AS WELL AS HAND-TO-HAND COMBAT WITH PRE-COGNITIVE SPEED.
BE RIGHT BACK, HANG TIGHT.
HURRY, THERE'S A CRAZY AMOUNT OF KINETIC ENERGY COMING OUR WAY.
WEE MAD MAC (CODE NAME: TRAVELER. AGE 14)
CAN BRIEFLY OPEN AND TRAVERSE A PLANE OF EXISTENCE NOT YET IDENTIFIED BY P.R.S. SCIENTISTS...
ALLOWING SHORT JUMPS ACROSS OUR OWN SPACE. AS IF UTILIZING SECRET PASSAGEWAYS.
AGH! I HATE THAT! CLOSING YOUR EYES DOESN'T HELP AT ALL.
THE PATTERNS IN TRAVELER'S TUNNELS ARE TOTALLY INSANE. I CAN BARELY TAKE IT.
YOU SEE THAT DOOR OVER THERE, CRONUS?
GET READY...

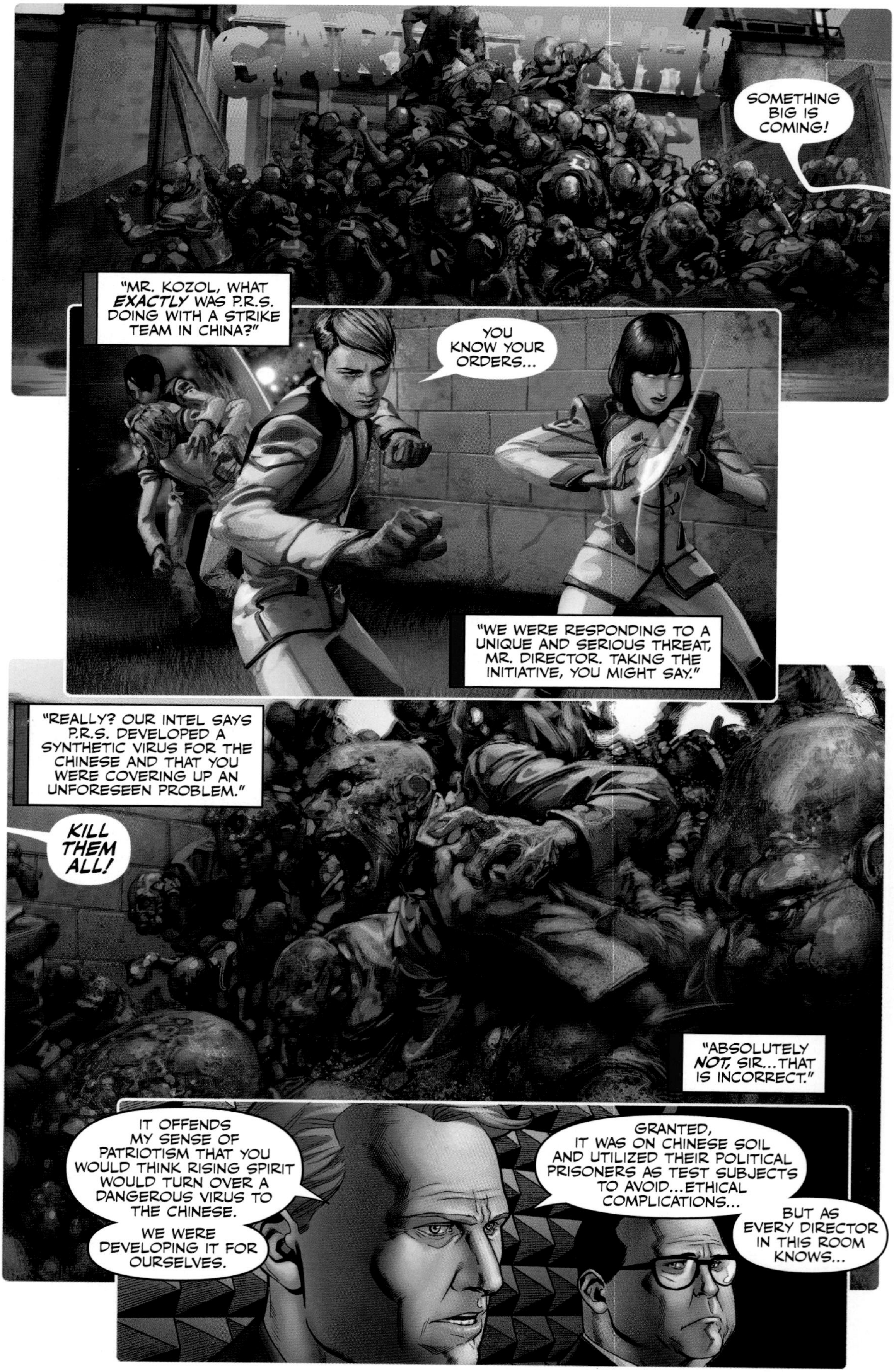
SOMETHING BIG IS COMING!
"MR. KOZOL, WHAT EXACTLY WAS P.R.S. DOING WITH A STRIKE TEAM IN CHINA?"
YOU KNOW YOUR ORDERS...
"WE WERE RESPONDING TO A UNIQUE AND SERIOUS THREAT, MR. DIRECTOR. TAKING THE INITIATIVE, YOU MIGHT SAY."
"REALLY? OUR INTEL SAYS P.R.S. DEVELOPED A SYNTHETIC VIRUS FOR THE CHINESE AND THAT YOU WERE COVERING UP AN UNFORESEEN PROBLEM."
KILL THEM ALL!
"ABSOLUTELY NOT, SIR...THAT IS INCORRECT."
IT OFFENDS MY SENSE OF PATRIOTISM THAT YOU WOULD THINK RISING SPIRIT WOULD TURN OVER A DANGEROUS VIRUS TO THE CHINESE.
WE WERE DEVELOPING IT FOR OURSELVES.
GRANTED, IT WAS ON CHINESE SOIL AND UTILIZED THEIR POLITICAL PRISONERS AS TEST SUBJECTS TO AVOID...ETHICAL COMPLICATIONS...
BUT AS EVERY DIRECTOR IN THIS ROOM KNOWS...

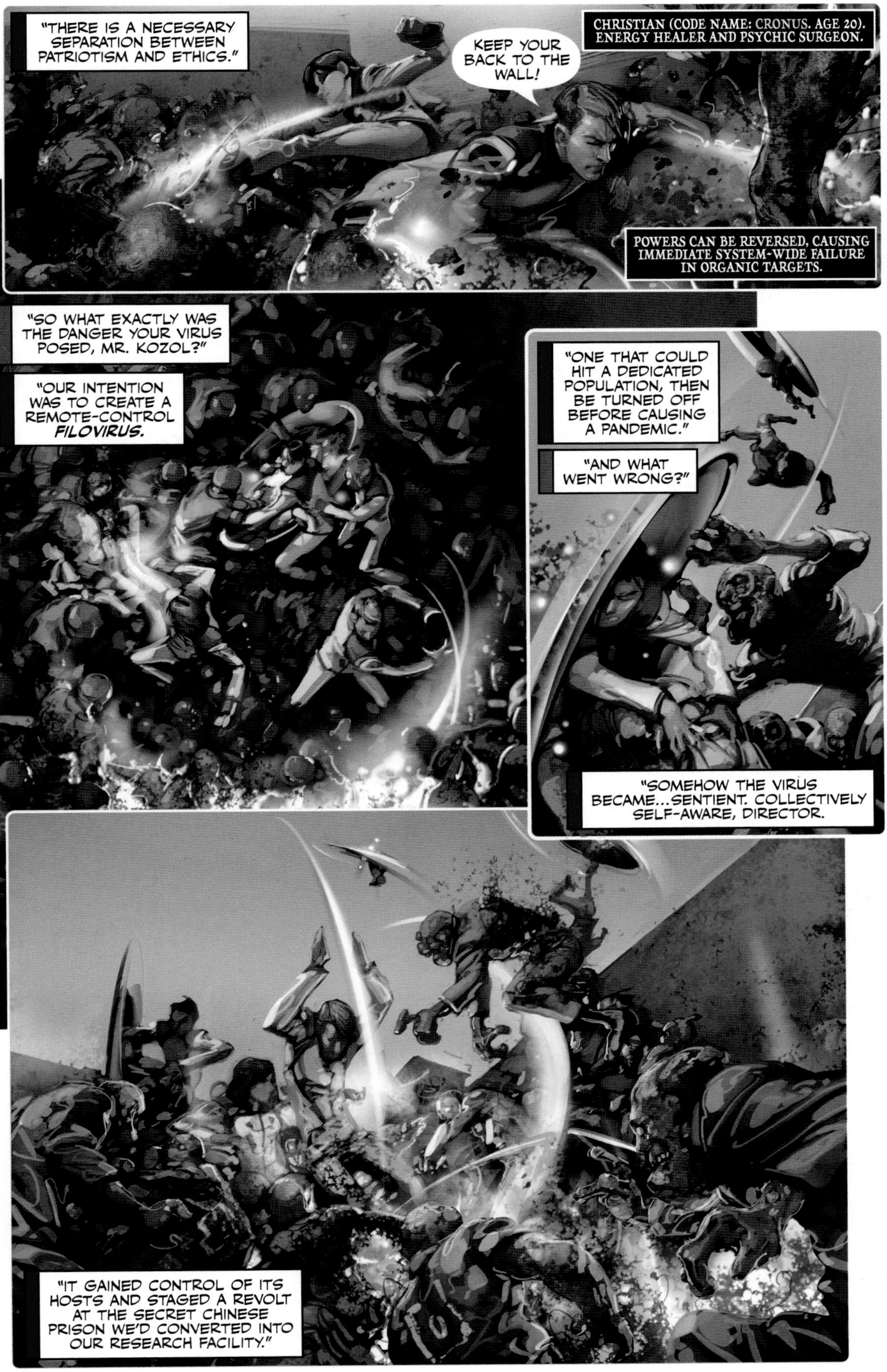
"THERE IS A NECESSARY SEPARATION BETWEEN PATRIOTISM AND ETHICS."
KEEP YOUR BACK TO THE WALL!
CHRISTIAN (CODE NAME: CRONUS. AGE 20). ENERGY HEALER AND PSYCHIC SURGEON.
POWERS CAN BE REVERSED, CAUSING IMMEDIATE SYSTEM-WIDE FAILURE IN ORGANIC TARGETS.
"SO WHAT EXACTLY WAS THE DANGER YOUR VIRUS POSED, MR. KOZOL?"
"OUR INTENTION WAS TO CREATE A REMOTE-CONTROL FILOVIRUS.
"ONE THAT COULD HIT A DEDICATED POPULATION, THEN BE TURNED OFF BEFORE CAUSING A PANDEMIC."
"AND WHAT WENT WRONG?"
"SOMEHOW THE VIRUS BECAME...SENTIENT. COLLECTIVELY SELF-AWARE, DIRECTOR.
"IT GAINED CONTROL OF ITS HOSTS AND STAGED A REVOLT AT THE SECRET CHINESE PRISON WE'D CONVERTED INTO OUR RESEARCH FACILITY."

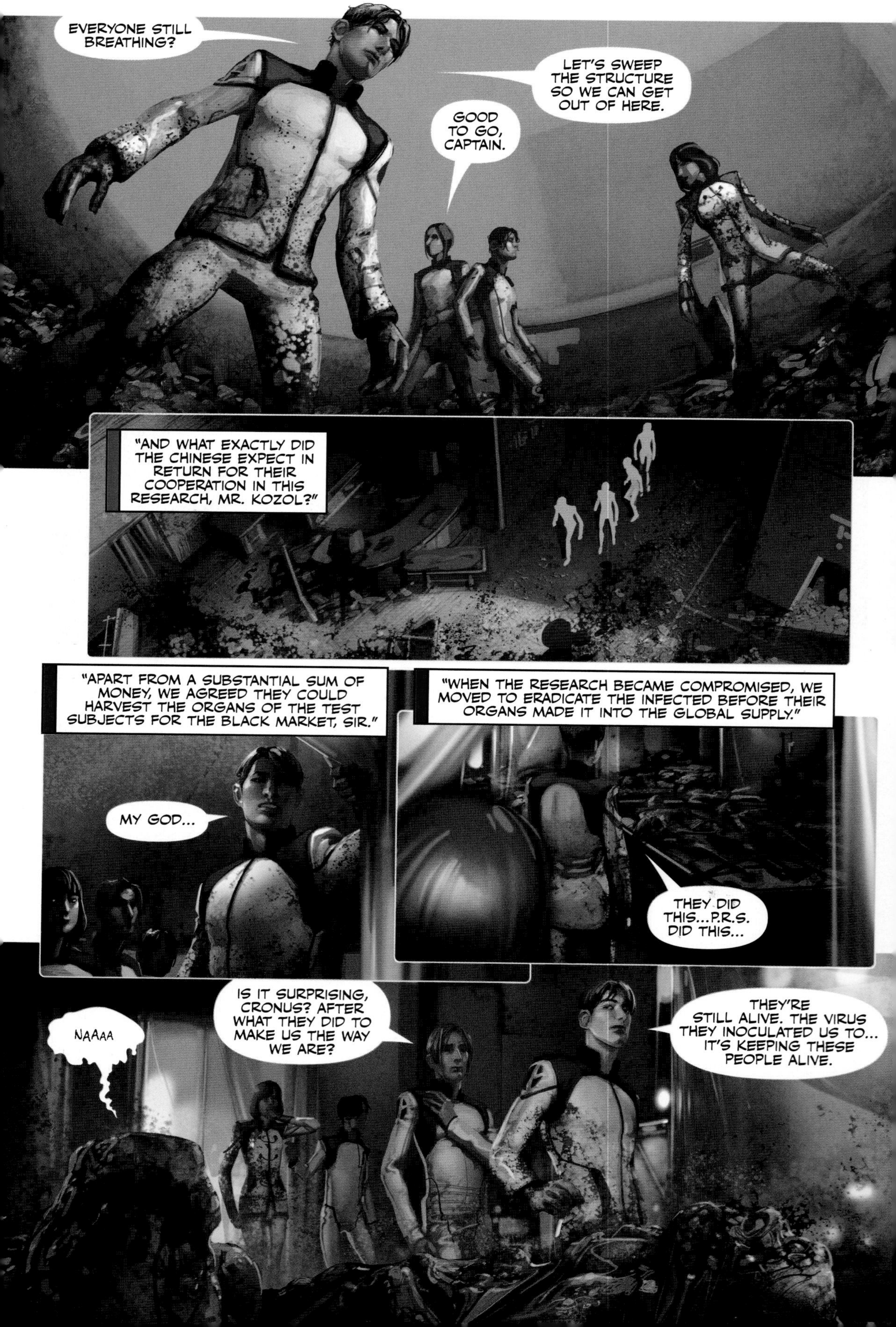
EVERYONE STILL BREATHING?
LET'S SWEEP THE STRUCTURE SO WE CAN GET OUT OF HERE.
GOOD TO GO, CAPTAIN.
"AND WHAT EXACTLY DID THE CHINESE EXPECT IN RETURN FOR THEIR COOPERATION IN THIS RESEARCH, MR. KOZOL?"
"APART FROM A SUBSTANTIAL SUM OF MONEY, WE AGREED THEY COULD HARVEST THE ORGANS OF THE TEST SUBJECTS FOR THE BLACK MARKET, SIR."
MY GOD...
"WHEN THE RESEARCH BECAME COMPROMISED, WE MOVED TO ERADICATE THE INFECTED BEFORE THEIR ORGANS MADE IT INTO THE GLOBAL SUPPLY."
THEY DID THIS...P.R.S. DID THIS...
NAAAA
IS IT SURPRISING, CRONUS? AFTER WHAT THEY DID TO MAKE US THE WAY WE ARE?
THEY'RE STILL ALIVE. THE VIRUS THEY INOCULATED US TO... IT'S KEEPING THESE PEOPLE ALIVE.

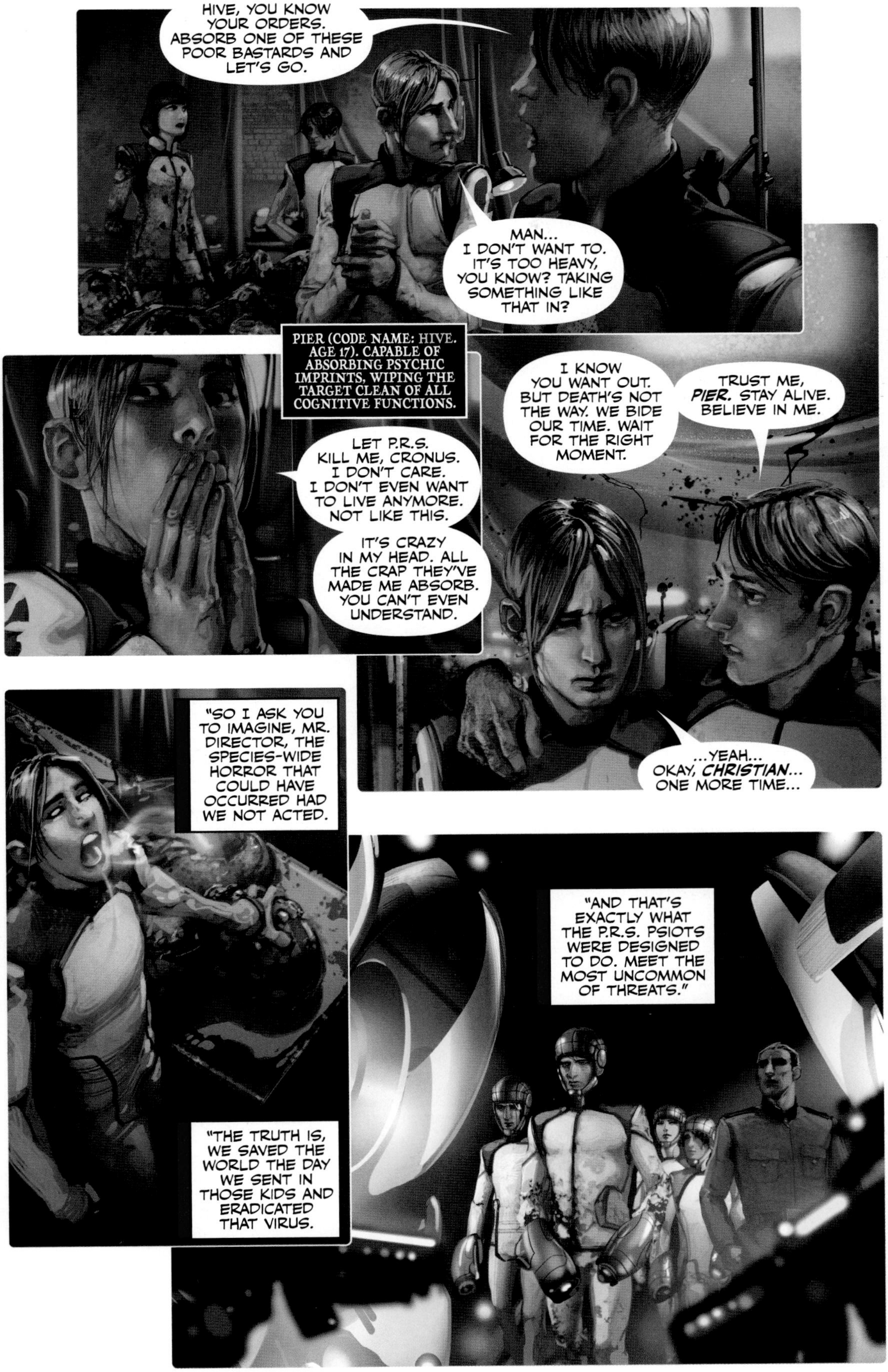
HIVE, YOU KNOW YOUR ORDERS. ABSORB ONE OF THESE POOR BASTARDS AND LET'S GO.
MAN... I DON'T WANT TO. IT'S TOO HEAVY, YOU KNOW? TAKING SOMETHING LIKE THAT IN?
PIER (CODE NAME: HIVE. AGE 17). CAPABLE OF ABSORBING PSYCHIC IMPRINTS, WIPING THE TARGET CLEAN OF ALL COGNITIVE FUNCTIONS.
LET P.R.S. KILL ME, CRONUS. I DON'T CARE. I DON'T EVEN WANT TO LIVE ANYMORE. NOT LIKE THIS.
IT'S CRAZY IN MY HEAD. ALL THE CRAP THEY'VE MADE ME ABSORB. YOU CAN'T EVEN UNDERSTAND.
I KNOW YOU WANT OUT. BUT DEATH'S NOT THE WAY. WE BIDE OUR TIME. WAIT FOR THE RIGHT MOMENT.
TRUST ME, PIER. STAY ALIVE. BELIEVE IN ME.
...YEAH... OKAY, CHRISTIAN... ONE MORE TIME...
"SO I ASK YOU TO IMAGINE, MR. DIRECTOR, THE SPECIES-WIDE HORROR THAT COULD HAVE OCCURRED HAD WE NOT ACTED.
"THE TRUTH IS, WE SAVED THE WORLD THE DAY WE SENT IN THOSE KIDS AND ERADICATED THAT VIRUS.
"AND THAT'S EXACTLY WHAT THE P.R.S. PSIOTS WERE DESIGNED TO DO. MEET THE MOST UNCOMMON OF THREATS."

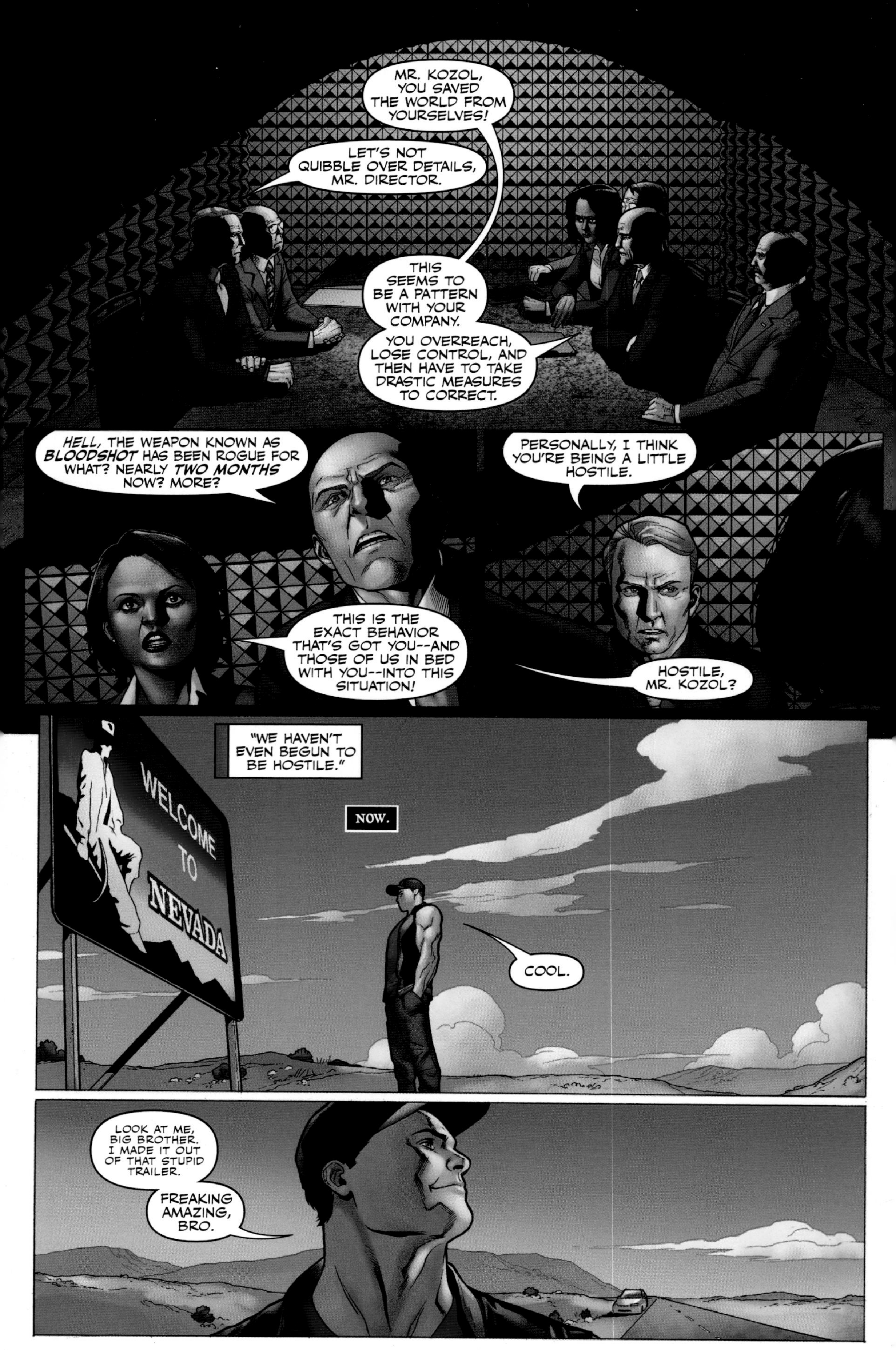
MR. KOZOL, YOU SAVED THE WORLD FROM YOURSELVES!
LET'S NOT QUIBBLE OVER DETAILS, MR. DIRECTOR.
THIS SEEMS TO BE A PATTERN WITH YOUR COMPANY.
YOU OVERREACH, LOSE CONTROL, AND THEN HAVE TO TAKE DRASTIC MEASURES TO CORRECT.
HELL, THE WEAPON KNOWN AS BLOODSHOT HAS BEEN ROGUE FOR WHAT? NEARLY TWO MONTHS NOW? MORE?
THIS IS THE EXACT BEHAVIOR THAT'S GOT YOU--AND THOSE OF US IN BED WITH YOU--INTO THIS SITUATION!
PERSONALLY, I THINK YOU'RE BEING A LITTLE HOSTILE.
HOSTILE, MR. KOZOL?
"WE HAVEN'T EVEN BEGUN TO BE HOSTILE."
NOW.
WELCOME TO NEVADA
COOL.
LOOK AT ME, BIG BROTHER. I MADE IT OUT OF THAT STUPID TRAILER.
FREAKING AMAZING, BRO.

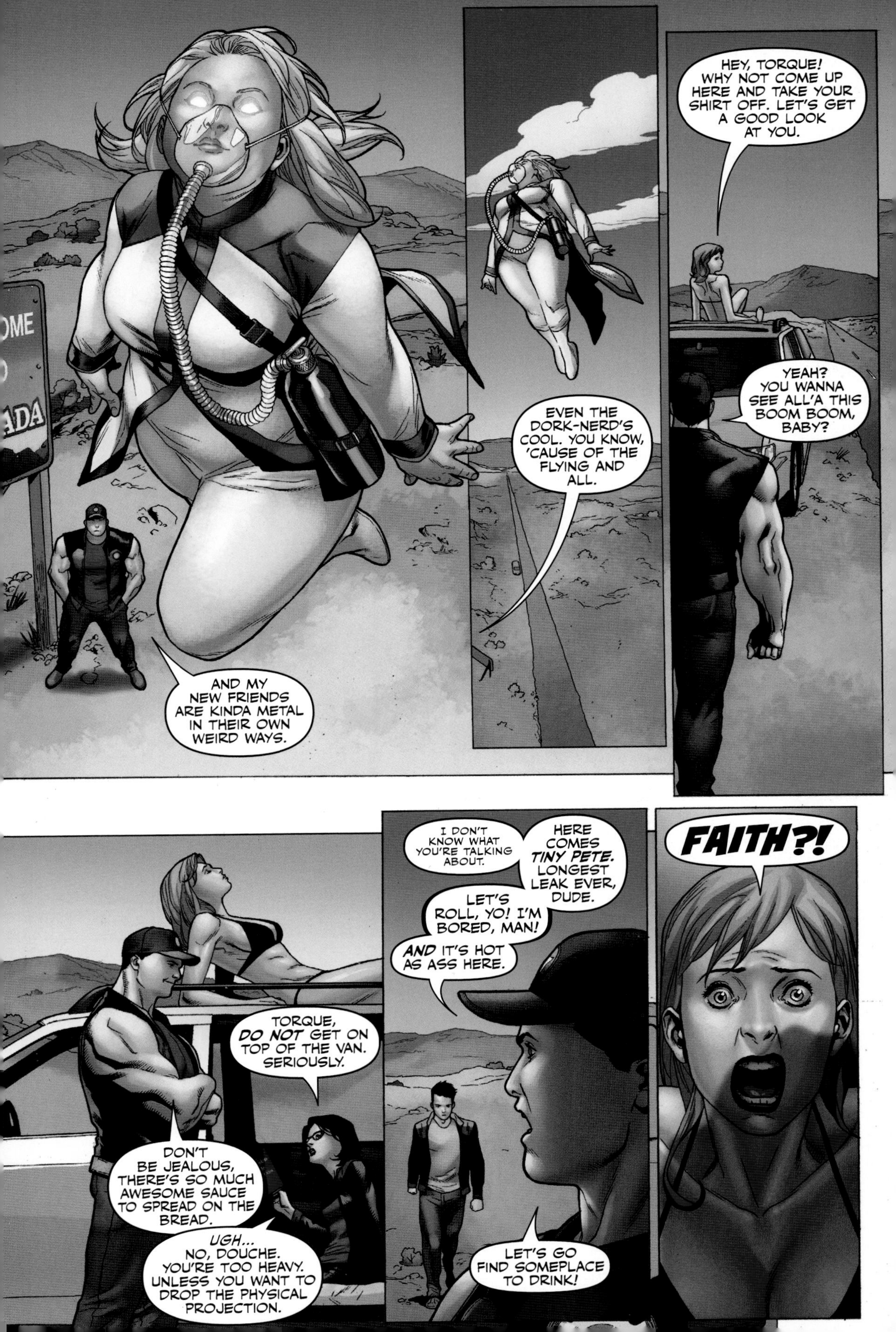
OME
ADA
AND MY NEW FRIENDS ARE KINDA METAL IN THEIR OWN WEIRD WAYS.
EVEN THE DORK-NERD'S COOL. YOU KNOW, 'CAUSE OF THE FLYING AND ALL.
HEY, TORQUE! WHY NOT COME UP HERE AND TAKE YOUR SHIRT OFF. LET'S GET A GOOD LOOK AT YOU.
YEAH? YOU WANNA SEE ALL'A THIS BOOM BOOM, BABY?
TORQUE, DO NOT GET ON TOP OF THE VAN. SERIOUSLY.
DON'T BE JEALOUS, THERE'S SO MUCH AWESOME SAUCE TO SPREAD ON THE BREAD.
UGH... NO, DOUCHE. YOU'RE TOO HEAVY. UNLESS YOU WANT TO DROP THE PHYSICAL PROJECTION.
I DON'T KNOW WHAT YOU'RE TALKING ABOUT.
HERE COMES TINY PETE. LONGEST LEAK EVER, DUDE.
LET'S ROLL, YO! I'M BORED, MAN!
AND IT'S HOT AS ASS HERE.
LET'S GO FIND SOMEPLACE TO DRINK!
FAITH?!

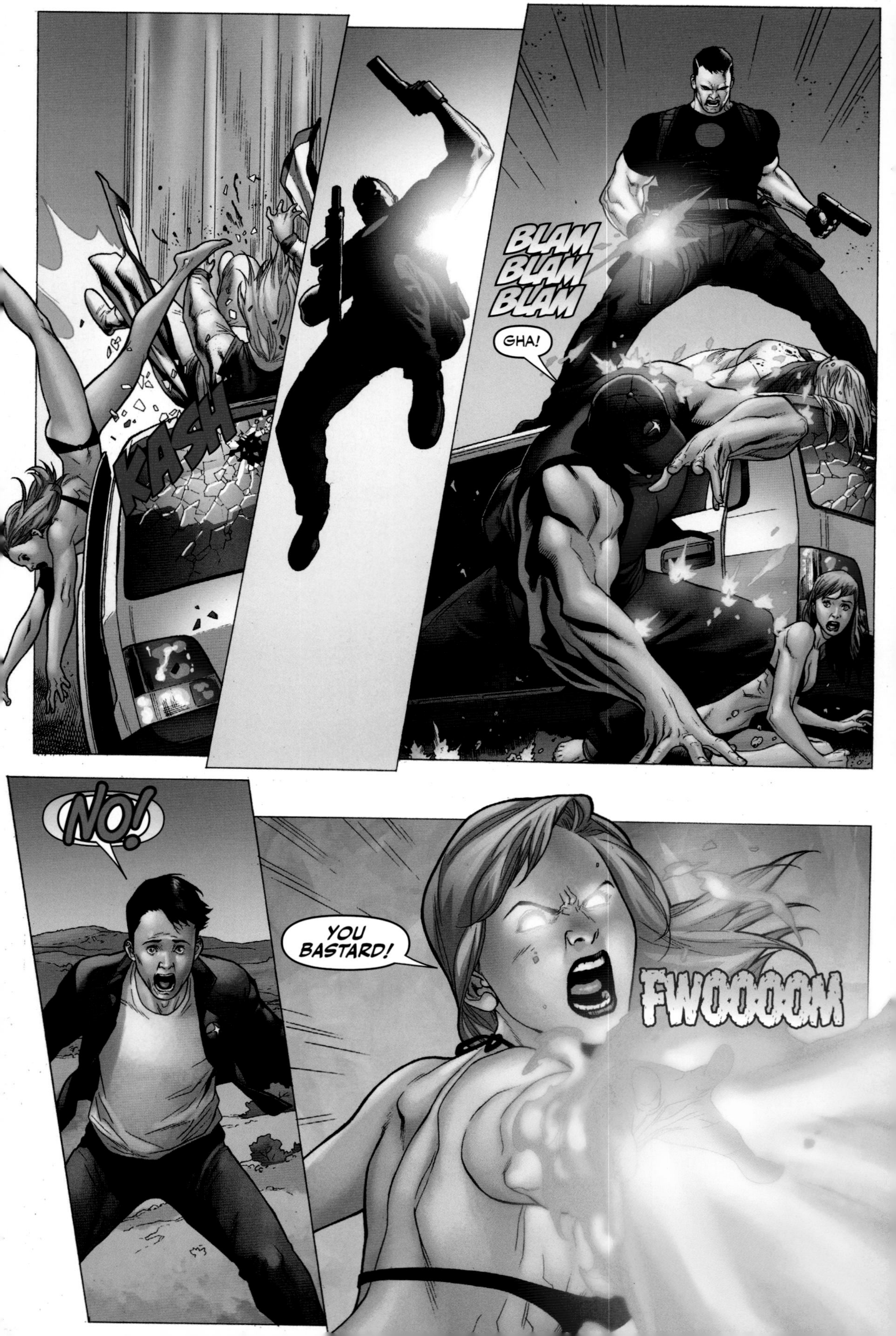
KASH
BLAM
BLAM
BLAM
GHA!
NO!
YOU BASTARD!
FWOOOOM

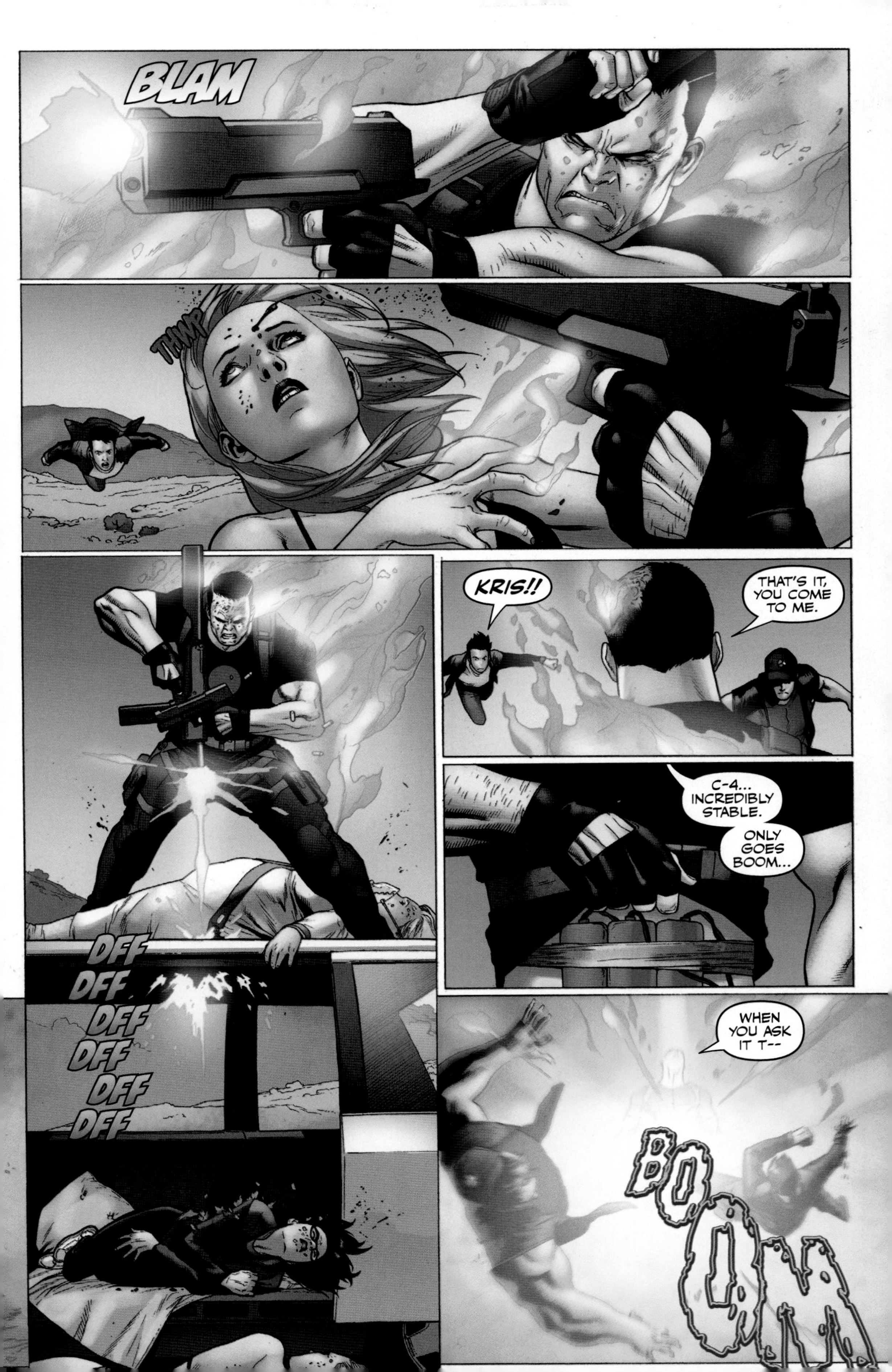
BLAM
THWP
KRIS!!
THAT'S IT, YOU COME TO ME.
C-4... INCREDIBLY STABLE.
ONLY GOES BOOM...
DFF DFF DFF DFF DFF DFF
WHEN YOU ASK IT T--
BOOM

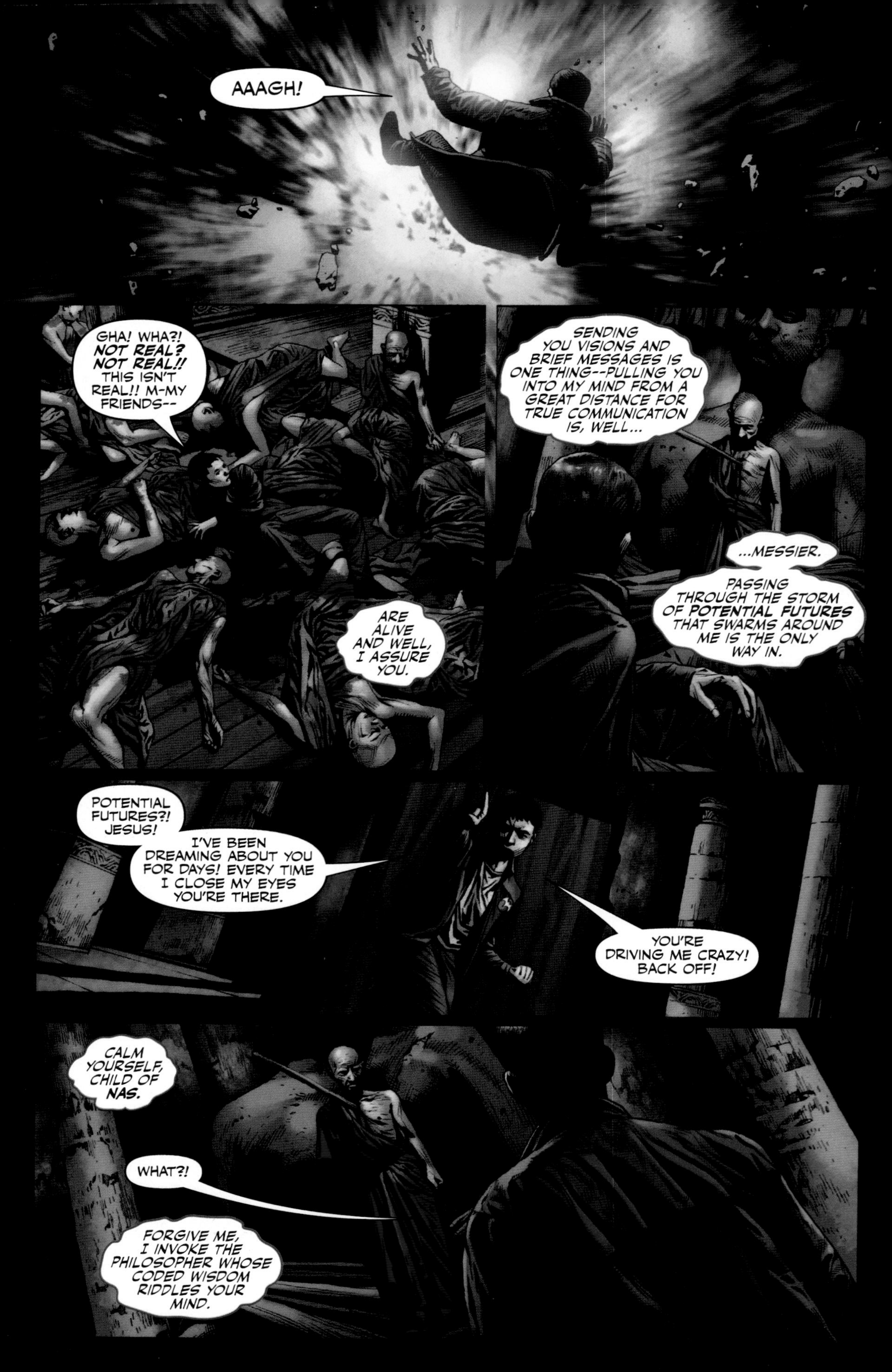
AAAGH!
GHA! WHA?! **NOT REAL? NOT REAL!!** THIS ISN'T REAL!! M-MY FRIENDS--
ARE ALIVE AND WELL, I ASSURE YOU.
SENDING YOU VISIONS AND BRIEF MESSAGES IS ONE THING--PULLING YOU INTO MY MIND FROM A GREAT DISTANCE FOR TRUE COMMUNICATION IS, WELL...
...MESSIER.
PASSING THROUGH THE STORM OF **POTENTIAL FUTURES** THAT SWARMS AROUND ME IS THE ONLY WAY IN.
POTENTIAL FUTURES?! JESUS!
I'VE BEEN DREAMING ABOUT YOU FOR DAYS! EVERY TIME I CLOSE MY EYES YOU'RE THERE.
YOU'RE DRIVING ME CRAZY! BACK OFF!
CALM YOURSELF, CHILD OF **NAS.**
WHAT?!
FORGIVE ME, I INVOKE THE PHILOSOPHER WHOSE CODED WISDOM RIDDLES YOUR MIND.

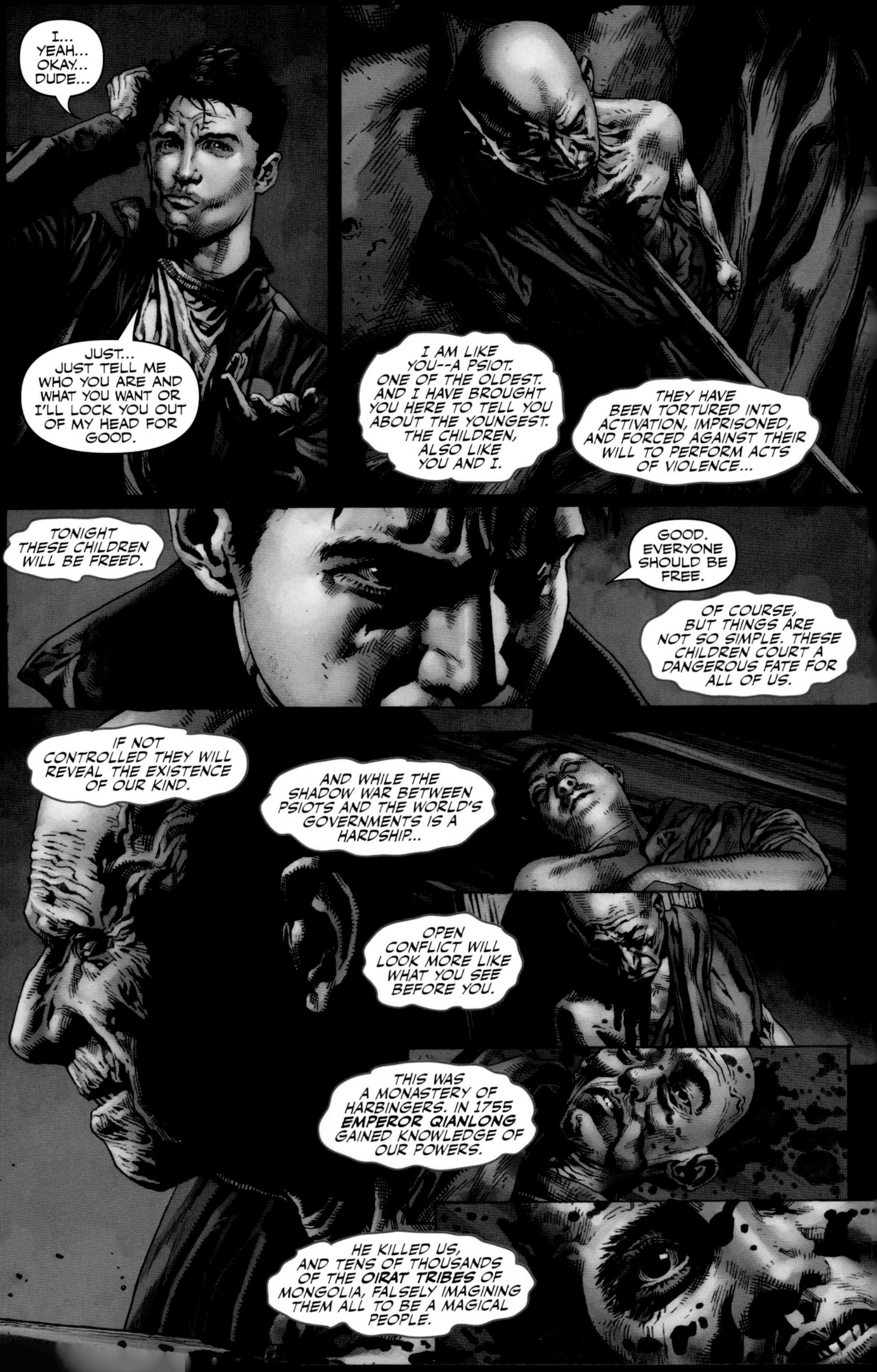

I... YEAH... OKAY... DUDE...
JUST... JUST TELL ME WHO YOU ARE AND WHAT YOU WANT OR I'LL LOCK YOU OUT OF MY HEAD FOR GOOD.
I AM LIKE YOU--A PSIOT. ONE OF THE OLDEST. AND I HAVE BROUGHT YOU HERE TO TELL YOU ABOUT THE YOUNGEST. THE CHILDREN, ALSO LIKE YOU AND I.
THEY HAVE BEEN TORTURED INTO ACTIVATION, IMPRISONED, AND FORCED AGAINST THEIR WILL TO PERFORM ACTS OF VIOLENCE...
TONIGHT THESE CHILDREN WILL BE FREED.
GOOD. EVERYONE SHOULD BE FREE.
OF COURSE, BUT THINGS ARE NOT SO SIMPLE. THESE CHILDREN COURT A DANGEROUS FATE FOR ALL OF US.
IF NOT CONTROLLED THEY WILL REVEAL THE EXISTENCE OF OUR KIND.
AND WHILE THE SHADOW WAR BETWEEN PSIOTS AND THE WORLD'S GOVERNMENTS IS A HARDSHIP...
OPEN CONFLICT WILL LOOK MORE LIKE WHAT YOU SEE BEFORE YOU.
THIS WAS A MONASTERY OF HARBINGERS. IN 1755 **EMPEROR QIANLONG** GAINED KNOWLEDGE OF OUR POWERS.
HE KILLED US, AND TENS OF THOUSANDS OF THE **OIRAT TRIBES** OF MONGOLIA, FALSELY IMAGINING THEM ALL TO BE A MAGICAL PEOPLE.

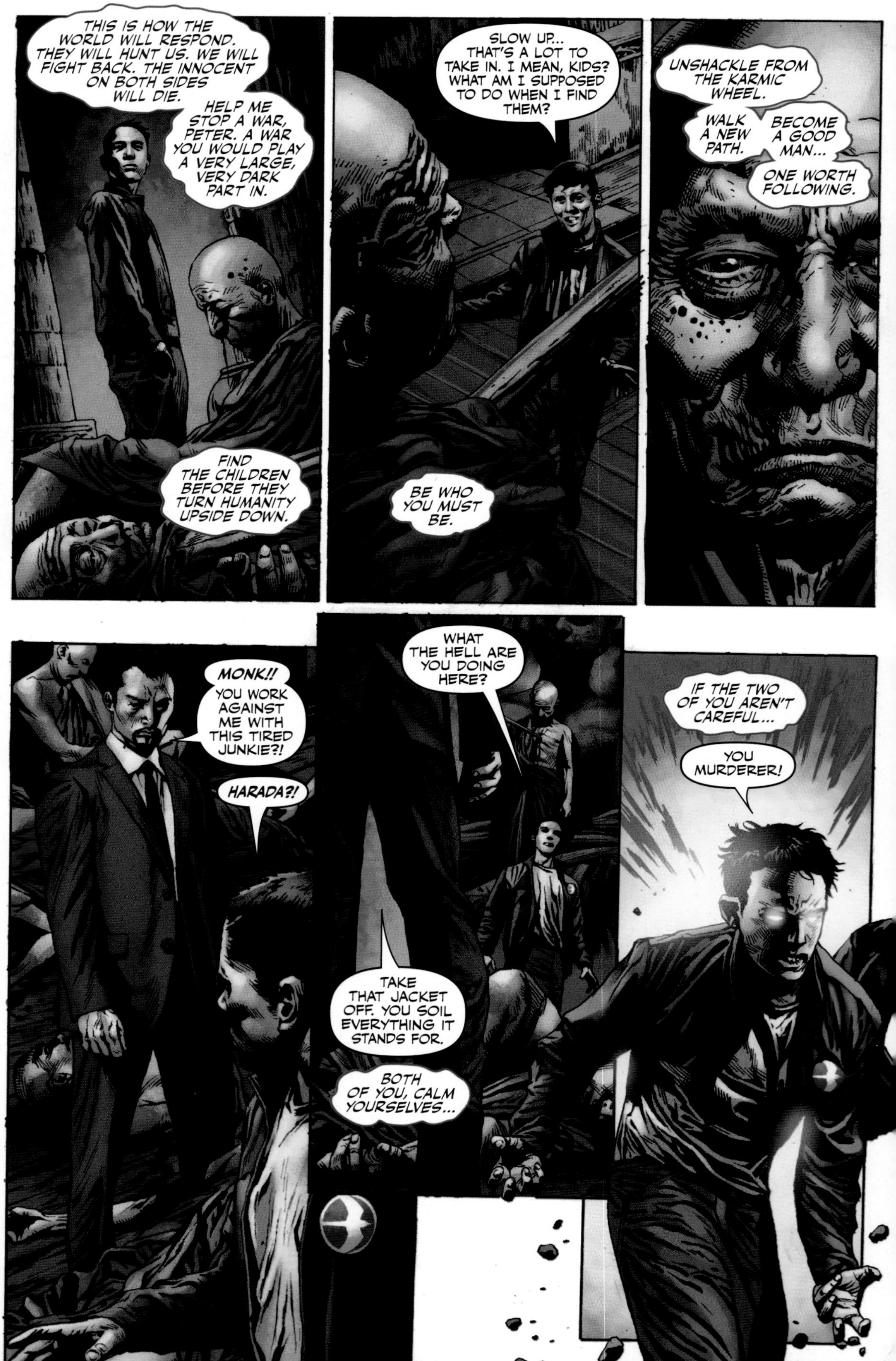
THIS IS HOW THE WORLD WILL RESPOND. THEY WILL HUNT US. WE WILL FIGHT BACK. THE INNOCENT ON BOTH SIDES WILL DIE.
HELP ME STOP A WAR, PETER. A WAR YOU WOULD PLAY A VERY LARGE, VERY DARK PART IN.
FIND THE CHILDREN BEFORE THEY TURN HUMANITY UPSIDE DOWN.
SLOW UP... THAT'S A LOT TO TAKE IN. I MEAN, KIDS? WHAT AM I SUPPOSED TO DO WHEN I FIND THEM?
BE WHO YOU MUST BE.
UNSHACKLE FROM THE KARMIC WHEEL.
WALK A NEW PATH.
BECOME A GOOD MAN...
ONE WORTH FOLLOWING.
MONK!! YOU WORK AGAINST ME WITH THIS TIRED JUNKIE?!
HARADA?!
WHAT THE HELL ARE YOU DOING HERE?
TAKE THAT JACKET OFF. YOU SOIL EVERYTHING IT STANDS FOR.
BOTH OF YOU, CALM YOURSELVES...
IF THE TWO OF YOU AREN'T CAREFUL...
YOU MURDERER!

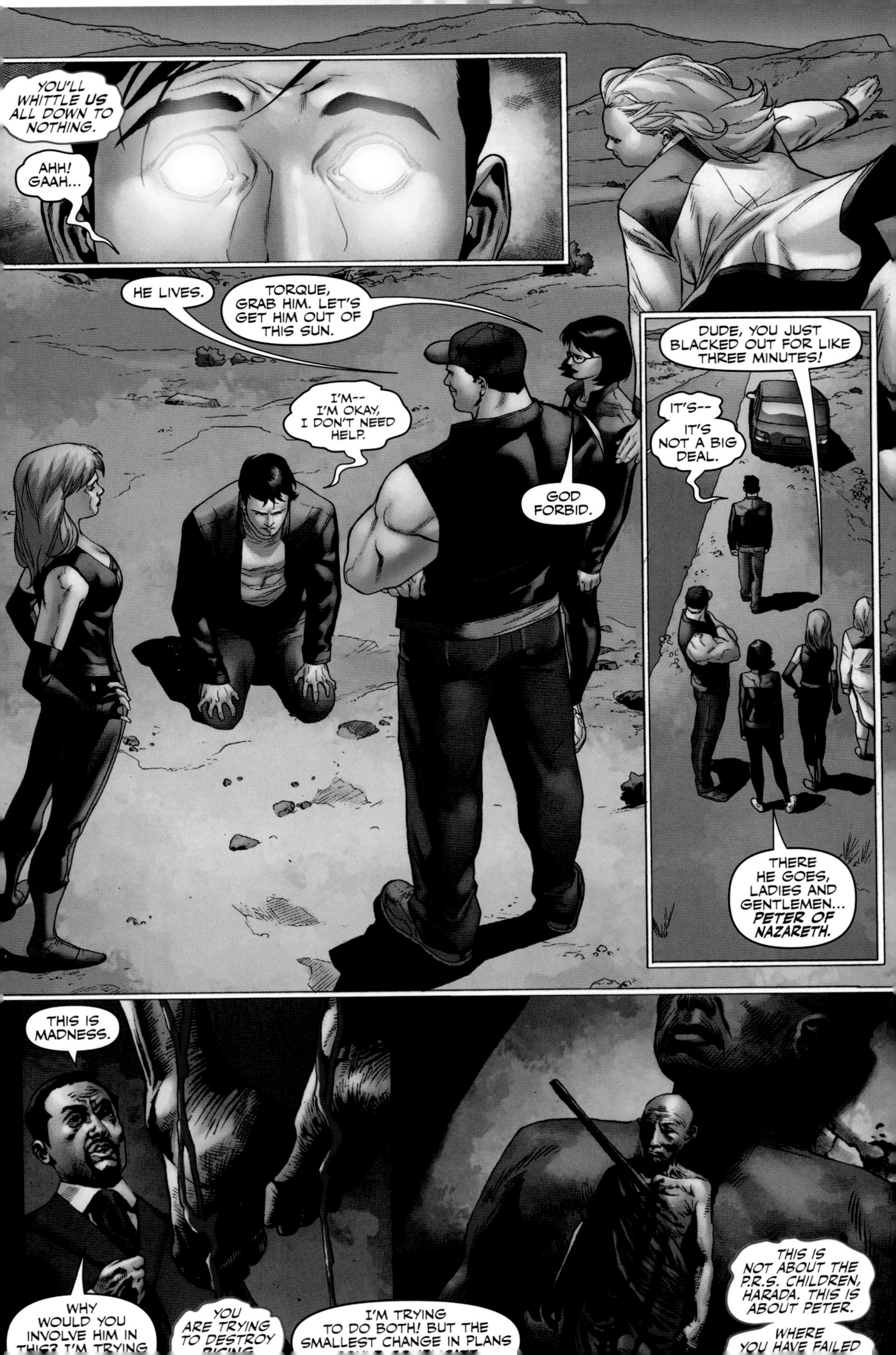

YOU'LL WHITTLE US ALL DOWN TO NOTHING.
AHH! GAAH...
HE LIVES.
TORQUE, GRAB HIM. LET'S GET HIM OUT OF THIS SUN.
I'M-- I'M OKAY, I DON'T NEED HELP.
GOD FORBID.
DUDE, YOU JUST BLACKED OUT FOR LIKE THREE MINUTES!
IT'S--
IT'S NOT A BIG DEAL.
THERE HE GOES, LADIES AND GENTLEMEN... PETER OF NAZARETH.
THIS IS MADNESS.
WHY WOULD YOU INVOLVE HIM IN THIS? I'M TRYING
YOU ARE TRYING TO DESTROY
I'M TRYING TO DO BOTH! BUT THE SMALLEST CHANGE IN PLANS
THIS IS NOT ABOUT THE P.R.S. CHILDREN, HARADA. THIS IS ABOUT PETER.
WHERE YOU HAVE FAILED

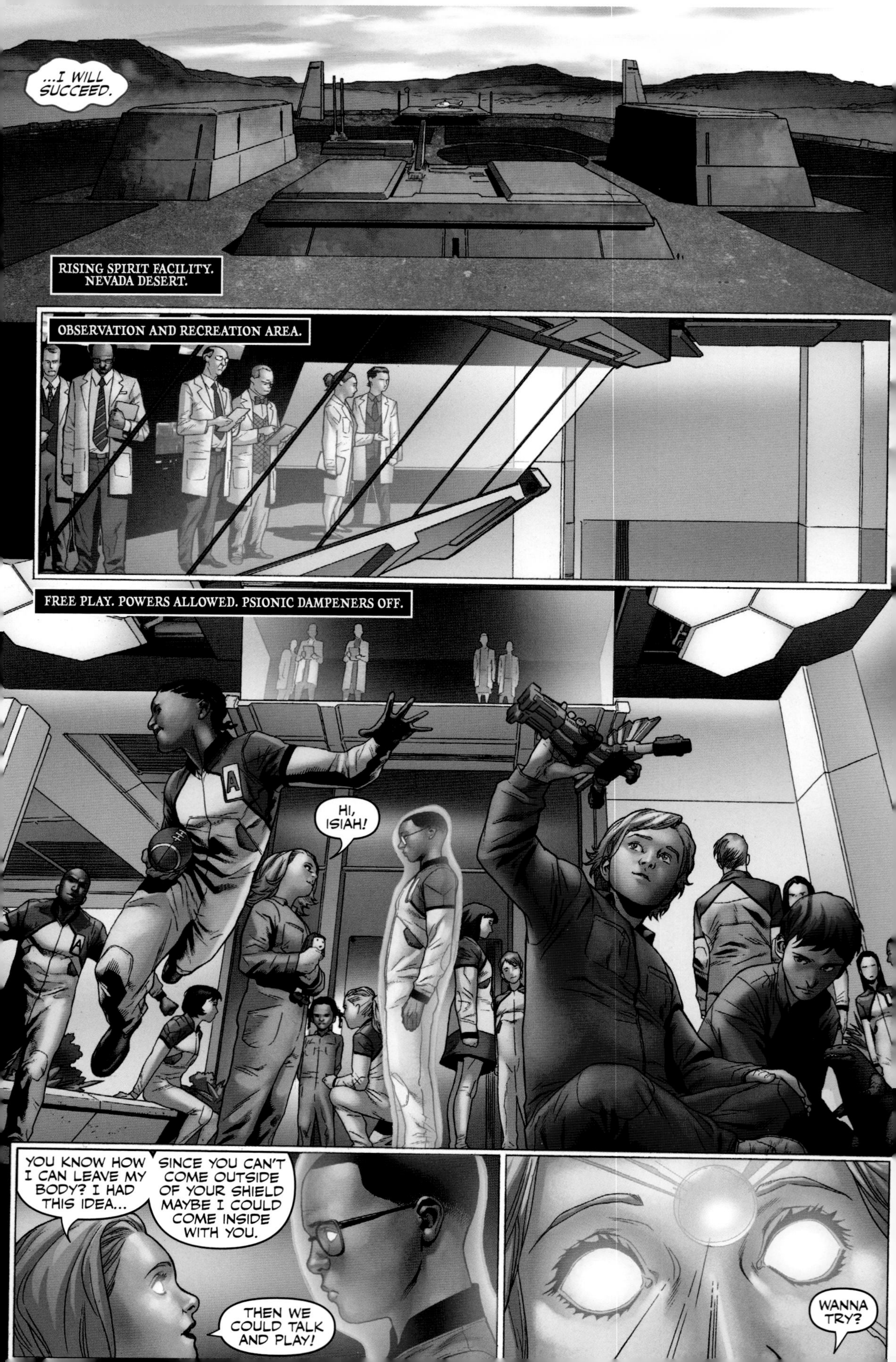
...I WILL SUCCEED.
RISING SPIRIT FACILITY. NEVADA DESERT.
OBSERVATION AND RECREATION AREA.
FREE PLAY. POWERS ALLOWED. PSIONIC DAMPENERS OFF.
HI, ISIAH!
YOU KNOW HOW I CAN LEAVE MY BODY? I HAD THIS IDEA...
SINCE YOU CAN'T COME OUTSIDE OF YOUR SHIELD MAYBE I COULD COME INSIDE WITH YOU.
THEN WE COULD TALK AND PLAY!
WANNA TRY?

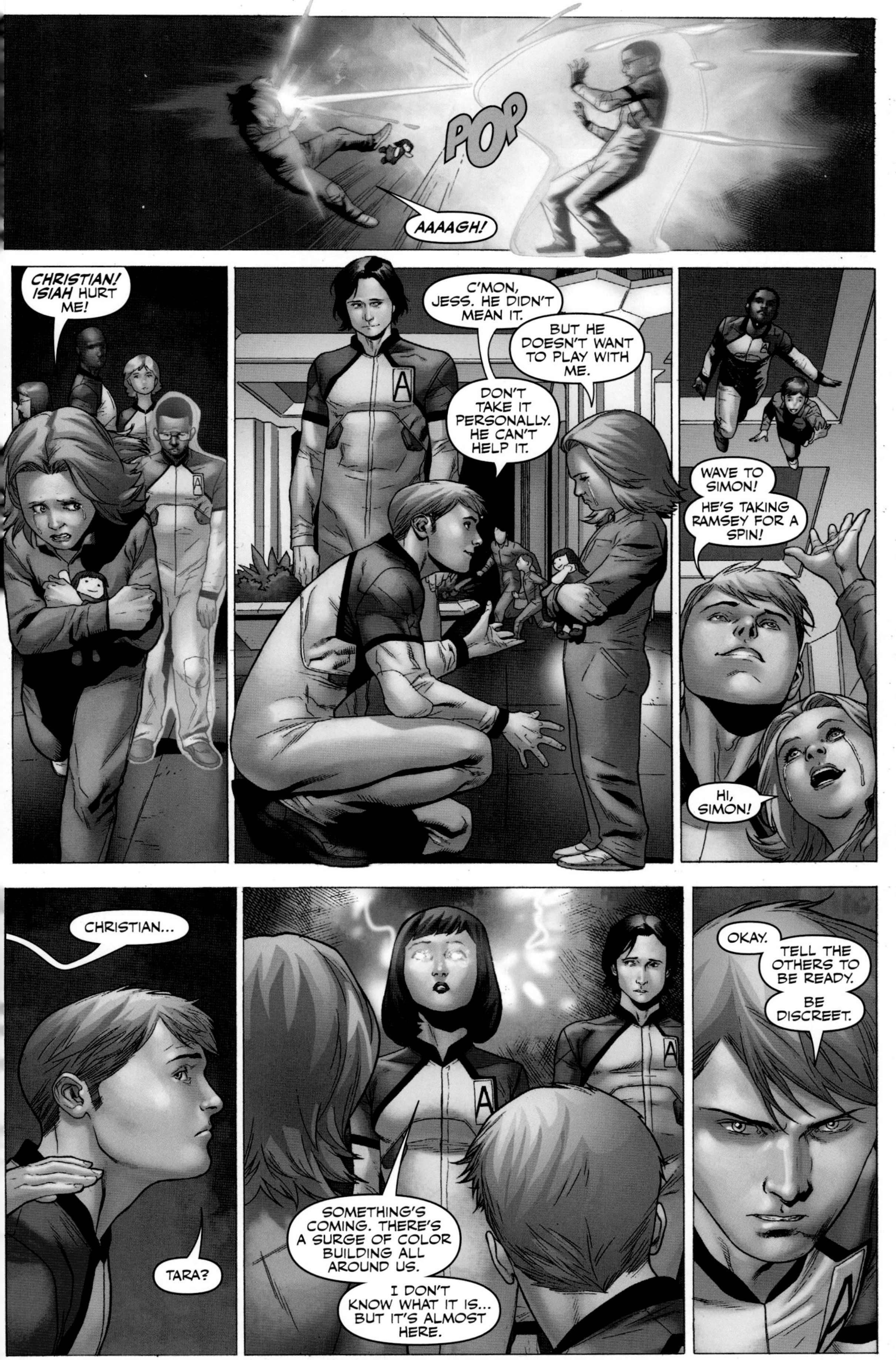
POP
AAAAGH!
CHRISTIAN! ISIAH HURT ME!
C'MON, JESS. HE DIDN'T MEAN IT.
BUT HE DOESN'T WANT TO PLAY WITH ME.
DON'T TAKE IT PERSONALLY. HE CAN'T HELP IT.
WAVE TO SIMON!
HE'S TAKING RAMSEY FOR A SPIN!
HI, SIMON!
CHRISTIAN...
TARA?
SOMETHING'S COMING. THERE'S A SURGE OF COLOR BUILDING ALL AROUND US.
I DON'T KNOW WHAT IT IS... BUT IT'S ALMOST HERE.
OKAY.
TELL THE OTHERS TO BE READY.
BE DISCREET.

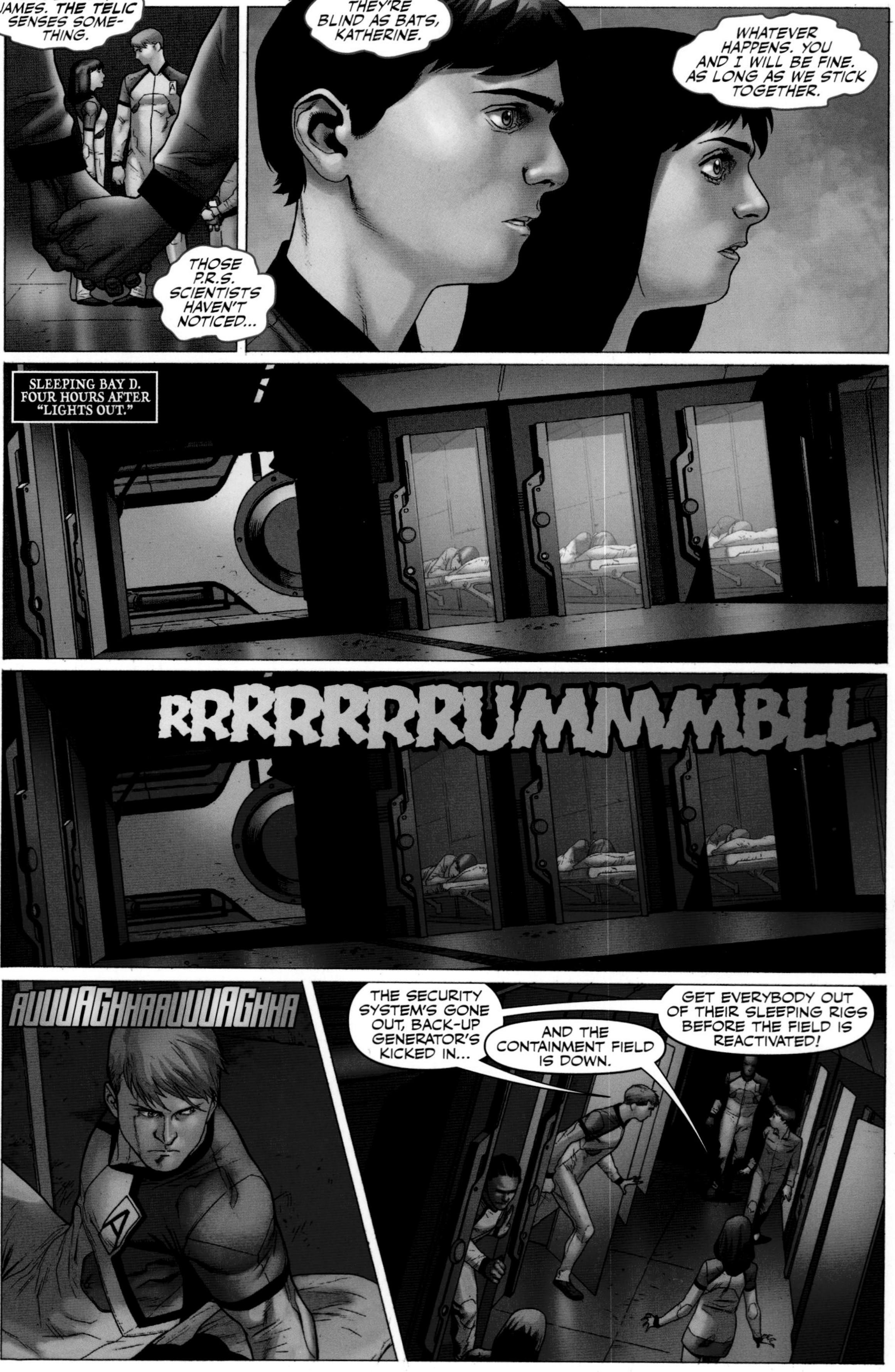
I TOLD YOU, JAMES. THE TELIC SENSES SOMETHING.
THEY'RE BLIND AS BATS, KATHERINE.
WHATEVER HAPPENS. YOU AND I WILL BE FINE. AS LONG AS WE STICK TOGETHER.
THOSE P.R.S. SCIENTISTS HAVEN'T NOTICED...
SLEEPING BAY D. FOUR HOURS AFTER "LIGHTS OUT."
RRRRRRRRUMMMMBLL
AUUUAGHHAAUUUAGHHA
THE SECURITY SYSTEM'S GONE OUT, BACK-UP GENERATOR'S KICKED IN...
AND THE CONTAINMENT FIELD IS DOWN.
GET EVERYBODY OUT OF THEIR SLEEPING RIGS BEFORE THE FIELD IS REACTIVATED!

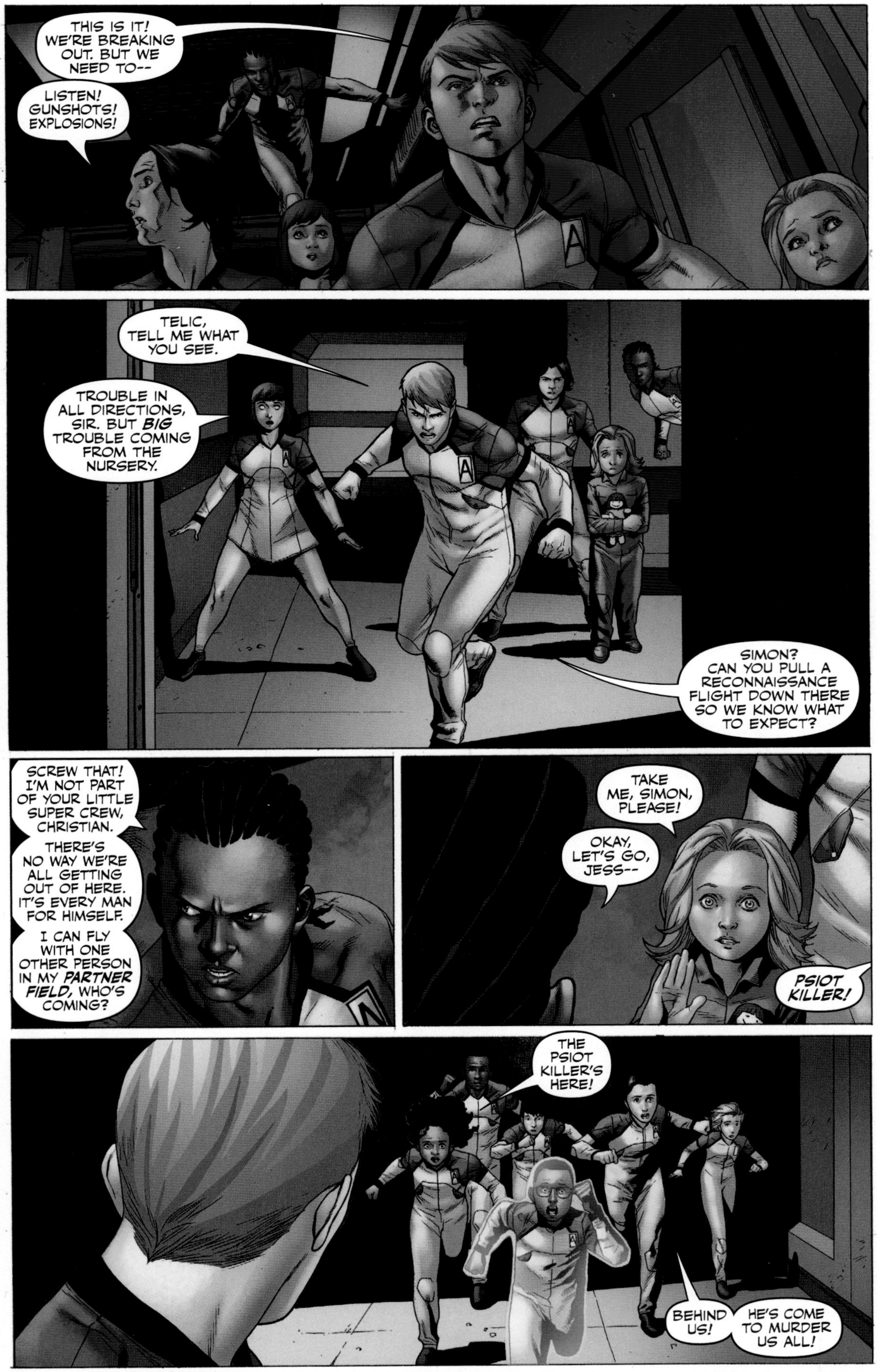
THIS IS IT! WE'RE BREAKING OUT. BUT WE NEED TO--
LISTEN! GUNSHOTS! EXPLOSIONS!
TELIC, TELL ME WHAT YOU SEE.
TROUBLE IN ALL DIRECTIONS, SIR. BUT BIG TROUBLE COMING FROM THE NURSERY.
SIMON? CAN YOU PULL A RECONNAISSANCE FLIGHT DOWN THERE SO WE KNOW WHAT TO EXPECT?
SCREW THAT! I'M NOT PART OF YOUR LITTLE SUPER CREW, CHRISTIAN.
THERE'S NO WAY WE'RE ALL GETTING OUT OF HERE. IT'S EVERY MAN FOR HIMSELF.
I CAN FLY WITH ONE OTHER PERSON IN MY PARTNER FIELD, WHO'S COMING?
TAKE ME, SIMON, PLEASE!
OKAY, LET'S GO, JESS--
PSIOT KILLER!
THE PSIOT KILLER'S HERE!
BEHIND US!
HE'S COME TO MURDER US ALL!

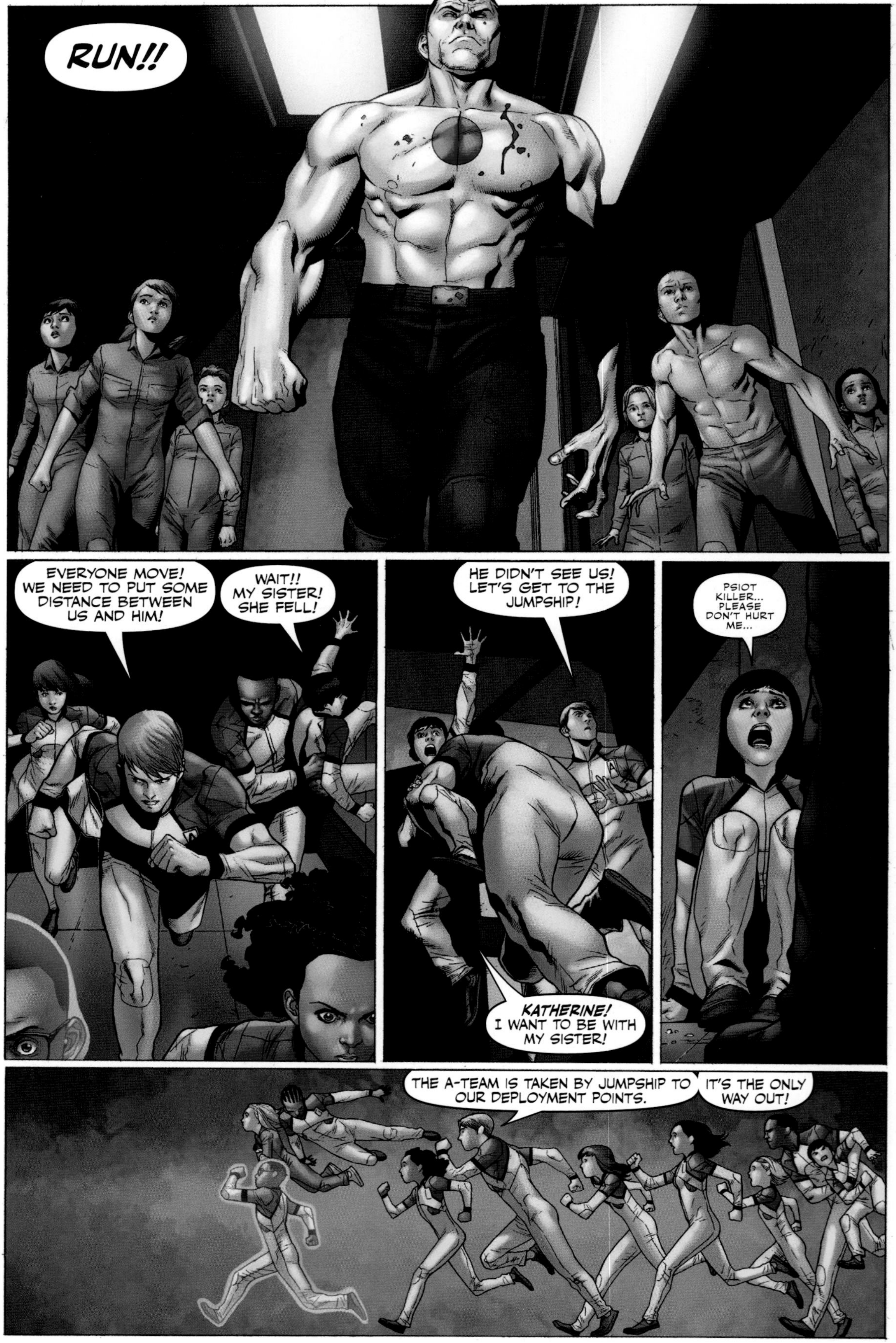
RUN!!
EVERYONE MOVE! WE NEED TO PUT SOME DISTANCE BETWEEN US AND HIM!
WAIT!! MY SISTER! SHE FELL!
HE DIDN'T SEE US! LET'S GET TO THE JUMPSHIP!
KATHERINE! I WANT TO BE WITH MY SISTER!
PSIOT KILLER... PLEASE DON'T HURT ME...
THE A-TEAM IS TAKEN BY JUMPSHIP TO OUR DEPLOYMENT POINTS.
IT'S THE ONLY WAY OUT!

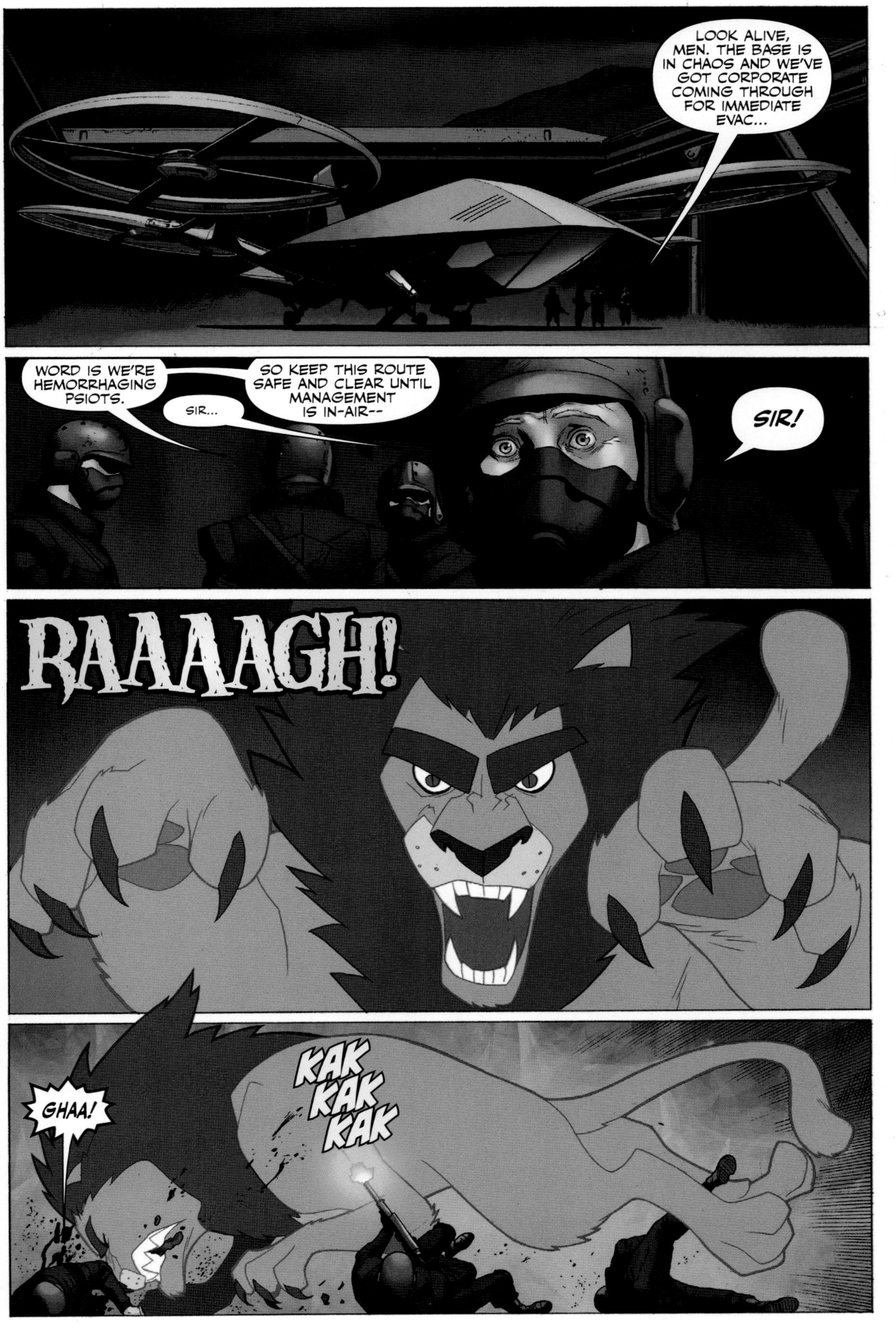
LOOK ALIVE, MEN. THE BASE IS IN CHAOS AND WE'VE GOT CORPORATE COMING THROUGH FOR IMMEDIATE EVAC...
WORD IS WE'RE HEMORRHAGING PSIOTS.
SO KEEP THIS ROUTE SAFE AND CLEAR UNTIL MANAGEMENT IS IN-AIR--
SIR...
SIR!
RAAAAGH!
GHAA!
KAK KAK KAK

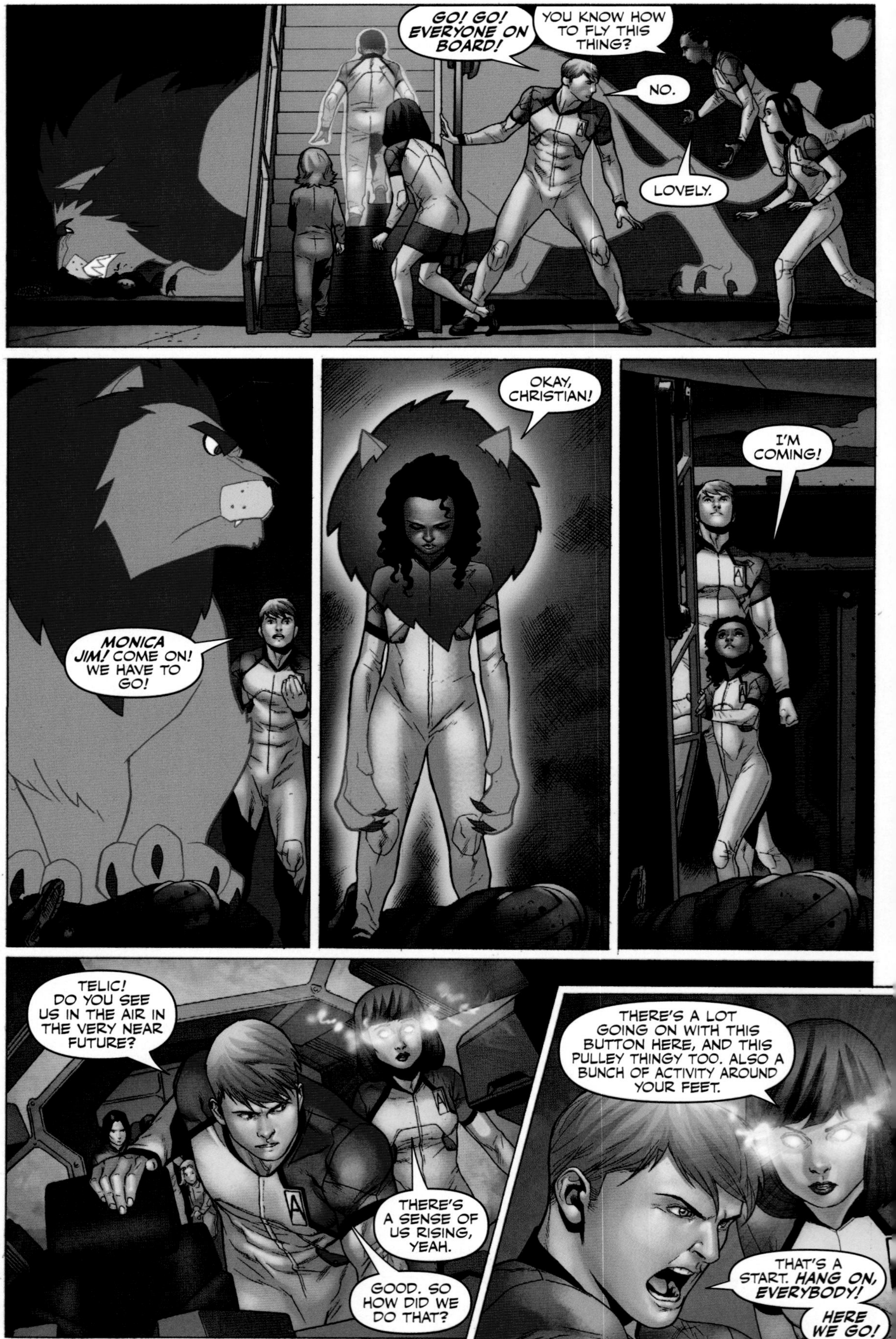
GO! GO! EVERYONE ON BOARD!
YOU KNOW HOW TO FLY THIS THING?
NO.
LOVELY.
MONICA JIM! COME ON! WE HAVE TO GO!
OKAY, CHRISTIAN!
I'M COMING!
TELIC! DO YOU SEE US IN THE AIR IN THE VERY NEAR FUTURE?
THERE'S A SENSE OF US RISING, YEAH.
GOOD. SO HOW DID WE DO THAT?
THERE'S A LOT GOING ON WITH THIS BUTTON HERE, AND THIS PULLEY THINGY TOO. ALSO A BUNCH OF ACTIVITY AROUND YOUR FEET.
THAT'S A START. HANG ON, EVERYBODY!
HERE WE GO!

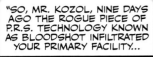

"SO, MR. KOZOL, NINE DAYS AGO THE ROGUE PIECE OF P.R.S. TECHNOLOGY KNOWN AS BLOODSHOT INFILTRATED YOUR PRIMARY FACILITY..."

FFFFFFFFF

"WHERE HE MANAGED TO COMPROMISE YOUR SECURITY SYSTEMS AND BYPASS YOUR SPECIALIZED PERSONNEL..."

"WHICH ENABLED THE ESCAPE OF ALL YOUR ACTIVATED PSIOTS."

CHRISTIAN! THE *ZYGOS TWIN* IS FREAKING OUT!

NO! NO! MY *BROTHER!!!* HE'S LEAVING ME!!

HEY! I NEED YOU TO SETTLE DOWN, KID!

"YOU EVEN ALLOWED BLOODSHOT HIMSELF TO LEAVE THE BASE WITH SOME OF THESE DANGEROUS CHILDREN UNDER HIS OWN CARE..."

LISTEN TO ME! I'M NOT GOING TO HURT YOU.

I PROMISE. YOU'RE SAFE WITH ME.

"DOES THAT ABOUT SUM IT UP, MR. KOZOL?"

YOU'RE ALL SAFE WITH ME.

I'M NOT WHAT YOU THINK I AM.

YES, SIR. THAT'S AN ACCURATE ASSESSMENT OF THE INSTIGATING INCIDENT, DIRECTOR.

THIS LEADS US TO BELIEVE YOUR SECURITY WAS EXTREMELY LACKING.

YOUR STATEMENT LEADS ME TO BELIEVE YOU'VE NO IDEA HOW EFFECTIVE BLOODSHOT IS.

AND TOYO HARADA? HOW DOES HE FIT INTO THIS?

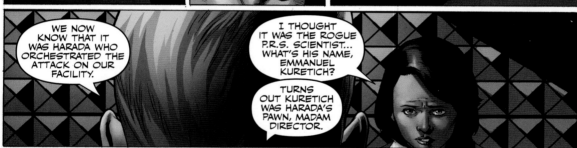

WE NOW KNOW THAT IT WAS HARADA WHO ORCHESTRATED THE ATTACK ON OUR FACILITY.

I THOUGHT IT WAS THE ROGUE P.R.S. SCIENTIST... WHAT'S HIS NAME, EMMANUEL KURETICH?

TURNS OUT KURETICH WAS HARADA'S PAWN, MADAM DIRECTOR.

"SEVERAL MONTHS AGO HARADA SENT ONE OF HIS HARBINGER FOUNDATION STUDENTS TO THE MIDDLE EAST TO BAIT US.

"UNFORTUNATELY, WE BIT AND DEPLOYED BLOODSHOT TO THE LOCATION.

"BY USING KURETICH, HARADA WAS ABLE TO TAKE BLOODSHOT OFFLINE AND TURN HIM AGAINST US."

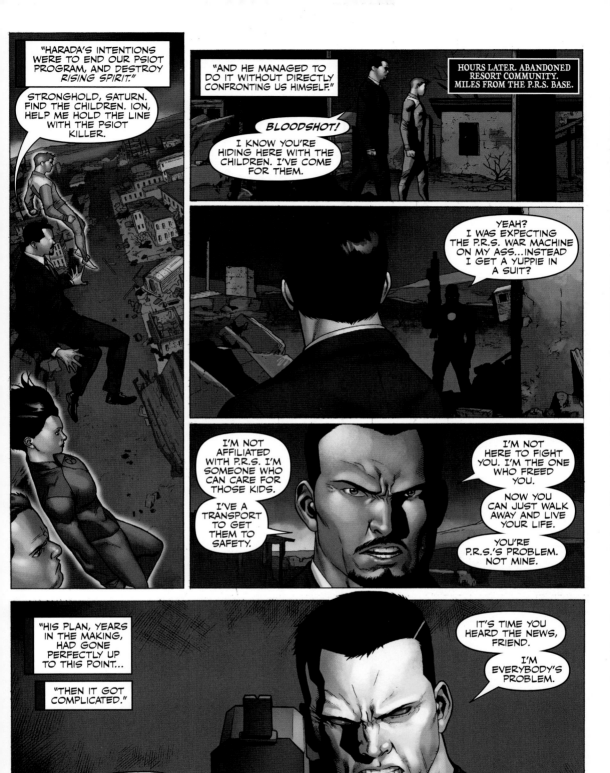

"HARADA'S INTENTIONS WERE TO END OUR PSIOT PROGRAM, AND DESTROY *RISING SPIRIT*."

STRONGHOLD, SATURN. FIND THE CHILDREN. ION, HELP ME HOLD THE LINE WITH THE PSIOT KILLER.

"AND HE MANAGED TO DO IT WITHOUT DIRECTLY CONFRONTING US HIMSELF."

HOURS LATER. ABANDONED RESORT COMMUNITY. MILES FROM THE P.R.S. BASE.

BLOODSHOT! I KNOW YOU'RE HIDING HERE WITH THE CHILDREN. I'VE COME FOR THEM.

YEAH? I WAS EXPECTING THE P.R.S. WAR MACHINE ON MY ASS...INSTEAD I GET A YUPPIE IN A SUIT?

I'M NOT AFFILIATED WITH P.R.S. I'M SOMEONE WHO CAN CARE FOR THOSE KIDS.

I'VE A TRANSPORT TO GET THEM TO SAFETY.

I'M NOT HERE TO FIGHT YOU. I'M THE ONE WHO FREED YOU.

NOW YOU CAN JUST WALK AWAY AND LIVE YOUR LIFE.

YOU'RE P.R.S.'S PROBLEM. NOT MINE.

"HIS PLAN, YEARS IN THE MAKING, HAD GONE PERFECTLY UP TO THIS POINT...

"THEN IT GOT COMPLICATED."

IT'S TIME YOU HEARD THE NEWS, FRIEND.

I'M EVERYBODY'S PROBLEM.

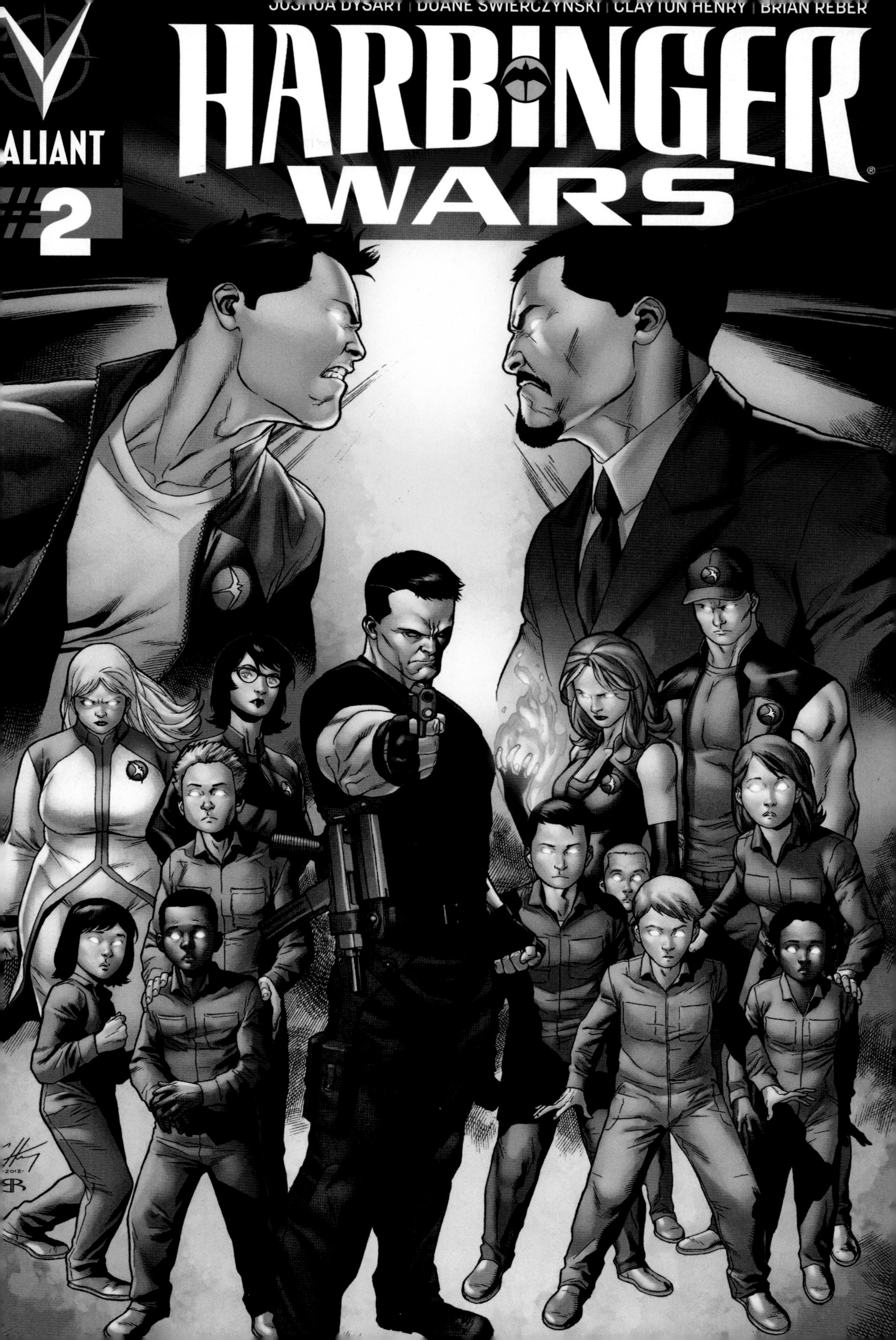

JOSHUA DYSART | DUANE SWIERCZYNSKI | CLAYTON HENRY | BRIAN REBER
VALIANT
HARBINGER WARS
#2

HARBINGER WARS

Project Rising Spirit created **Bloodshot** to be the perfect weapon. They infused him with nanites that provided him with an extraordinary array of powers, allowing him to accomplish missions with lethal accuracy. He was frequently sent to capture super-powered individuals known as **psiots**, many of them children. However, **Bloodshot** freed himself from his programming and turned on his masters, assaulting the P.R.S. facility where many of the psiots were held. During the conflagration, **Bloodshot** liberated many psiots, but the children were separated into two groups amid the chaos. One is led by **Bloodshot**, who has led them to an abandoned town in the Nevada desert. A second group – led by a psiot named **Cronus** and calling themselves **Generation Zero** – has taken over the Bellagio in Las Vegas.

Project Rising Spirit, however, want the psiots back, and they aren't the only ones. **Toyo Harada** – leader of the **Harbinger Foundation**, which trains psiots for a private army, has led a team of his top soldiers to confront **Bloodshot** in the ghost town.

Meanwhile, **Peter Stancheck** – a former Harada pupil who had a falling-out with his would-be mentor – has been sent by the enigmatic precog known as the **Bleeding Monk** to save the children. He leads his **Renegades** on a mission to recover them...

THE RENEGADES

Leader
- **Peter Stanchek** – *Troubled youth in possession of vast telepathic and telekinetic powers*

Members
- **Torque** – *A disabled young man now blessed with an immensely strong body thanks to the psychic projection he surrounds himself with*
- **Flamingo** – *Beautiful firestarter that can create and control flame*
- **Kris** – *A non-psiot and brilliant team tactician*
- **Zephyr** – *The heart of the team with the ability to fly*

Peter Stanchek **Torque** **Flamingo** **Kris** **Zephyr**

THE HARBINGER FOUNDATION

Leader
- **Toyo Harada** – *Billionaire founder of the Harbinger Foundation in possession of vast telepathic and telekinetic powers*

Members
- **Ion** – *Can produce and control electricity*
- **Stronghold** – *Is able to gather kinetic energy and then expel it with tremendous force*
- **Saturn** – *Possesses the ability to create and control powerful tornadoes and cyclones*

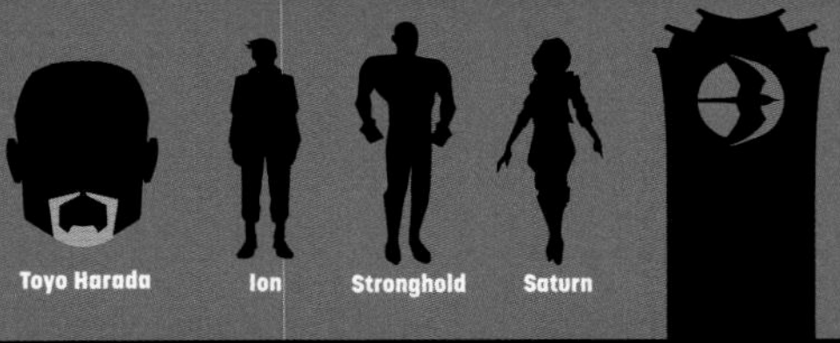

Toyo Harada **Ion** **Stronghold** **Saturn**

BLOODSHOT & ESCAPED PSIOTS

Leader
- **Bloodshot** – *The perfect soldier. His bloodstream is infused with nanite technology giving him a range of post-human abilities*

Members
- **Clem** – *Can control the minds of living beings*
- **Cloud** – *Obscures peoples' thoughts, allowing Clem to take them over*
- **Serenade** – *Is able to manipulate the emotions of others via pheromone emission*
- **Ramsey** – *Possesses the ability to control and manipulate hard light objects*
- **Graham** – *Can psychically project a father, mother, and sister that appear real to onlookers*
- **Baxter** – *Is able to unleash a terrifying monster conjured from deep within his imagination*
- **Katherine** – *Holds a powerful telepathic link with her brother, James*
- **Maggie** – *Powers unknown*

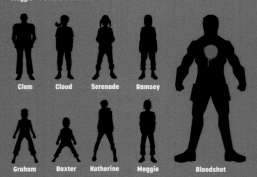

Clem **Cloud** **Serenade** **Ramsey**
Graham **Baxter** **Katherine** **Maggie** **Bloodshot**

GENERATION ZERO

Leader
- **Cronus** – *Militant leader of Generation Zero. Possesses vast healing abilities that can be used to destroy cells as well*

Members
- **The Telic** – *Possesses precognitive abilities, allowing her to see into the immediate future*
- **Traveler** – *Can teleport by quickly slipping into and out of an unknown space*
- **Isiah** – *Projects an impenetrable shield around himself at all times*
- **Hive** – *Can absorb the thoughts and memories of others, storing them in his mind*
- **Astral** – *Can project her consciousness outside of her own body*
- **Atomus** – *An extremely fast flyer*
- **James** – *Holds a powerful telepathic link with his sister, Katherine*
- **Howl** – *Ability to raise the dead*
- **Eliphas** – *Can mimic any power, talent, or ability that he sees*

Cronus **The Telic** **Traveler** **Isiah** **Hive**
Astral **Atomus** **James** **Howl** **Eliphas**

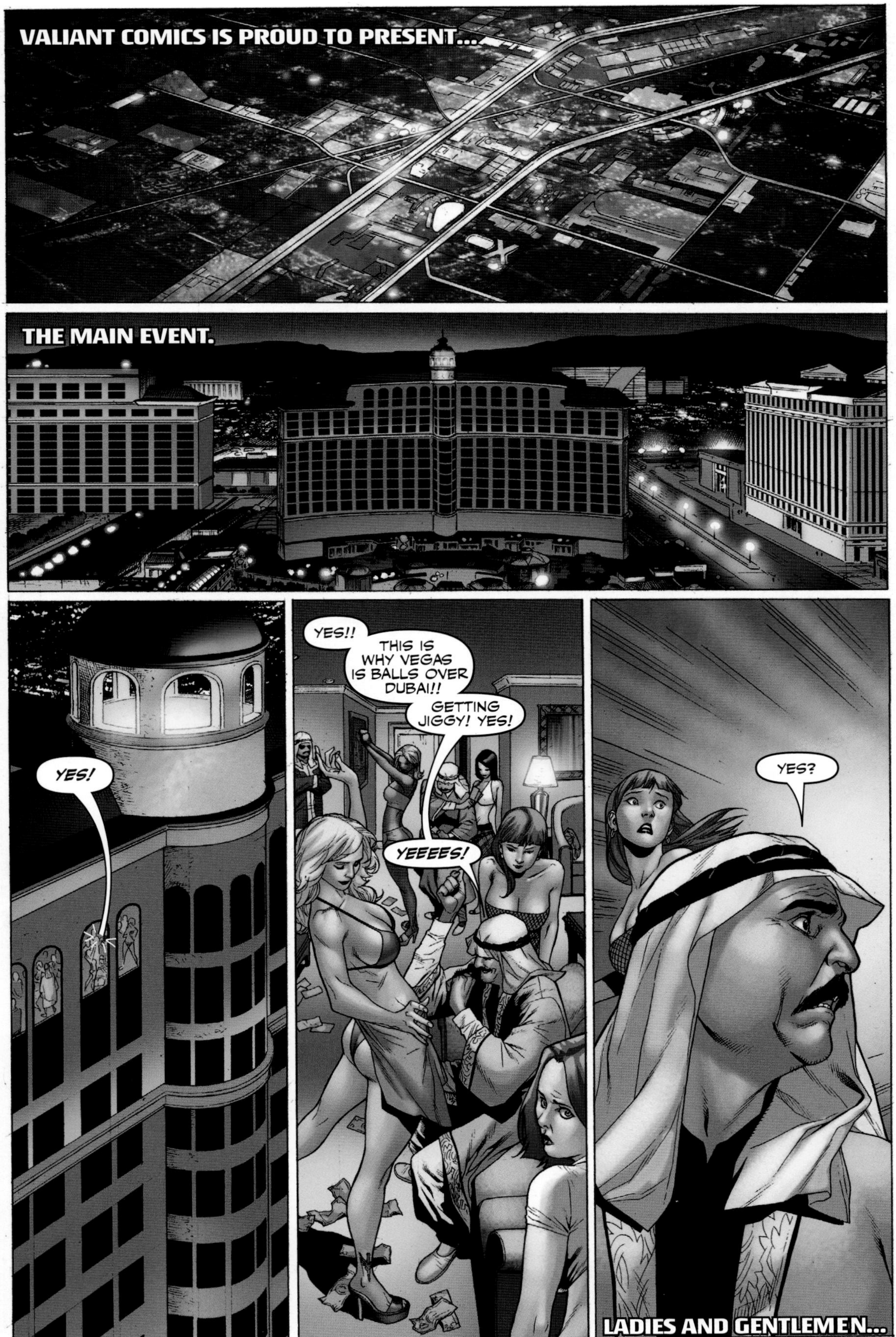
VALIANT COMICS IS PROUD TO PRESENT...
THE MAIN EVENT.
YES!
YES!!
THIS IS WHY VEGAS IS BALLS OVER DUBAI!!
GETTING JIGGY! YES!
YEEEES!
YES?
LADIES AND GENTLEMEN...

LET'S GET READY TO
RUUUUMBLE...

NO.

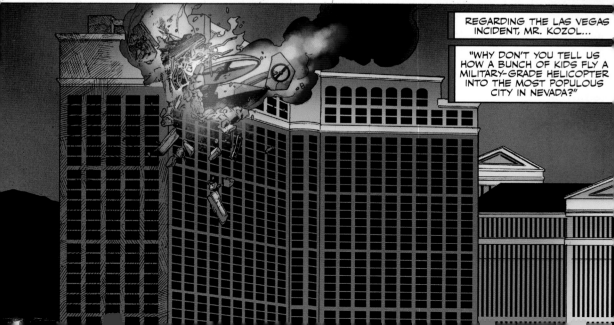

REGARDING THE LAS VEGAS
INCIDENT, MR. KOZOL...

"WHY DON'T YOU TELL US
HOW A BUNCH OF KIDS FLY A
MILITARY-GRADE HELICOPTER
INTO THE MOST POPULOUS
CITY IN NEVADA?"

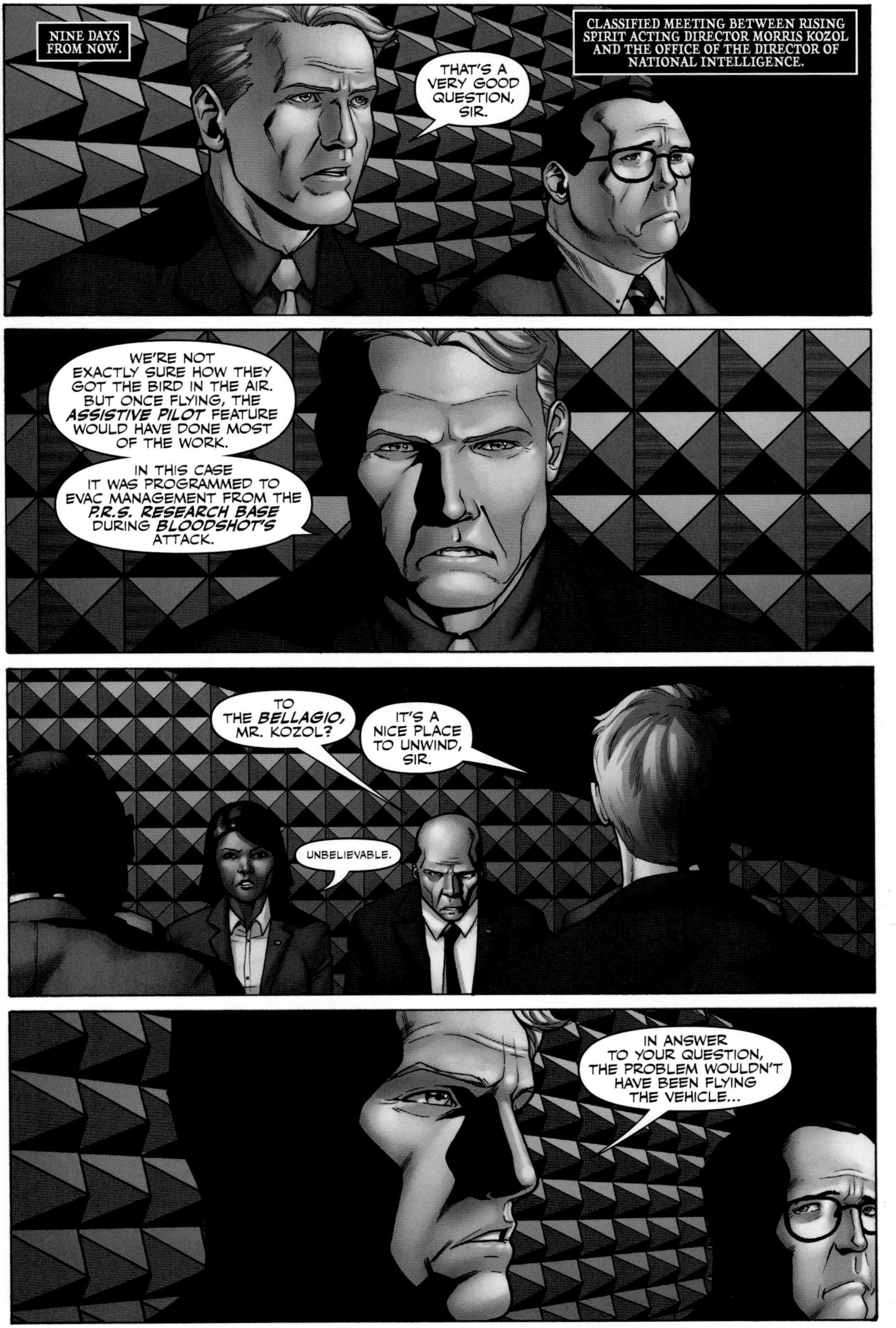
NINE DAYS FROM NOW.
CLASSIFIED MEETING BETWEEN RISING SPIRIT ACTING DIRECTOR MORRIS KOZOL AND THE OFFICE OF THE DIRECTOR OF NATIONAL INTELLIGENCE.
THAT'S A VERY GOOD QUESTION, SIR.
WE'RE NOT EXACTLY SURE HOW THEY GOT THE BIRD IN THE AIR. BUT ONCE FLYING, THE *ASSISTIVE PILOT* FEATURE WOULD HAVE DONE MOST OF THE WORK.
IN THIS CASE IT WAS PROGRAMMED TO EVAC MANAGEMENT FROM THE *P.R.S. RESEARCH BASE* DURING *BLOODSHOT'S* ATTACK.
TO THE *BELLAGIO*, MR. KOZOL?
IT'S A NICE PLACE TO UNWIND, SIR.
UNBELIEVABLE.
IN ANSWER TO YOUR QUESTION, THE PROBLEM WOULDN'T HAVE BEEN FLYING THE VEHICLE...

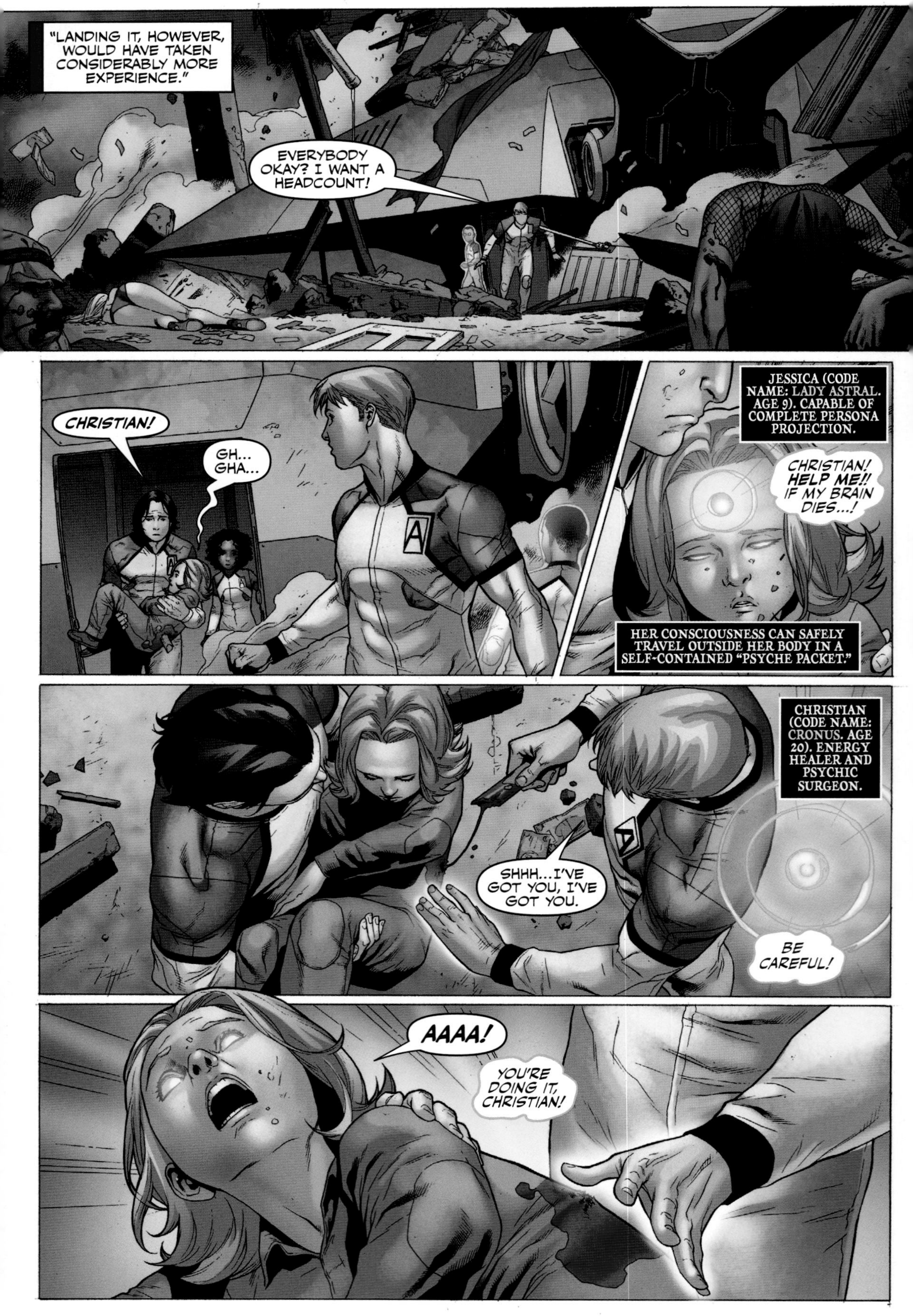
"LANDING IT, HOWEVER, WOULD HAVE TAKEN CONSIDERABLY MORE EXPERIENCE."
EVERYBODY OKAY? I WANT A HEADCOUNT!
CHRISTIAN!
GH... GHA...
JESSICA (CODE NAME: LADY ASTRAL. AGE 9). CAPABLE OF COMPLETE PERSONA PROJECTION.
CHRISTIAN! HELP ME!! IF MY BRAIN DIES...!
HER CONSCIOUSNESS CAN SAFELY TRAVEL OUTSIDE HER BODY IN A SELF-CONTAINED "PSYCHE PACKET."
CHRISTIAN (CODE NAME: CRONUS. AGE 20). ENERGY HEALER AND PSYCHIC SURGEON.
SHHH...I'VE GOT YOU, I'VE GOT YOU.
BE CAREFUL!
AAAA!
YOU'RE DOING IT, CHRISTIAN!

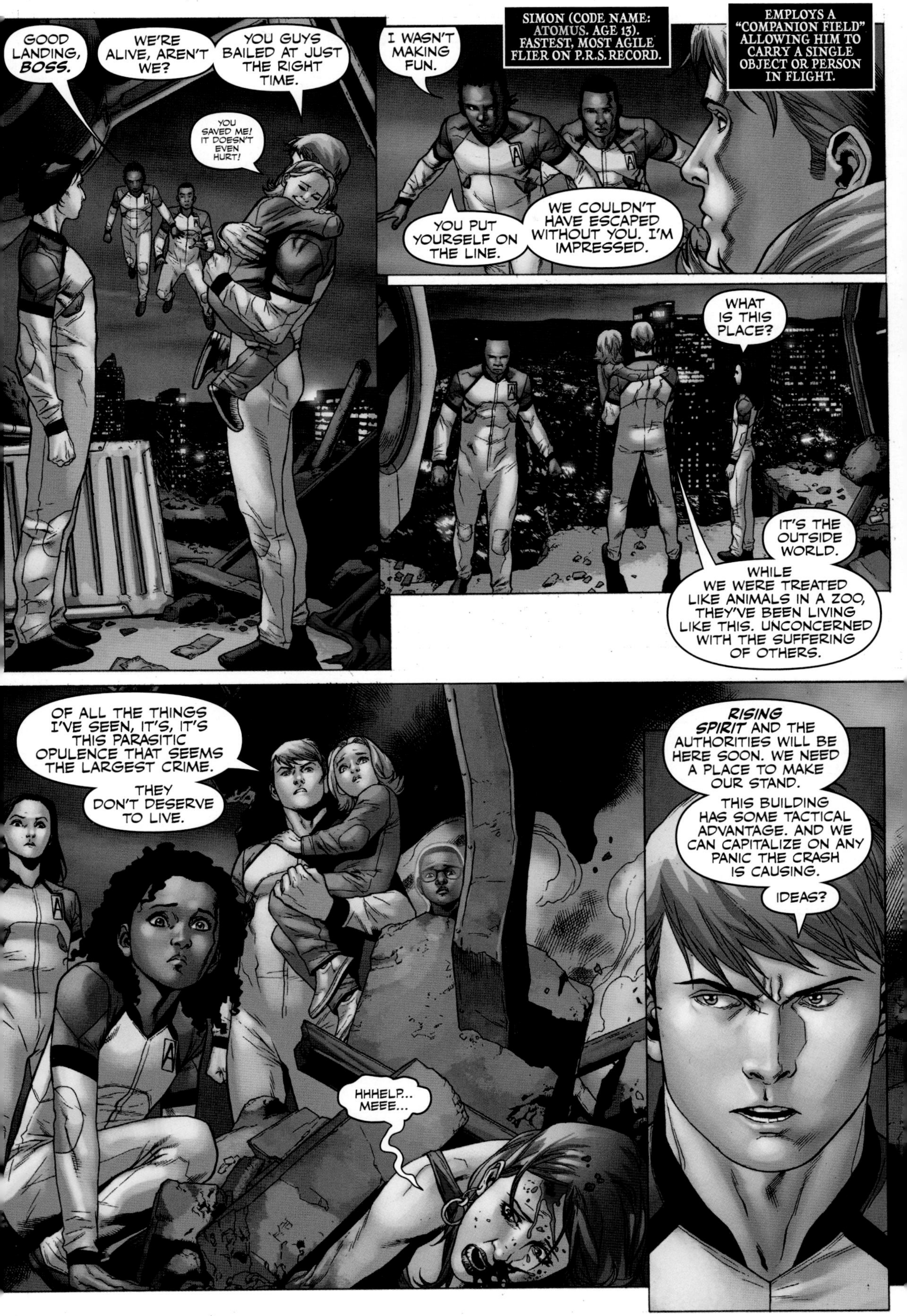
GOOD LANDING, *BOSS.*
WE'RE ALIVE, AREN'T WE?
YOU GUYS BAILED AT JUST THE RIGHT TIME.
YOU SAVED ME! IT DOESN'T EVEN HURT!
I WASN'T MAKING FUN.
SIMON (CODE NAME: ATOMUS. AGE 13). FASTEST, MOST AGILE FLIER ON P.R.S. RECORD.
EMPLOYS A "COMPANION FIELD" ALLOWING HIM TO CARRY A SINGLE OBJECT OR PERSON IN FLIGHT.
YOU PUT YOURSELF ON THE LINE.
WE COULDN'T HAVE ESCAPED WITHOUT YOU. I'M IMPRESSED.
WHAT IS THIS PLACE?
IT'S THE OUTSIDE WORLD.
WHILE WE WERE TREATED LIKE ANIMALS IN A ZOO, THEY'VE BEEN LIVING LIKE THIS. UNCONCERNED WITH THE SUFFERING OF OTHERS.
OF ALL THE THINGS I'VE SEEN, IT'S, IT'S THIS PARASITIC OPULENCE THAT SEEMS THE LARGEST CRIME.
THEY DON'T DESERVE TO LIVE.
RISING SPIRIT AND THE AUTHORITIES WILL BE HERE SOON. WE NEED A PLACE TO MAKE OUR STAND.
THIS BUILDING HAS SOME TACTICAL ADVANTAGE. AND WE CAN CAPITALIZE ON ANY PANIC THE CRASH IS CAUSING.
IDEAS?
HHHELP... MEEE...

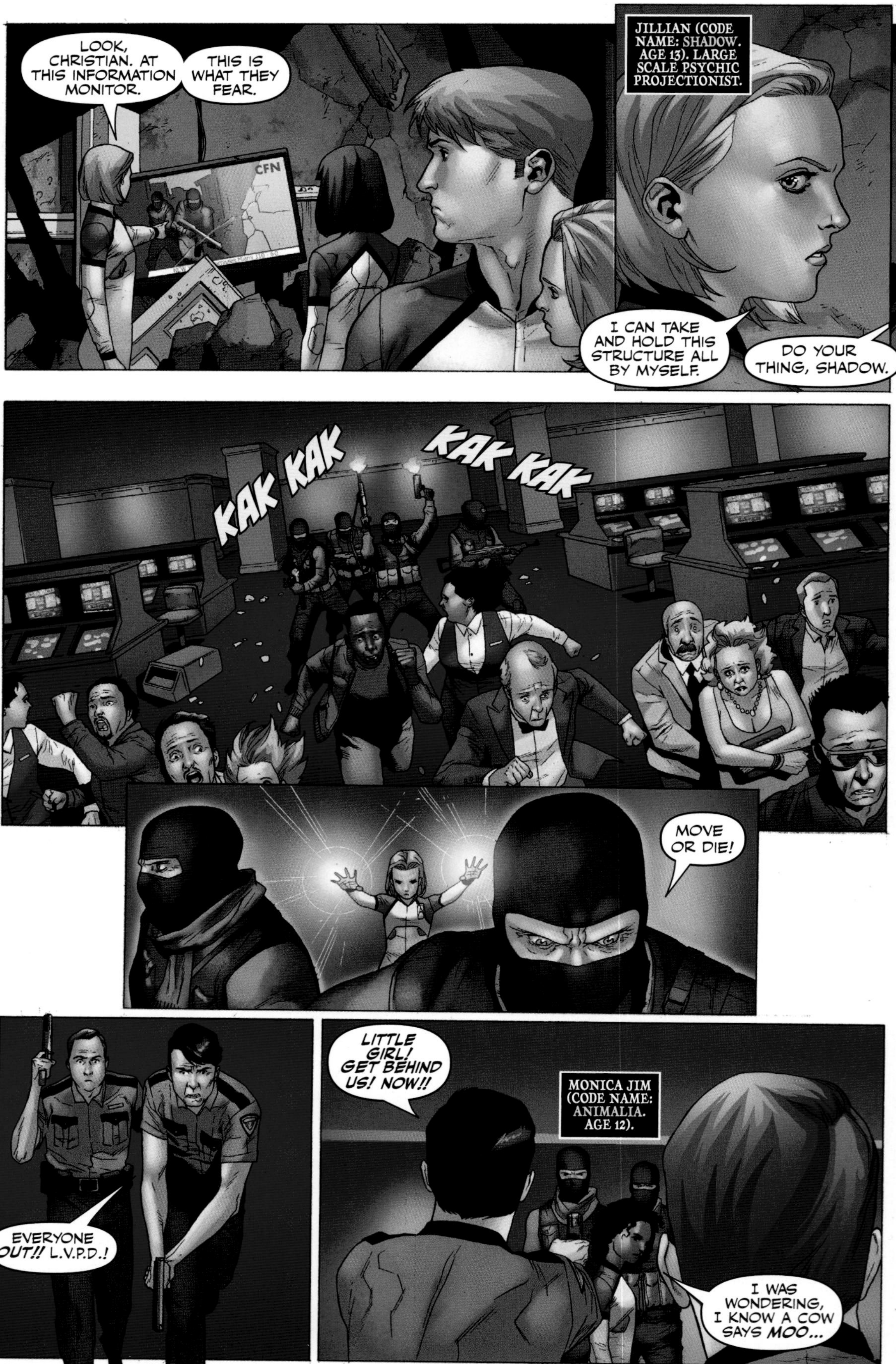
LOOK, CHRISTIAN. AT THIS INFORMATION MONITOR.
THIS IS WHAT THEY FEAR.
CFN
JILLIAN (CODE NAME: SHADOW. AGE 13). LARGE SCALE PSYCHIC PROJECTIONIST.
I CAN TAKE AND HOLD THIS STRUCTURE ALL BY MYSELF.
DO YOUR THING, SHADOW.
KAK KAK
KAK KAK
MOVE OR DIE!
EVERYONE OUT!! L.V.P.D.!
LITTLE GIRL! GET BEHIND US! NOW!!
MONICA JIM (CODE NAME: ANIMALIA. AGE 12).
I WAS WONDERING, I KNOW A COW SAYS MOO...

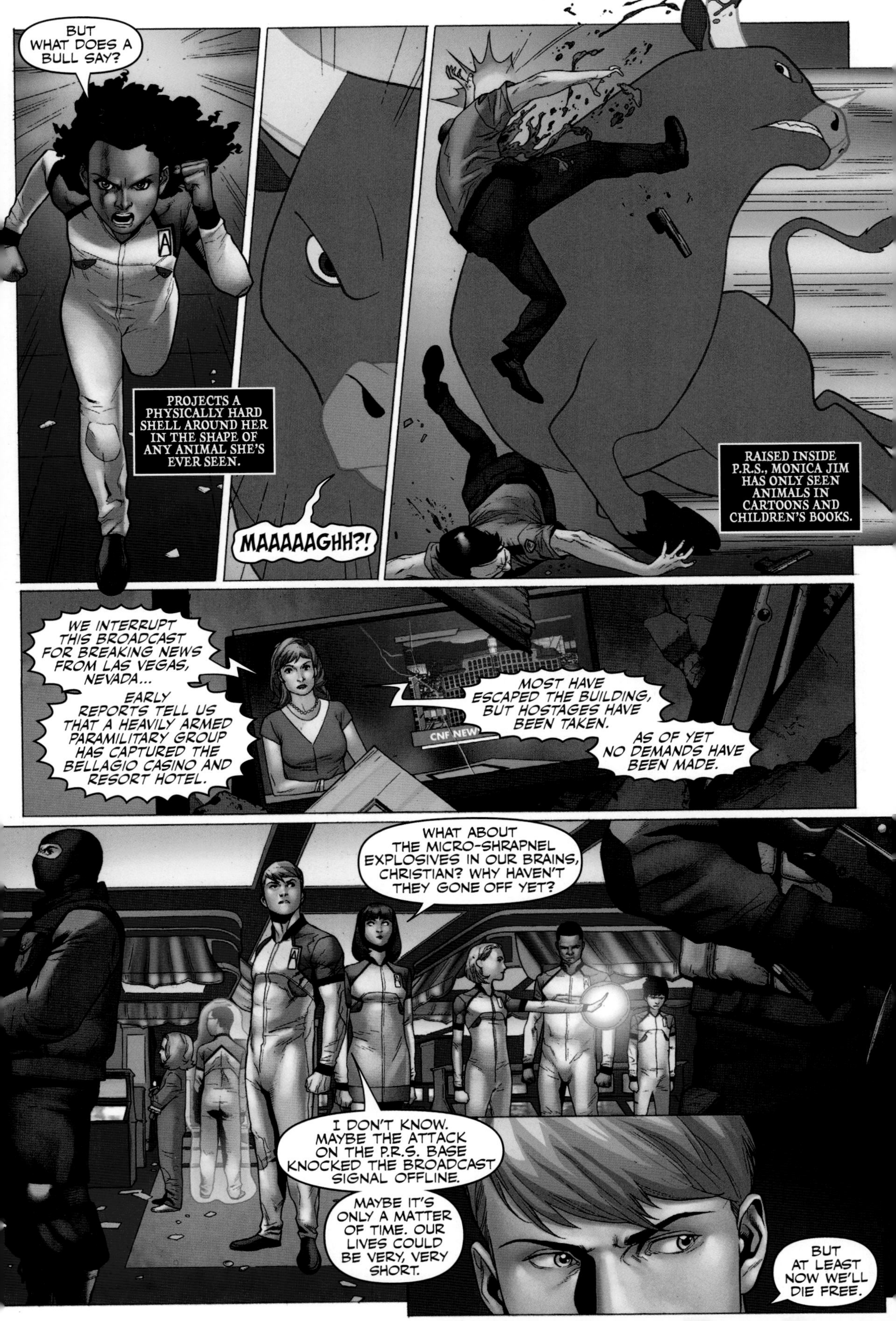

BUT WHAT DOES A BULL SAY?
PROJECTS A PHYSICALLY HARD SHELL AROUND HER IN THE SHAPE OF ANY ANIMAL SHE'S EVER SEEN.
MAAAAAGHH?!
RAISED INSIDE P.R.S., MONICA JIM HAS ONLY SEEN ANIMALS IN CARTOONS AND CHILDREN'S BOOKS.
WE INTERRUPT THIS BROADCAST FOR BREAKING NEWS FROM LAS VEGAS, NEVADA...
EARLY REPORTS TELL US THAT A HEAVILY ARMED PARAMILITARY GROUP HAS CAPTURED THE BELLAGIO CASINO AND RESORT HOTEL.
MOST HAVE ESCAPED THE BUILDING, BUT HOSTAGES HAVE BEEN TAKEN.
AS OF YET NO DEMANDS HAVE BEEN MADE.
WHAT ABOUT THE MICRO-SHRAPNEL EXPLOSIVES IN OUR BRAINS, CHRISTIAN? WHY HAVEN'T THEY GONE OFF YET?
I DON'T KNOW. MAYBE THE ATTACK ON THE P.R.S. BASE KNOCKED THE BROADCAST SIGNAL OFFLINE.
MAYBE IT'S ONLY A MATTER OF TIME. OUR LIVES COULD BE VERY, VERY SHORT.
BUT AT LEAST NOW WE'LL DIE FREE.

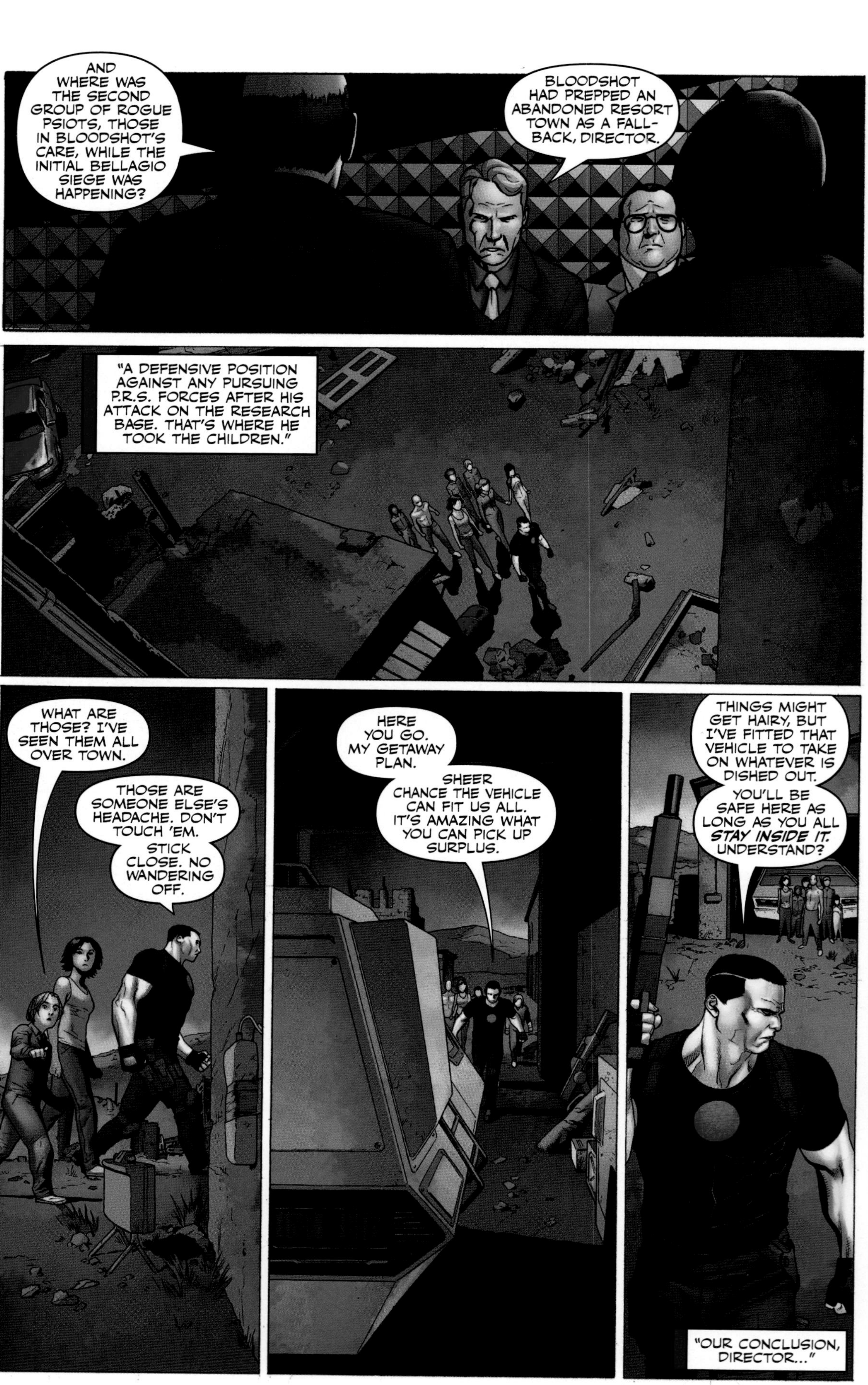

AND WHERE WAS THE SECOND GROUP OF ROGUE PSIOTS, THOSE IN BLOODSHOT'S CARE, WHILE THE INITIAL BELLAGIO SIEGE WAS HAPPENING?
BLOODSHOT HAD PREPPED AN ABANDONED RESORT TOWN AS A FALL-BACK, DIRECTOR.
"A DEFENSIVE POSITION AGAINST ANY PURSUING P.R.S. FORCES AFTER HIS ATTACK ON THE RESEARCH BASE. THAT'S WHERE HE TOOK THE CHILDREN."
WHAT ARE THOSE? I'VE SEEN THEM ALL OVER TOWN.
THOSE ARE SOMEONE ELSE'S HEADACHE. DON'T TOUCH 'EM.
STICK CLOSE. NO WANDERING OFF.
HERE YOU GO. MY GETAWAY PLAN.
SHEER CHANCE THE VEHICLE CAN FIT US ALL. IT'S AMAZING WHAT YOU CAN PICK UP SURPLUS.
THINGS MIGHT GET HAIRY, BUT I'VE FITTED THAT VEHICLE TO TAKE ON WHATEVER IS DISHED OUT.
YOU'LL BE SAFE HERE AS LONG AS YOU ALL ***STAY INSIDE IT.*** UNDERSTAND?
"OUR CONCLUSION, DIRECTOR..."

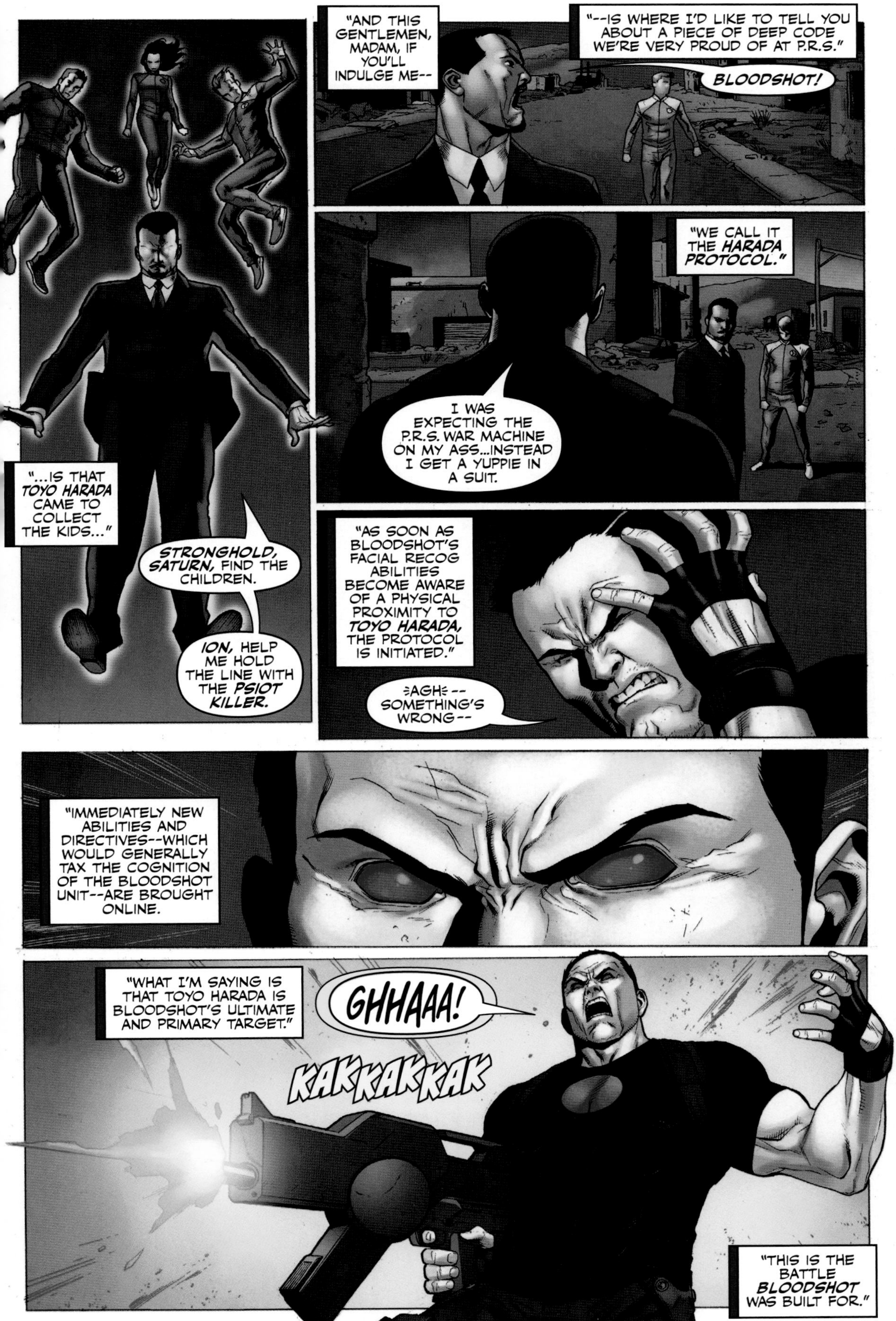
"...IS THAT TOYO HARADA CAME TO COLLECT THE KIDS..."
STRONGHOLD, SATURN, FIND THE CHILDREN.
ION, HELP ME HOLD THE LINE WITH THE PSIOT KILLER.
"AND THIS GENTLEMEN, MADAM, IF YOU'LL INDULGE ME--
"--IS WHERE I'D LIKE TO TELL YOU ABOUT A PIECE OF DEEP CODE WE'RE VERY PROUD OF AT P.R.S."
BLOODSHOT!
"WE CALL IT THE HARADA PROTOCOL."
I WAS EXPECTING THE P.R.S. WAR MACHINE ON MY ASS...INSTEAD I GET A YUPPIE IN A SUIT.
"AS SOON AS BLOODSHOT'S FACIAL RECOG ABILITIES BECOME AWARE OF A PHYSICAL PROXIMITY TO TOYO HARADA, THE PROTOCOL IS INITIATED."
AGH-- SOMETHING'S WRONG--
"IMMEDIATELY NEW ABILITIES AND DIRECTIVES--WHICH WOULD GENERALLY TAX THE COGNITION OF THE BLOODSHOT UNIT--ARE BROUGHT ONLINE.
"WHAT I'M SAYING IS THAT TOYO HARADA IS BLOODSHOT'S ULTIMATE AND PRIMARY TARGET."
GHHAAA!
KAKKAKKAK
"THIS IS THE BATTLE BLOODSHOT WAS BUILT FOR."

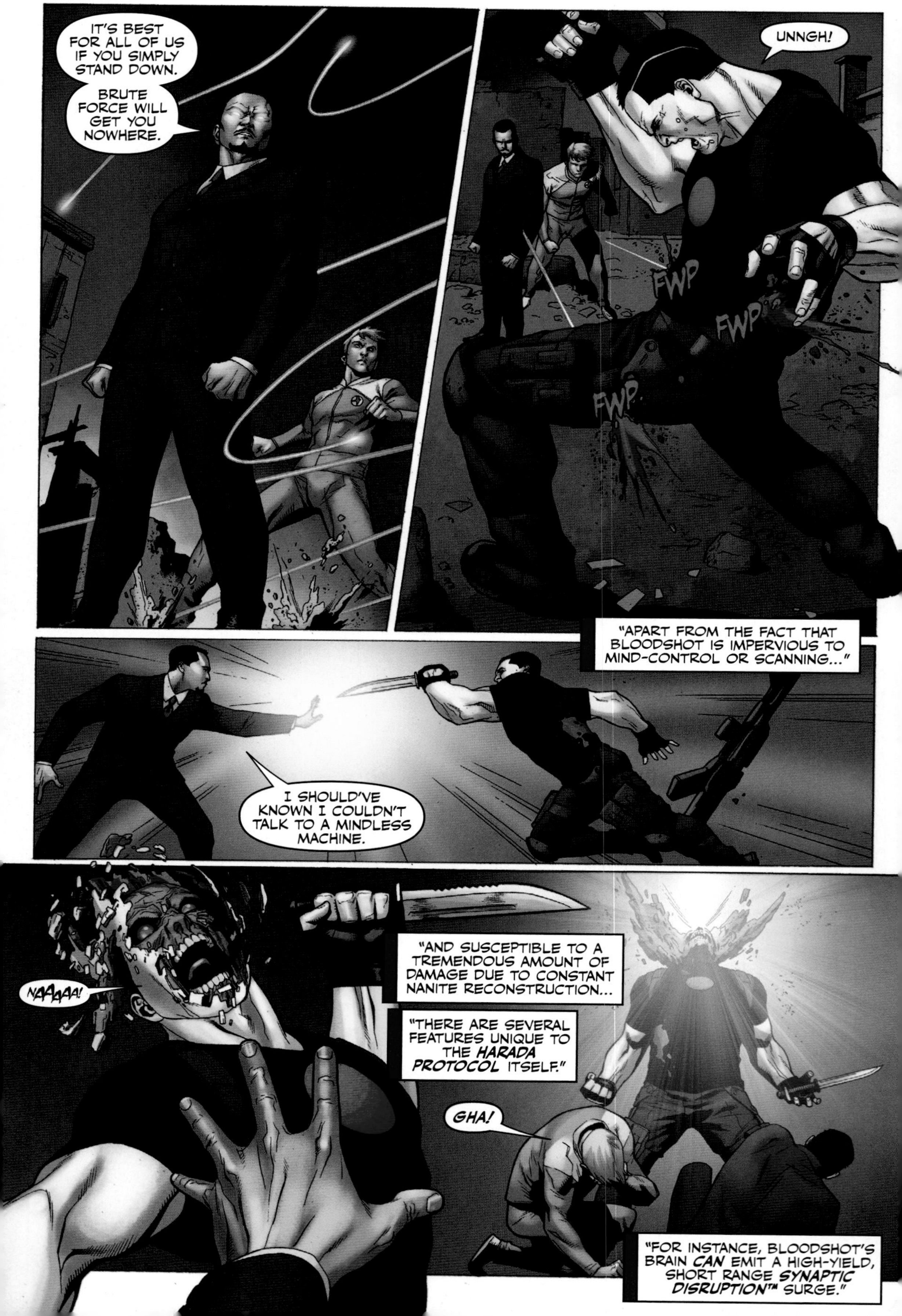
IT'S BEST FOR ALL OF US IF YOU SIMPLY STAND DOWN.
BRUTE FORCE WILL GET YOU NOWHERE.
UNNGH!
FWP
FWP
FWP
"APART FROM THE FACT THAT BLOODSHOT IS IMPERVIOUS TO MIND-CONTROL OR SCANNING..."
I SHOULD'VE KNOWN I COULDN'T TALK TO A MINDLESS MACHINE.
NAAAAA!
"AND SUSCEPTIBLE TO A TREMENDOUS AMOUNT OF DAMAGE DUE TO CONSTANT NANITE RECONSTRUCTION...
"THERE ARE SEVERAL FEATURES UNIQUE TO THE HARADA PROTOCOL ITSELF."
GHA!
"FOR INSTANCE, BLOODSHOT'S BRAIN CAN EMIT A HIGH-YIELD, SHORT RANGE SYNAPTIC DISRUPTION™ SURGE."

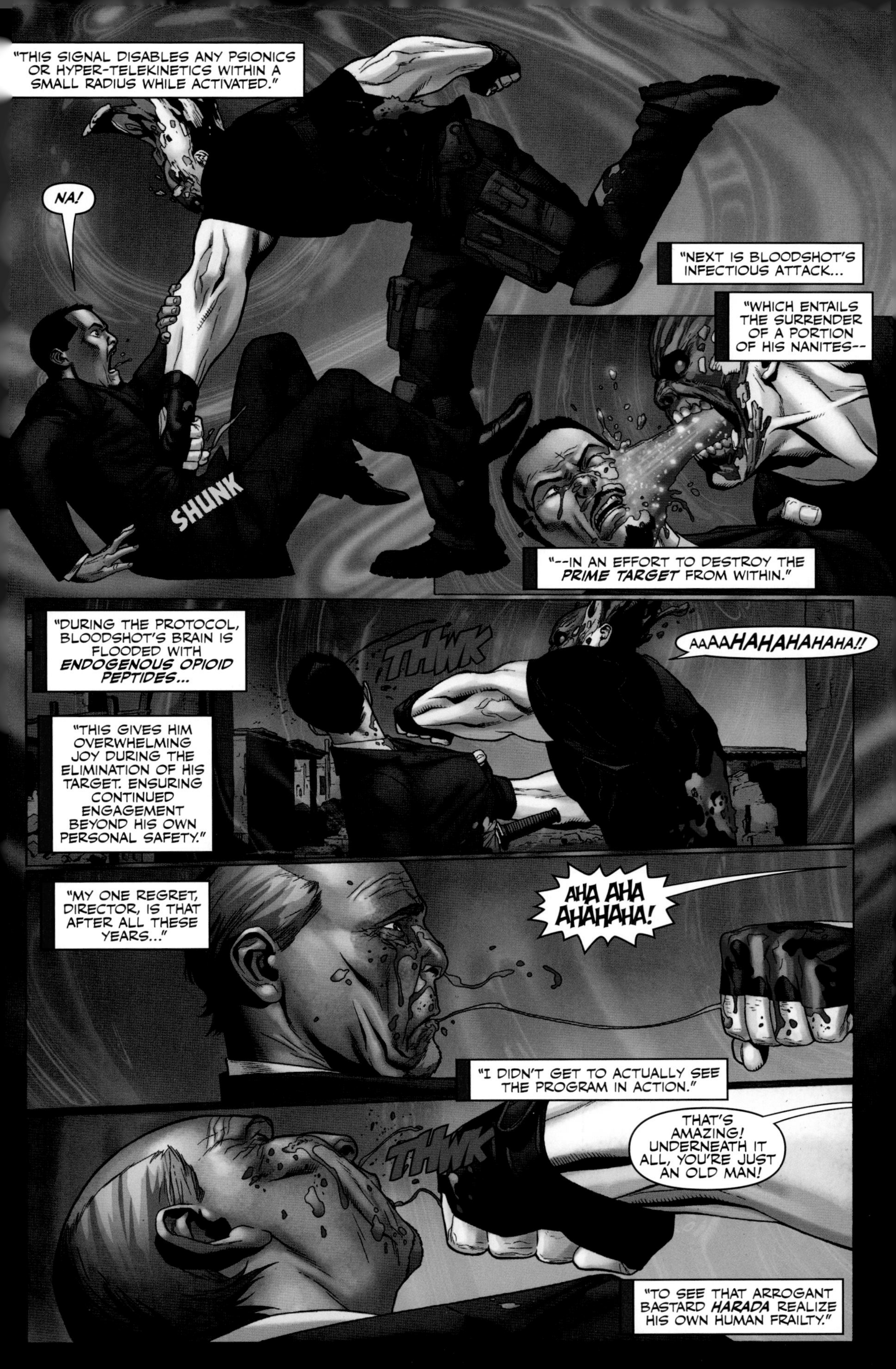
"THIS SIGNAL DISABLES ANY PSIONICS OR HYPER-TELEKINETICS WITHIN A SMALL RADIUS WHILE ACTIVATED."
NA!
SHUNK
"NEXT IS BLOODSHOT'S INFECTIOUS ATTACK...
"WHICH ENTAILS THE SURRENDER OF A PORTION OF HIS NANITES--
"--IN AN EFFORT TO DESTROY THE *PRIME TARGET* FROM WITHIN."
"DURING THE PROTOCOL, BLOODSHOT'S BRAIN IS FLOODED WITH *ENDOGENOUS OPIOID PEPTIDES*...
THWK
AAAAHAHAHAHAHA!!
"THIS GIVES HIM OVERWHELMING JOY DURING THE ELIMINATION OF HIS TARGET. ENSURING CONTINUED ENGAGEMENT BEYOND HIS OWN PERSONAL SAFETY."
"MY ONE REGRET, DIRECTOR, IS THAT AFTER ALL THESE YEARS..."
AHA AHA AHAHAHA!
"I DIDN'T GET TO ACTUALLY SEE THE PROGRAM IN ACTION."
THWK
THAT'S AMAZING! UNDERNEATH IT ALL, YOU'RE JUST AN OLD MAN!
"TO SEE THAT ARROGANT BASTARD *HARADA* REALIZE HIS OWN HUMAN FRAILTY."

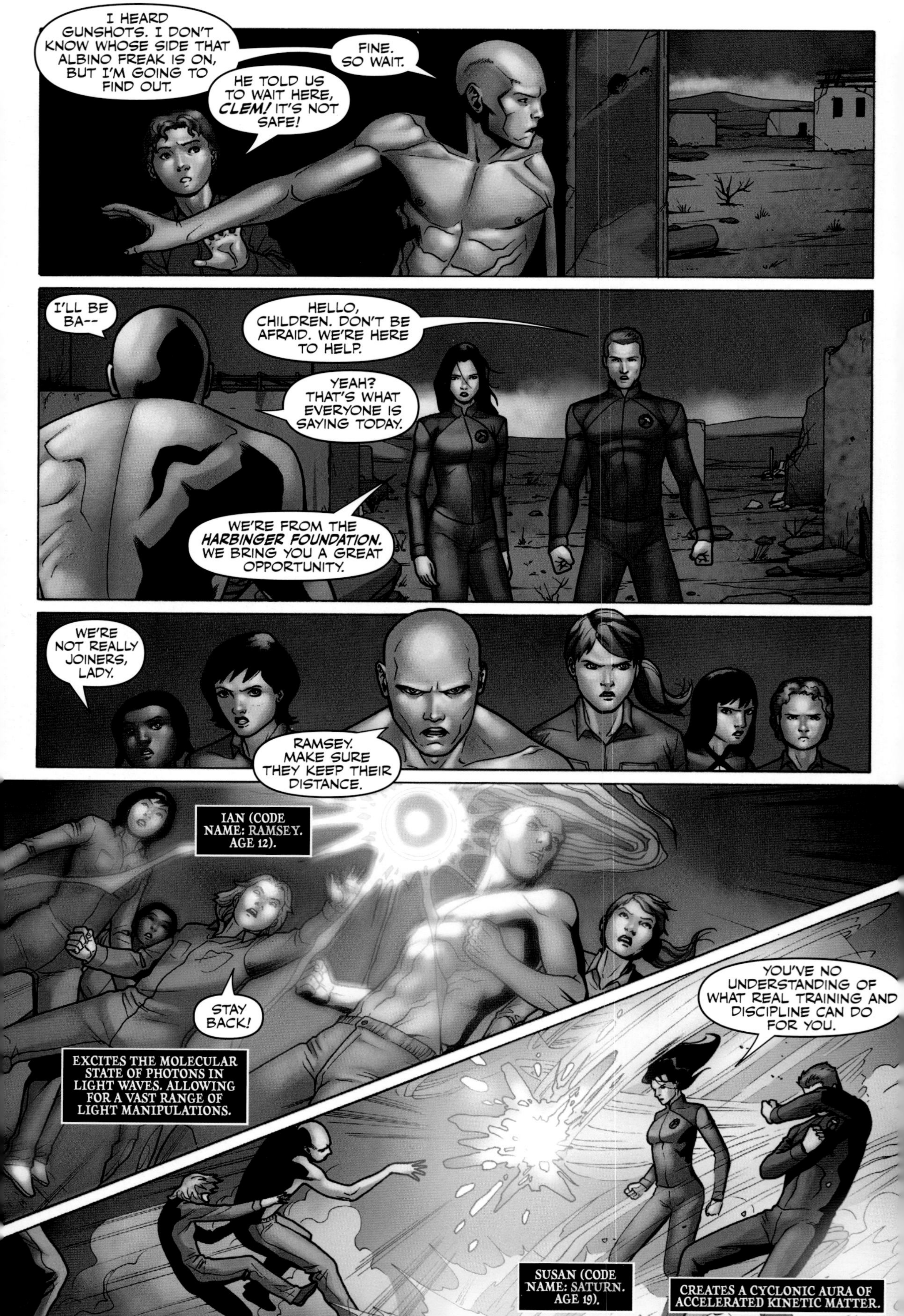
I HEARD GUNSHOTS. I DON'T KNOW WHOSE SIDE THAT ALBINO FREAK IS ON, BUT I'M GOING TO FIND OUT.
HE TOLD US TO WAIT HERE, CLEM! IT'S NOT SAFE!
FINE. SO WAIT.
I'LL BE BA--
HELLO, CHILDREN. DON'T BE AFRAID. WE'RE HERE TO HELP.
YEAH? THAT'S WHAT EVERYONE IS SAYING TODAY.
WE'RE FROM THE HARBINGER FOUNDATION. WE BRING YOU A GREAT OPPORTUNITY.
WE'RE NOT REALLY JOINERS, LADY.
RAMSEY. MAKE SURE THEY KEEP THEIR DISTANCE.
IAN (CODE NAME: RAMSEY. AGE 12).
STAY BACK!
EXCITES THE MOLECULAR STATE OF PHOTONS IN LIGHT WAVES. ALLOWING FOR A VAST RANGE OF LIGHT MANIPULATIONS.
YOU'VE NO UNDERSTANDING OF WHAT REAL TRAINING AND DISCIPLINE CAN DO FOR YOU.
SUSAN (CODE NAME: SATURN. AGE 19).
CREATES A CYCLONIC AURA OF ACCELERATED KINETIC MATTER.

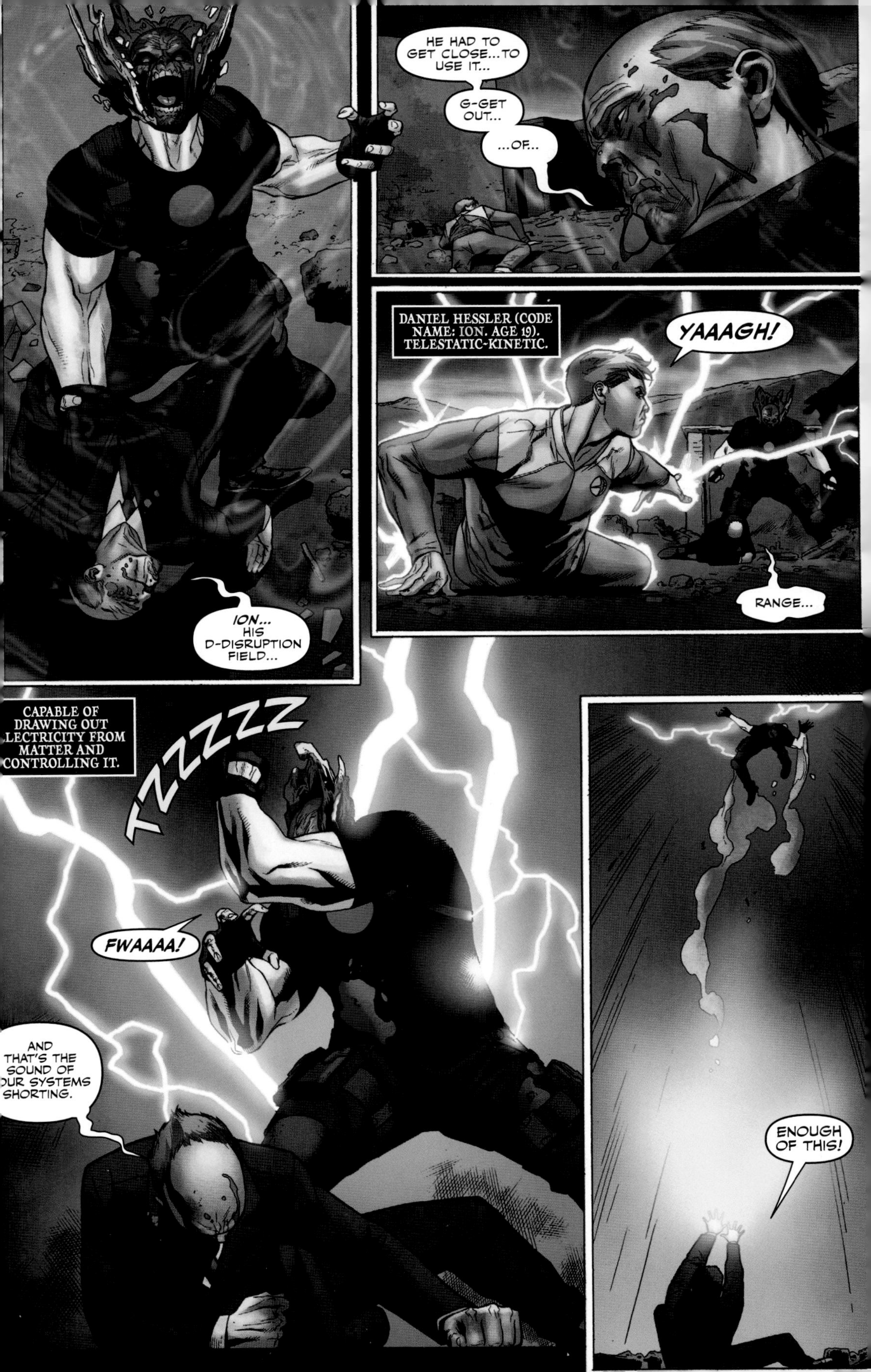
ION... HIS D-DISRUPTION FIELD...
HE HAD TO GET CLOSE...TO USE IT...
G-GET OUT...
...OF...
DANIEL HESSLER (CODE NAME: ION. AGE 19). TELESTATIC-KINETIC.
YAAAGH!
RANGE...
CAPABLE OF DRAWING OUT ELECTRICITY FROM MATTER AND CONTROLLING IT.
TZZZZZ
FWAAAA!
AND THAT'S THE SOUND OF OUR SYSTEMS SHORTING.
ENOUGH OF THIS!

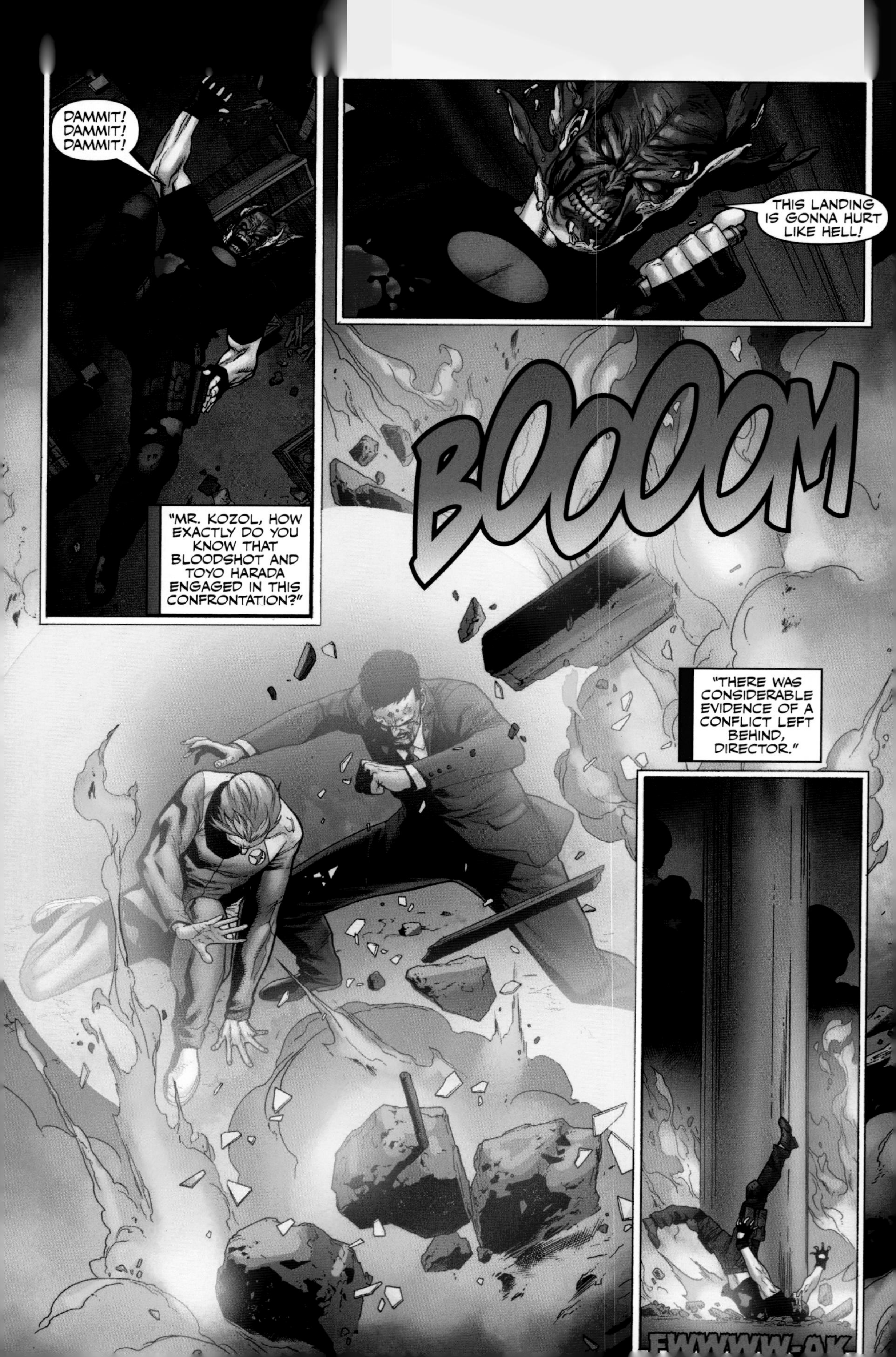

DAMMIT! DAMMIT! DAMMIT!
THIS LANDING IS GONNA HURT LIKE HELL!
"MR. KOZOL, HOW EXACTLY DO YOU KNOW THAT BLOODSHOT AND TOYO HARADA ENGAGED IN THIS CONFRONTATION?"
BOOOOM
"THERE WAS CONSIDERABLE EVIDENCE OF A CONFLICT LEFT BEHIND, DIRECTOR."

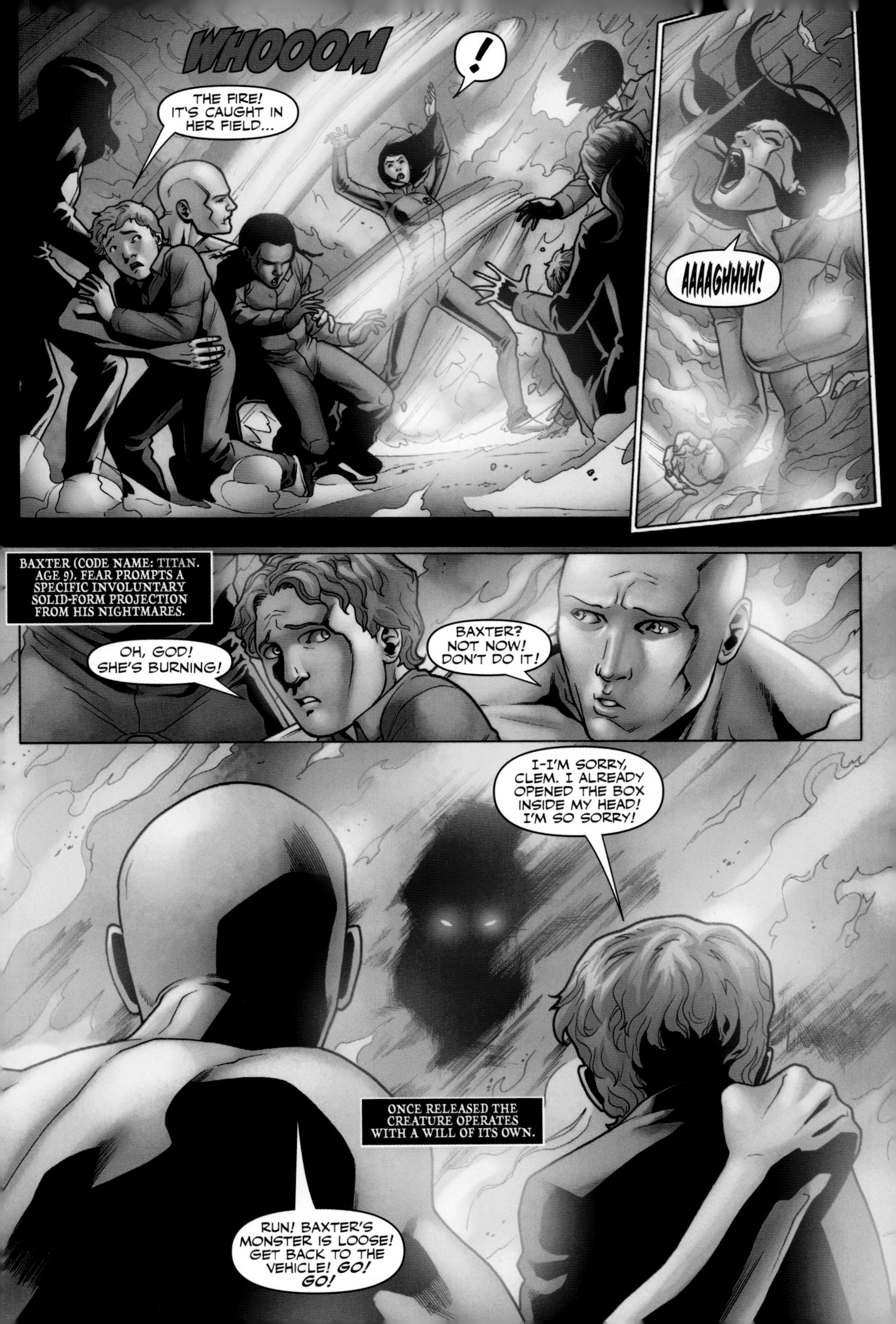
WHOOOM
THE FIRE! IT'S CAUGHT IN HER FIELD...
!
AAAAGHHHH!
BAXTER (CODE NAME: TITAN. AGE 9). FEAR PROMPTS A SPECIFIC INVOLUNTARY SOLID-FORM PROJECTION FROM HIS NIGHTMARES.
OH, GOD! SHE'S BURNING!
BAXTER? NOT NOW! DON'T DO IT!
I-I'M SORRY, CLEM. I ALREADY OPENED THE BOX INSIDE MY HEAD! I'M SO SORRY!
ONCE RELEASED THE CREATURE OPERATES WITH A WILL OF ITS OWN.
RUN! BAXTER'S MONSTER IS LOOSE! GET BACK TO THE VEHICLE! GO! GO!

SUCH AN IMPRESSIVE MACHINE. AND POSSESSING OF FEATURES I WASN'T PROPERLY WARNED ABOUT.

I—I'M NOT A MACHINE... I'M A M-MAN...

NOW I'M GOING TO GRIND YOU TO NOTHING AND SPEND YEARS STUDYING YOUR NANITES AS THEY STRUGGLE, ATOM BY ATOM, TO REBUILD--

?!

HOOONK

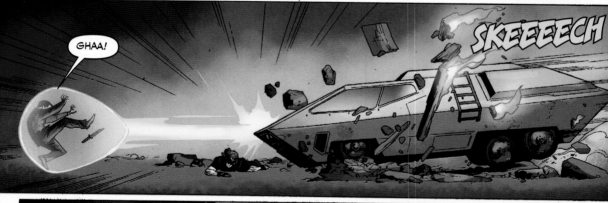

GHAA!

SKEEEECH

CLEM, YOU IDIOT! YOU RAN OVER HIM!

HE'S ALL RIGHT. REMEMBER ALL THE DAMAGE HE TOOK FROM GAMMA?

LET'S JUST GET HIM ONBOARD!

GUK

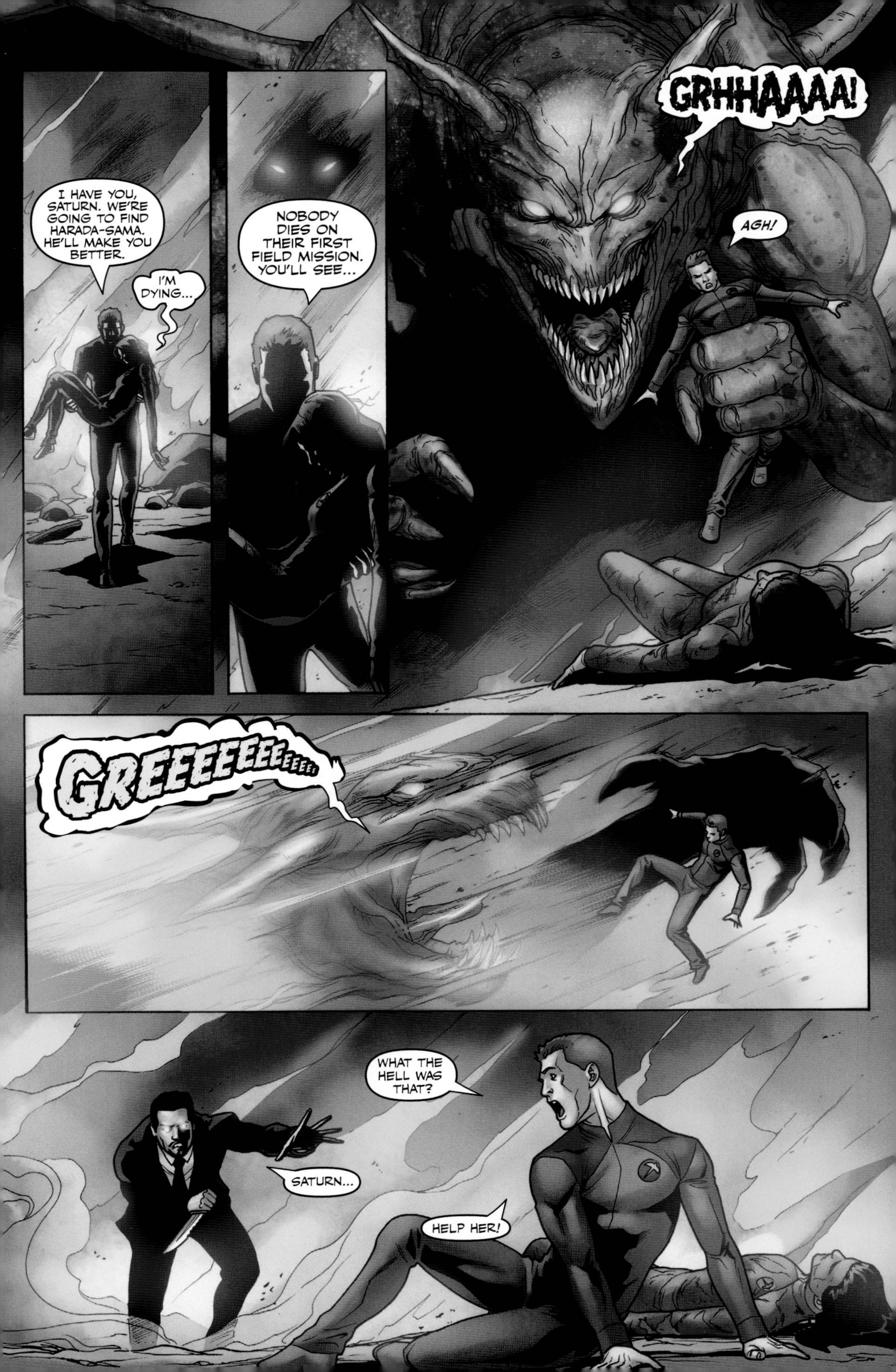
I HAVE YOU, SATURN. WE'RE GOING TO FIND HARADA-SAMA. HE'LL MAKE YOU BETTER.
I'M DYING...
NOBODY DIES ON THEIR FIRST FIELD MISSION. YOU'LL SEE...
GRHHAAAA!
AGH!
GREEEEEEEEEEE
WHAT THE HELL WAS THAT?
SATURN...
HELP HER!

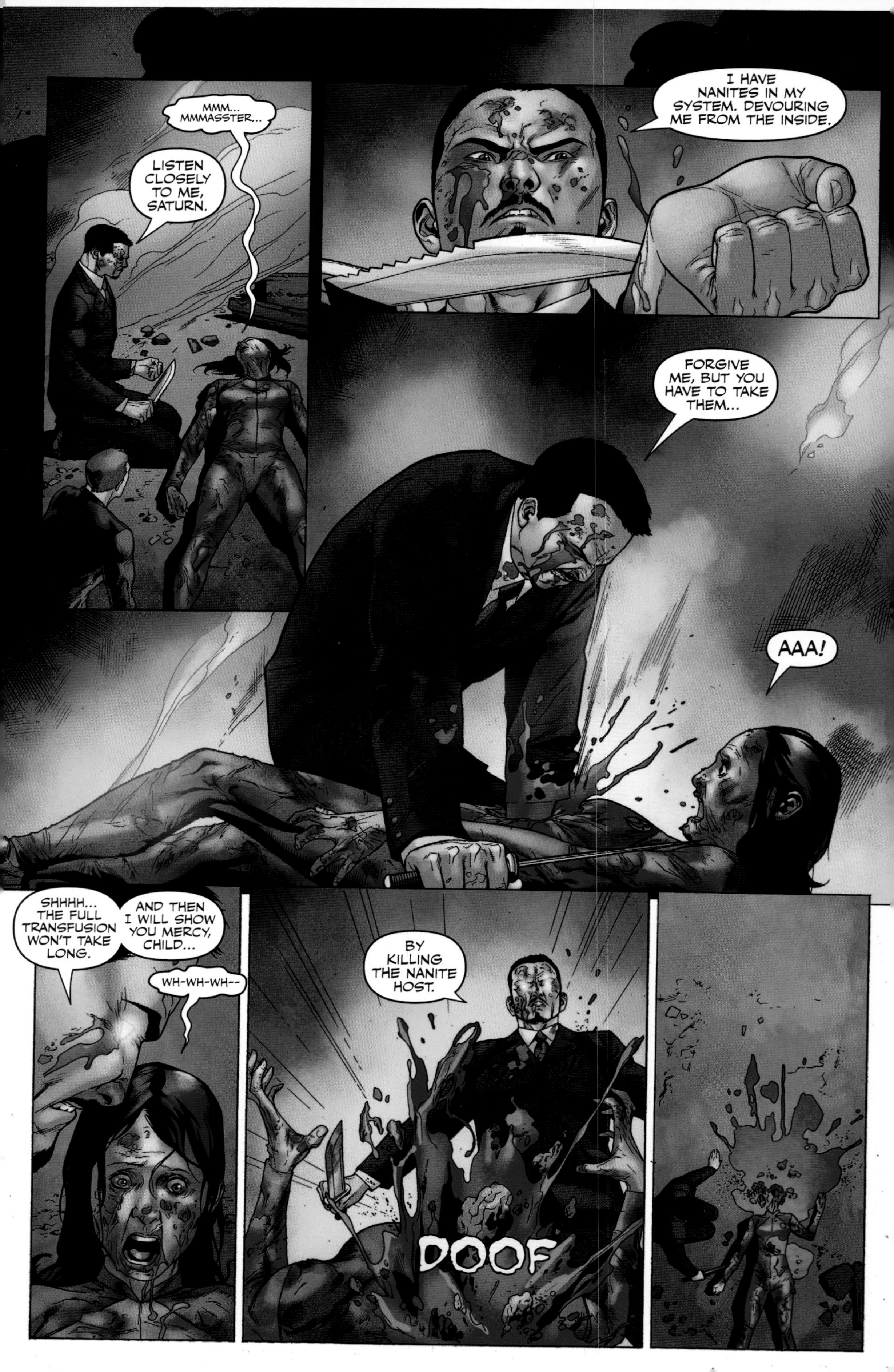
MMM... MMMASSTER...
LISTEN CLOSELY TO ME, SATURN.
I HAVE NANITES IN MY SYSTEM. DEVOURING ME FROM THE INSIDE.
FORGIVE ME, BUT YOU HAVE TO TAKE THEM...
AAA!
SHHHH... THE FULL TRANSFUSION WON'T TAKE LONG.
AND THEN I WILL SHOW YOU MERCY, CHILD...
WH-WH-WH--
BY KILLING THE NANITE HOST.
DOOF

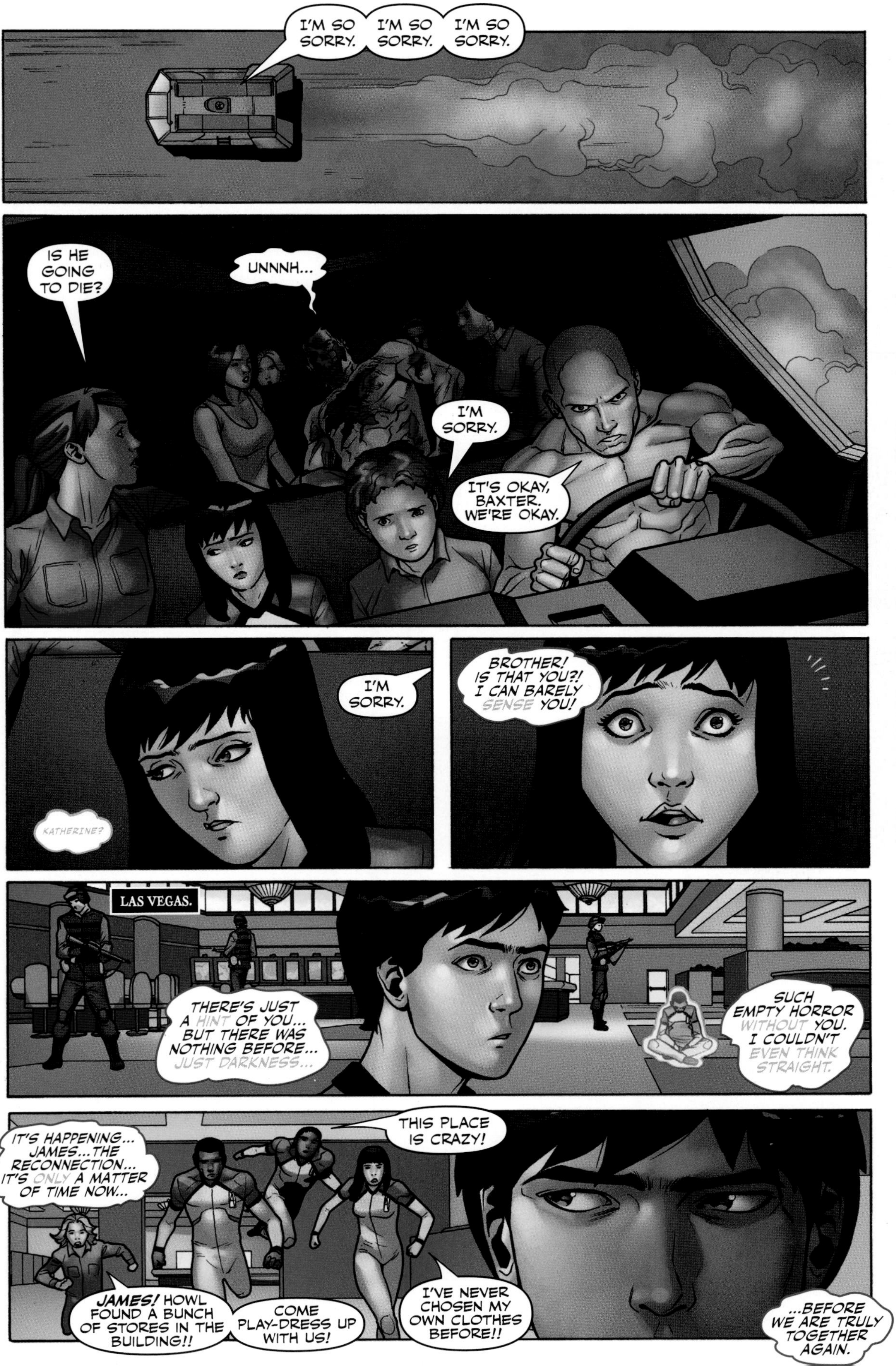
I'M SO SORRY.
I'M SO SORRY.
I'M SO SORRY.
IS HE GOING TO DIE?
UNNNH...
I'M SORRY.
IT'S OKAY, BAXTER. WE'RE OKAY.
I'M SORRY.
KATHERINE?
BROTHER! IS THAT YOU?! I CAN BARELY SENSE YOU!
LAS VEGAS.
THERE'S JUST A HINT OF YOU... BUT THERE WAS NOTHING BEFORE... JUST DARKNESS...
SUCH EMPTY HORROR WITHOUT YOU. I COULDN'T EVEN THINK STRAIGHT.
IT'S HAPPENING... JAMES... THE RECONNECTION... IT'S ONLY A MATTER OF TIME NOW...
THIS PLACE IS CRAZY!
JAMES! HOWL FOUND A BUNCH OF STORES IN THE BUILDING!!
COME PLAY-DRESS UP WITH US!
I'VE NEVER CHOSEN MY OWN CLOTHES BEFORE!!
...BEFORE WE ARE TRULY TOGETHER AGAIN.

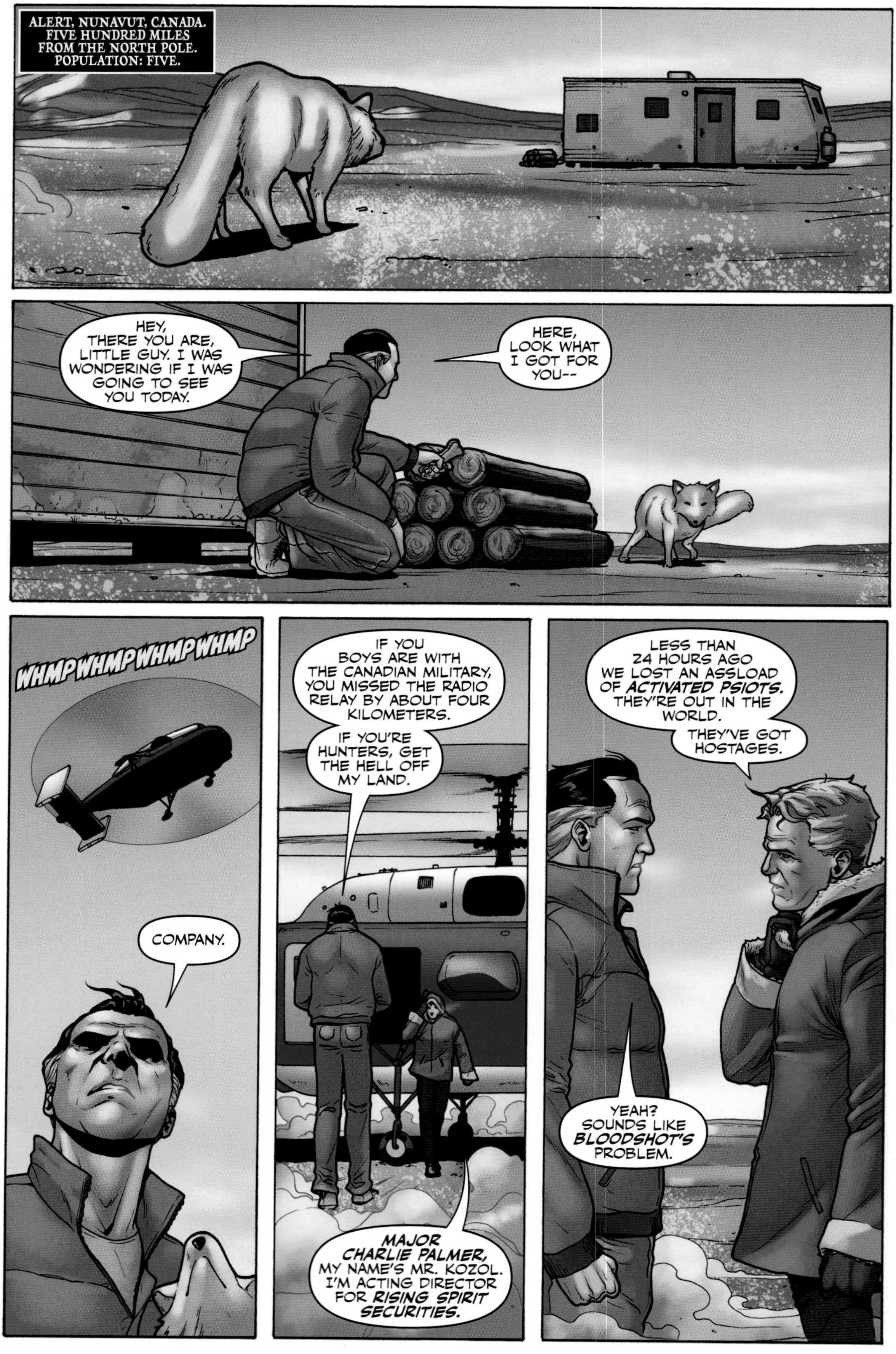
ALERT, NUNAVUT, CANADA. FIVE HUNDRED MILES FROM THE NORTH POLE. POPULATION: FIVE.
HEY, THERE YOU ARE, LITTLE GUY. I WAS WONDERING IF I WAS GOING TO SEE YOU TODAY.
HERE, LOOK WHAT I GOT FOR YOU--
WHMPWHMPWHMPWHMP
COMPANY.
IF YOU BOYS ARE WITH THE CANADIAN MILITARY, YOU MISSED THE RADIO RELAY BY ABOUT FOUR KILOMETERS.
IF YOU'RE HUNTERS, GET THE HELL OFF MY LAND.
MAJOR CHARLIE PALMER, MY NAME'S MR. KOZOL. I'M ACTING DIRECTOR FOR RISING SPIRIT SECURITIES.
LESS THAN 24 HOURS AGO WE LOST AN ASSLOAD OF ACTIVATED PSIOTS. THEY'RE OUT IN THE WORLD.
THEY'VE GOT HOSTAGES.
YEAH? SOUNDS LIKE BLOODSHOT'S PROBLEM.

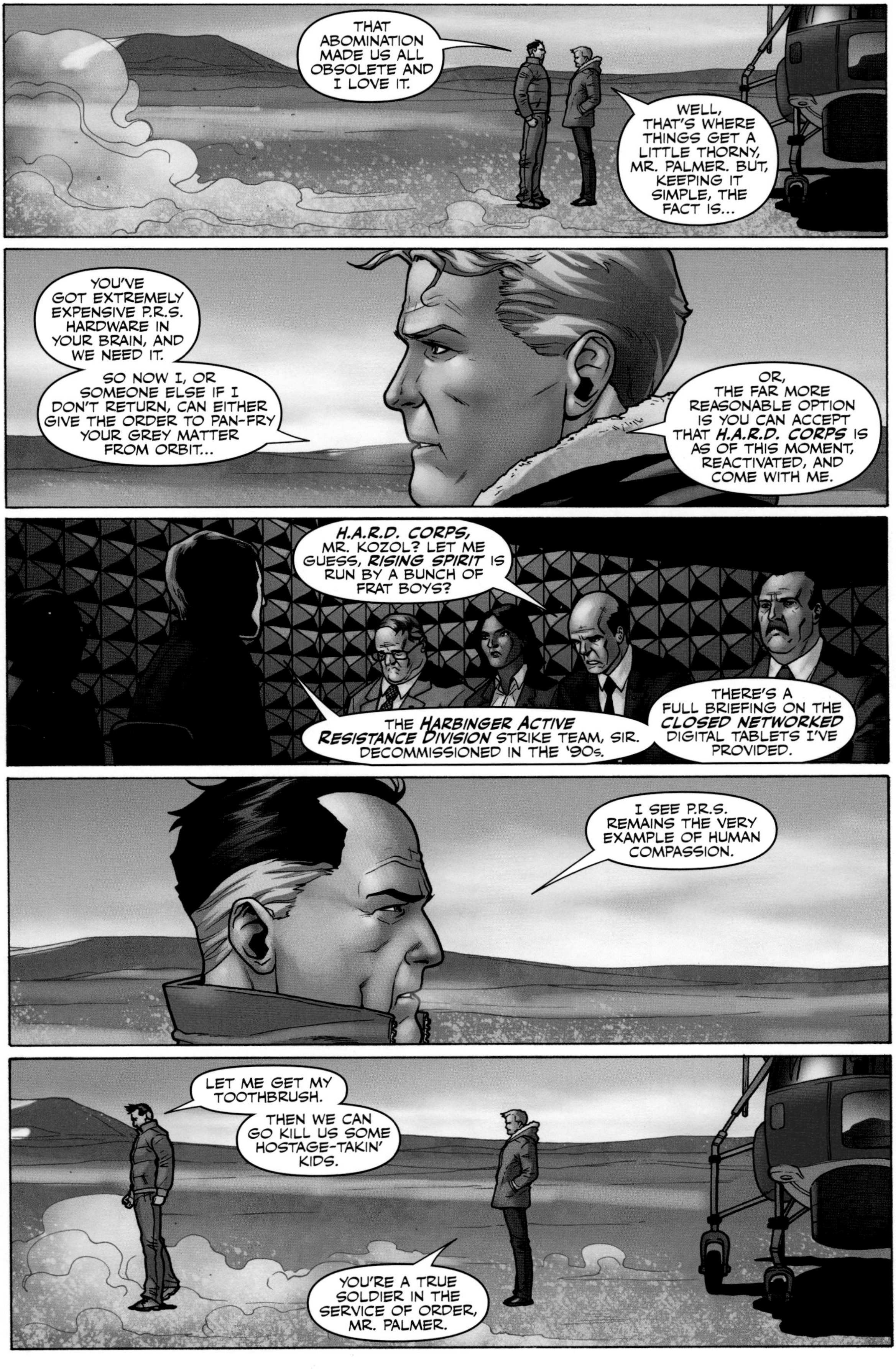
THAT ABOMINATION MADE US ALL OBSOLETE AND I LOVE IT.
WELL, THAT'S WHERE THINGS GET A LITTLE THORNY, MR. PALMER. BUT, KEEPING IT SIMPLE, THE FACT IS...
YOU'VE GOT EXTREMELY EXPENSIVE P.R.S. HARDWARE IN YOUR BRAIN, AND WE NEED IT.
SO NOW I, OR SOMEONE ELSE IF I DON'T RETURN, CAN EITHER GIVE THE ORDER TO PAN-FRY YOUR GREY MATTER FROM ORBIT...
OR, THE FAR MORE REASONABLE OPTION IS YOU CAN ACCEPT THAT H.A.R.D. CORPS IS AS OF THIS MOMENT, REACTIVATED, AND COME WITH ME.
H.A.R.D. CORPS, MR. KOZOL? LET ME GUESS, RISING SPIRIT IS RUN BY A BUNCH OF FRAT BOYS?
THE HARBINGER ACTIVE RESISTANCE DIVISION STRIKE TEAM, SIR. DECOMMISSIONED IN THE '90s.
THERE'S A FULL BRIEFING ON THE CLOSED NETWORKED DIGITAL TABLETS I'VE PROVIDED.
I SEE P.R.S. REMAINS THE VERY EXAMPLE OF HUMAN COMPASSION.
LET ME GET MY TOOTHBRUSH.
THEN WE CAN GO KILL US SOME HOSTAGE-TAKIN' KIDS.
YOU'RE A TRUE SOLDIER IN THE SERVICE OF ORDER, MR. PALMER.

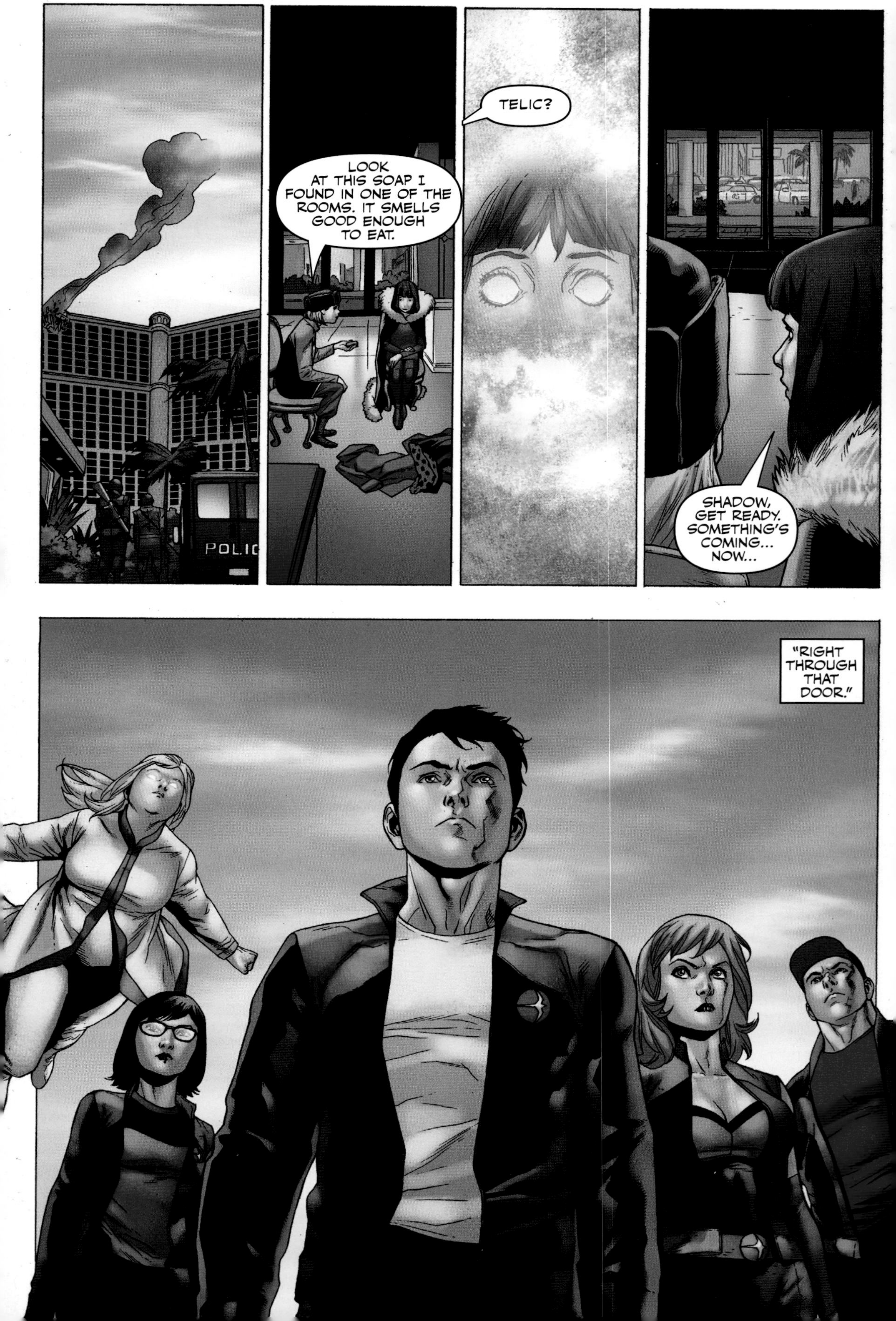
LOOK AT THIS SOAP I FOUND IN ONE OF THE ROOMS. IT SMELLS GOOD ENOUGH TO EAT.
TELIC?
SHADOW, GET READY. SOMETHING'S COMING... NOW...
POLIC
"RIGHT THROUGH THAT DOOR."

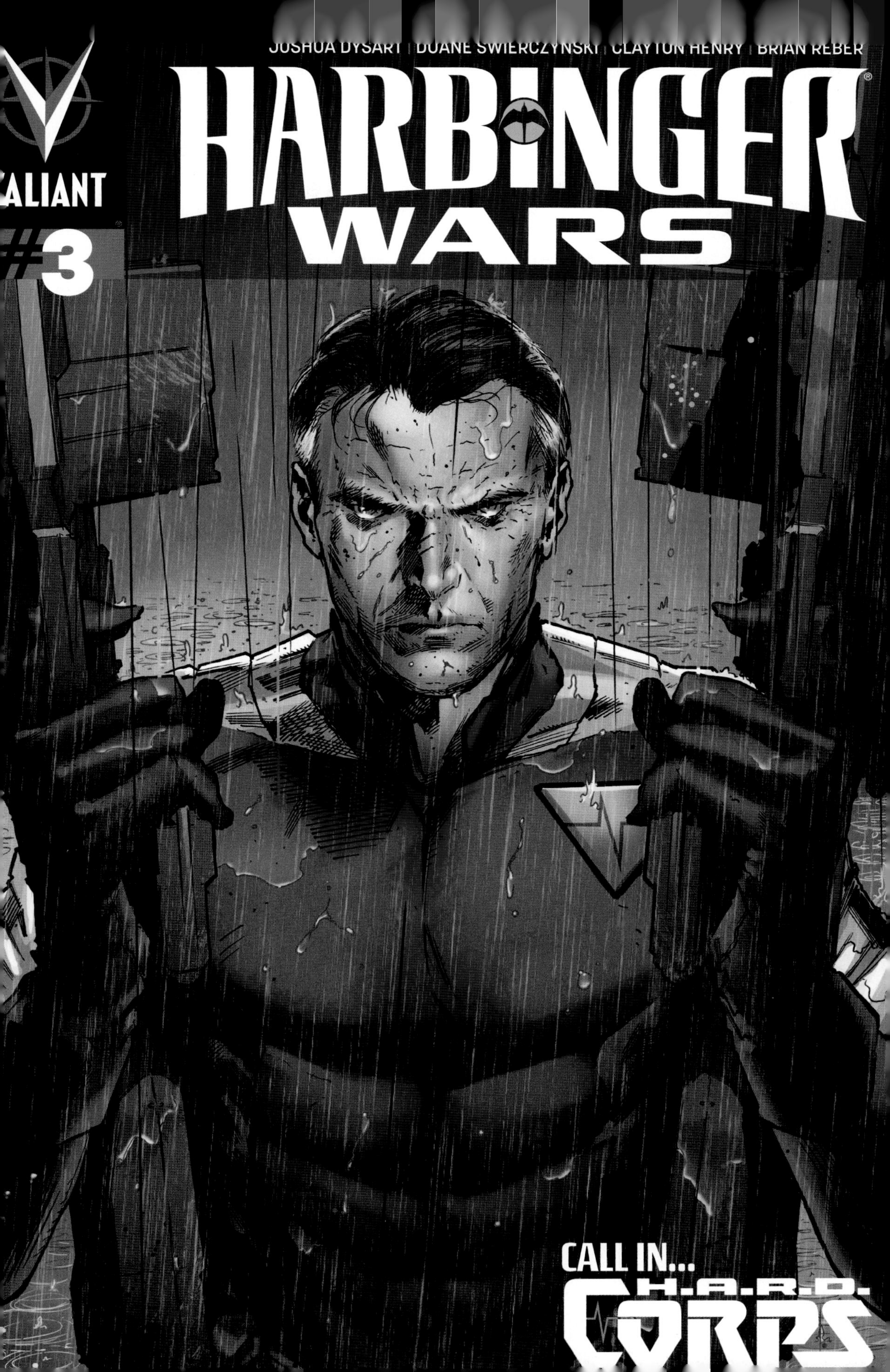

JOSHUA DYSART | DUANE SWIERCZYNSKI | CLAYTON HENRY | BRIAN REBER
VALIANT
HARBINGER WARS
#3
CALL IN...
H.A.R.D. CORPS

HARBINGER WARS

SHOWDOWN

PETER STANCHEK & THE RENEGADES

BLOODSHOT & ESCAPED PSIOTS

HARADA AND THE EGGBREAKERS

H.A.R.D. CORPS

OREGON
IDAHO
Winnemucca
NEVADA
Elko
Reno
Carson City
Project Rising Spirit
Kuretich's Mobile Lab
Ely
UTAH
Site of the Harada Protocols Incident
Fresno
Bakersfield
Military Blockade
Las Vegas
N
CALIFORNIA
ARIZONA

• **Project Rising Spirit** created **Bloodshot** to be the perfect weapon, providing him with an extraordinary array of powers that allow him to accomplish his primary mission - the capture of super-powered children known as **psiots** - with lethal accuracy. Now **Bloodshot** has freed himself from his programming and turned on his masters.

Upon assaulting the **P.R.S.** facility, **Bloodshot** liberated the psiots he helped capture, but the children were separated into two groups. The first group, calling itself **Generation Zero**, led by a psiot named Cronus, has taken over the Bellagio Hotel in Las Vegas.

Project Rising Spirit, Toyo Harada and **Bloodshot** all want control of the psiots. As the battle raged between **Harada** and **Bloodshot, Stanchek** and the **Renegades** have arrived in Vegas.

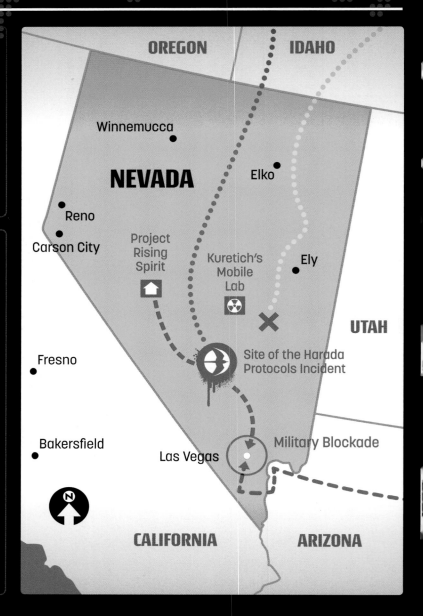

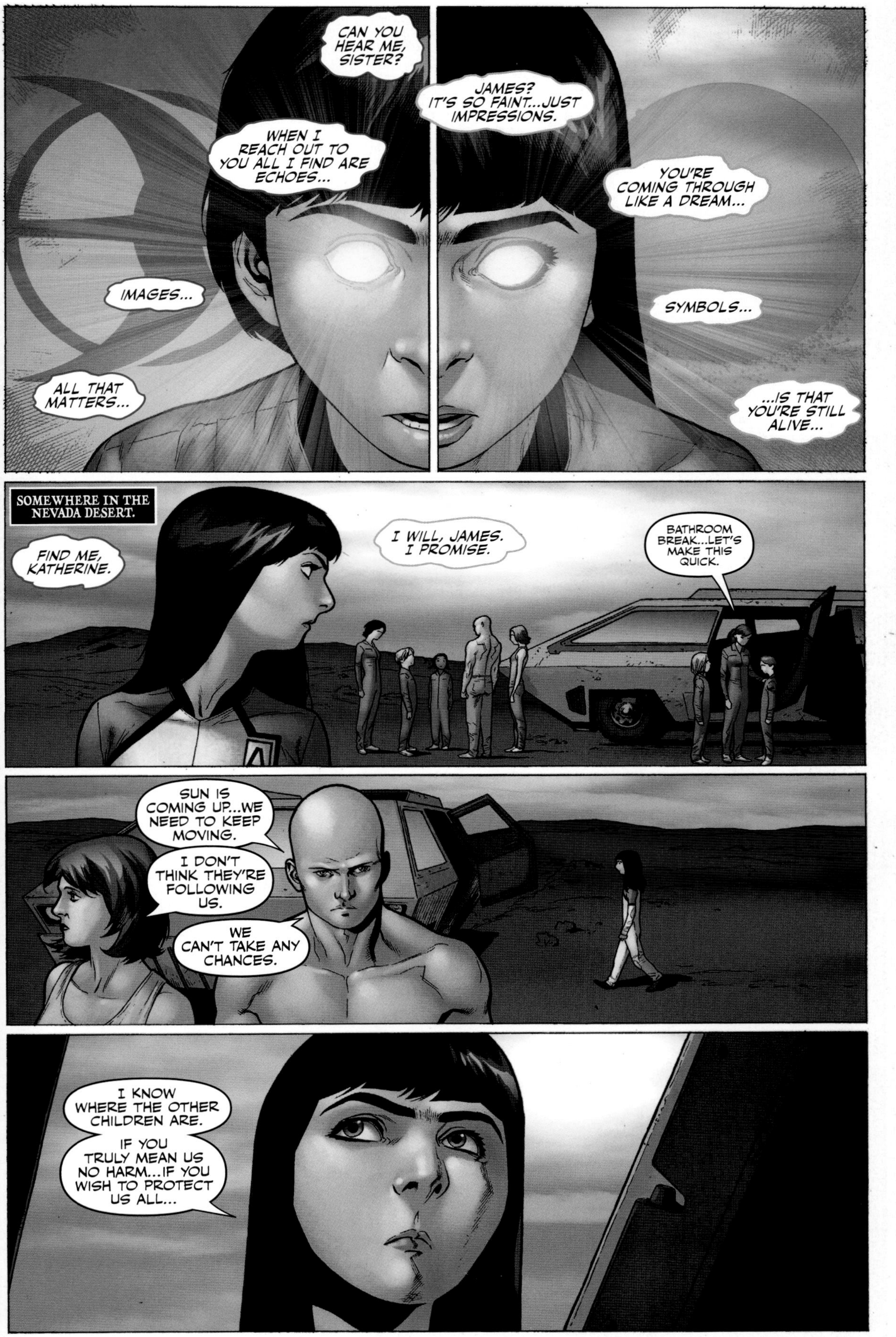
CAN YOU HEAR ME, SISTER?
WHEN I REACH OUT TO YOU ALL I FIND ARE ECHOES...
IMAGES...
ALL THAT MATTERS...
JAMES? IT'S SO FAINT...JUST IMPRESSIONS.
YOU'RE COMING THROUGH LIKE A DREAM...
SYMBOLS...
...IS THAT YOU'RE STILL ALIVE...
SOMEWHERE IN THE NEVADA DESERT.
FIND ME, KATHERINE.
I WILL, JAMES. I PROMISE.
BATHROOM BREAK...LET'S MAKE THIS QUICK.
SUN IS COMING UP...WE NEED TO KEEP MOVING.
I DON'T THINK THEY'RE FOLLOWING US.
WE CAN'T TAKE ANY CHANCES.
I KNOW WHERE THE OTHER CHILDREN ARE.
IF YOU TRULY MEAN US NO HARM...IF YOU WISH TO PROTECT US ALL...

...YOU'LL TAKE US TO THEM, PSIOT HUNTER.

"MR. KOZOL..."

...CAN YOU IDENTIFY THESE *HARBINGER FOUNDATION* STUDENTS FOR US?

EIGHT DAYS FROM NOW. MEETING BETWEEN RISING SPIRIT ACTING DIRECTOR MORRIS KOZOL AND THE DIRECTOR OF NATIONAL INTELLIGENCE.

NO, SIR.

ISN'T ONE OF YOUR CONTRACTS TO PROVIDE US DATA ON THE *HARBINGER FOUNDATION?*

THOSE ARE NOT *HARADA'S* STUDENTS.

THESE PHOTOS CLEARLY SHOW THEM WEARING FOUNDATION UNIFORMS.

WE'RE CHALKING THAT UP TO YOUTHFUL IRONY, SIR. HIPPIES IN CAMO, THAT SORT OF THING.

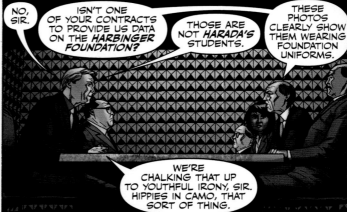

THESE ARE ACTUALLY FOUR NEWLY ACTIVATED, UNAFFILIATED PSIOTS AND ONE EX-STUDENT OF HARADA'S.

WE'VE BEEN TRACKING HIM FOR SOME TIME. A NASTY PIECE OF WORK, CONSTANTLY JACKED ON PILLS AND ADDICTED TO VIOLENCE.

ACCORDING TO OUR INTEL, HE KILLED HIS OWN BEST FRIEND.

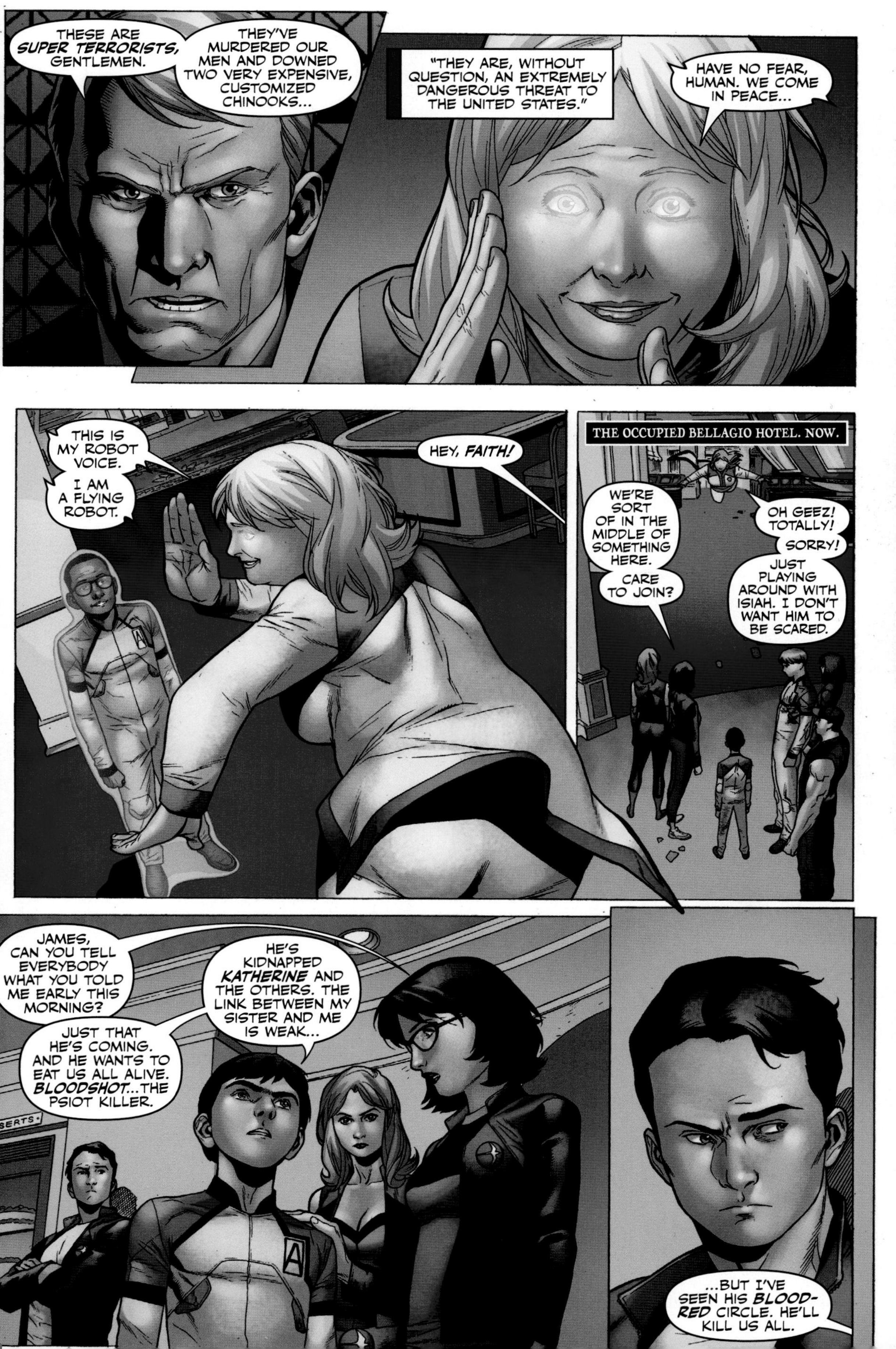
THESE ARE SUPER TERRORISTS, GENTLEMEN.
THEY'VE MURDERED OUR MEN AND DOWNED TWO VERY EXPENSIVE, CUSTOMIZED CHINOOKS...
"THEY ARE, WITHOUT QUESTION, AN EXTREMELY DANGEROUS THREAT TO THE UNITED STATES."
HAVE NO FEAR, HUMAN. WE COME IN PEACE...
THIS IS MY ROBOT VOICE.
I AM A FLYING ROBOT.
HEY, FAITH!
THE OCCUPIED BELLAGIO HOTEL. NOW.
WE'RE SORT OF IN THE MIDDLE OF SOMETHING HERE.
CARE TO JOIN?
OH GEEZ! TOTALLY!
SORRY!
JUST PLAYING AROUND WITH ISIAH. I DON'T WANT HIM TO BE SCARED.
JAMES, CAN YOU TELL EVERYBODY WHAT YOU TOLD ME EARLY THIS MORNING?
JUST THAT HE'S COMING. AND HE WANTS TO EAT US ALL ALIVE. BLOODSHOT...THE PSIOT KILLER.
HE'S KIDNAPPED KATHERINE AND THE OTHERS. THE LINK BETWEEN MY SISTER AND ME IS WEAK...
...BUT I'VE SEEN HIS BLOOD-RED CIRCLE. HE'LL KILL US ALL.

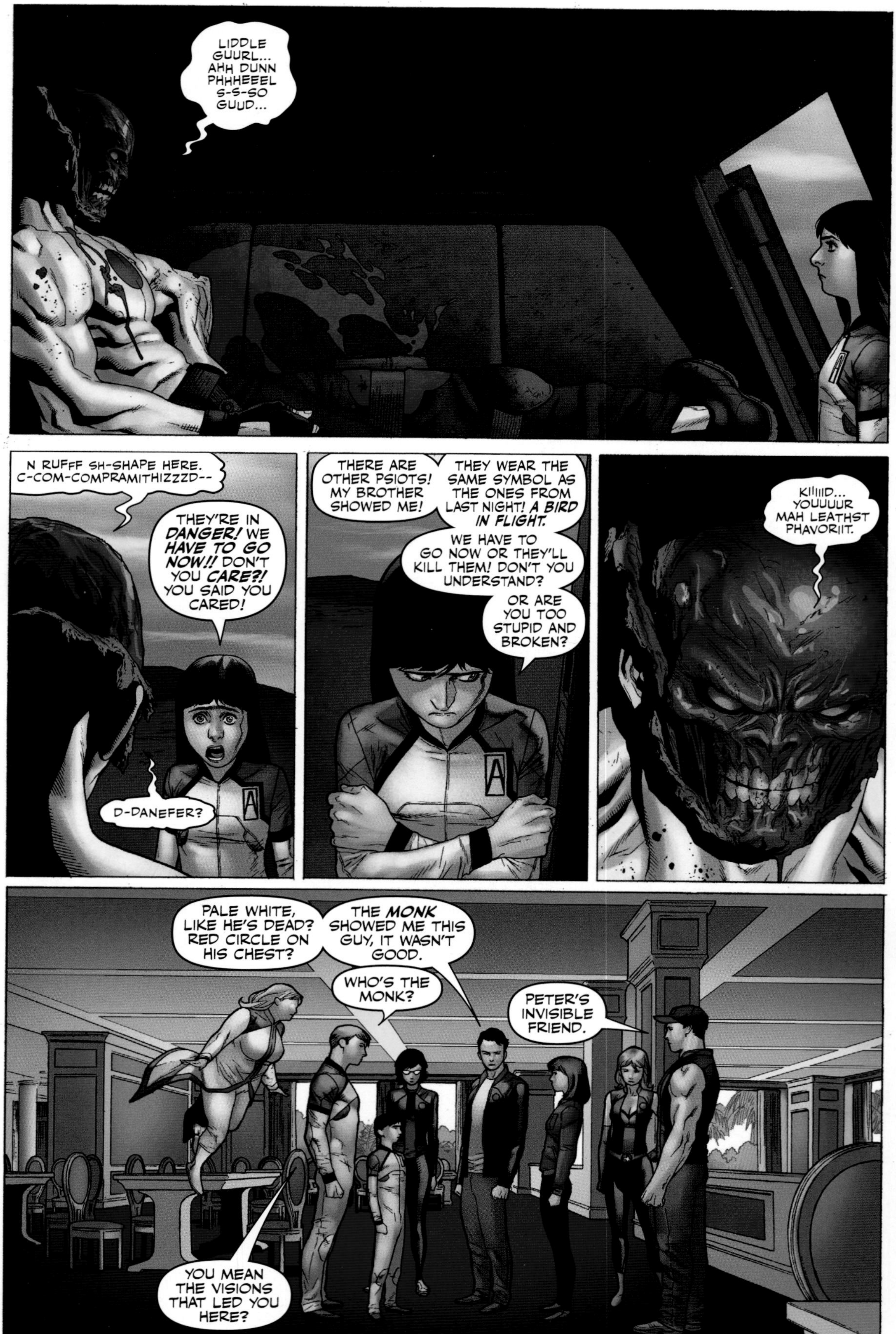
LIDDLE GUURL... AHH DUNN PHHHEEEL S-S-SO GUUD...
N RUFFF SH-SHAPE HERE. C-COM-COMPRAMITHIZZZD--
THEY'RE IN DANGER! WE HAVE TO GO NOW!! DON'T YOU CARE?! YOU SAID YOU CARED!
D-DANEFER?
THERE ARE OTHER PSIOTS! MY BROTHER SHOWED ME!
THEY WEAR THE SAME SYMBOL AS THE ONES FROM LAST NIGHT! A BIRD IN FLIGHT.
WE HAVE TO GO NOW OR THEY'LL KILL THEM! DON'T YOU UNDERSTAND?
OR ARE YOU TOO STUPID AND BROKEN?
KIIIIID... YOUUUUR MAH LEATHST PHAVORIIT.
PALE WHITE, LIKE HE'S DEAD? RED CIRCLE ON HIS CHEST?
THE MONK SHOWED ME THIS GUY, IT WASN'T GOOD.
WHO'S THE MONK?
PETER'S INVISIBLE FRIEND.
YOU MEAN THE VISIONS THAT LED YOU HERE?

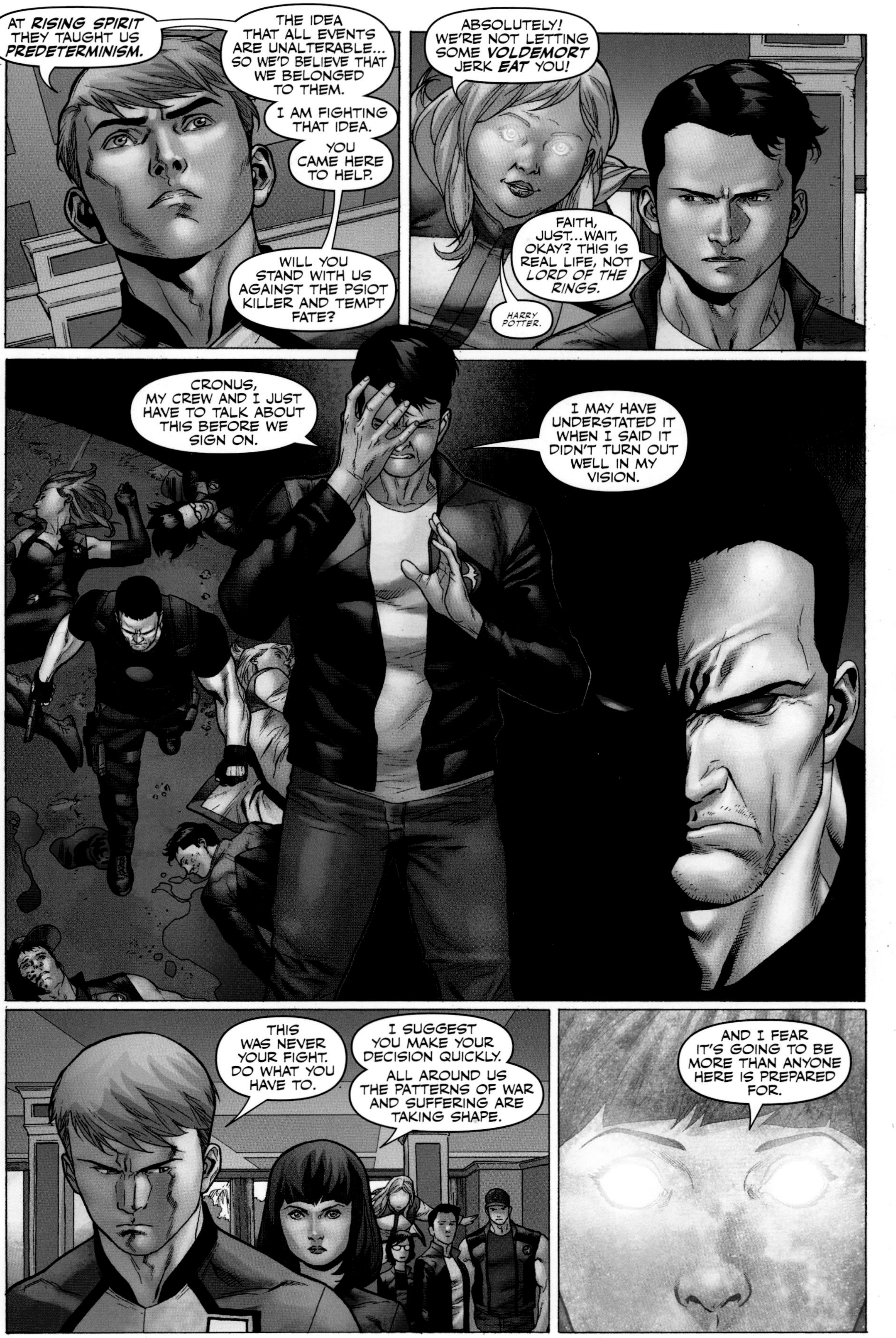
AT RISING SPIRIT THEY TAUGHT US PREDETERMINISM.
THE IDEA THAT ALL EVENTS ARE UNALTERABLE... SO WE'D BELIEVE THAT WE BELONGED TO THEM.
I AM FIGHTING THAT IDEA.
YOU CAME HERE TO HELP.
WILL YOU STAND WITH US AGAINST THE PSIOT KILLER AND TEMPT FATE?
ABSOLUTELY! WE'RE NOT LETTING SOME VOLDEMORT JERK EAT YOU!
FAITH, JUST...WAIT, OKAY? THIS IS REAL LIFE, NOT LORD OF THE RINGS.
HARRY POTTER.
CRONUS, MY CREW AND I JUST HAVE TO TALK ABOUT THIS BEFORE WE SIGN ON.
I MAY HAVE UNDERSTATED IT WHEN I SAID IT DIDN'T TURN OUT WELL IN MY VISION.
THIS WAS NEVER YOUR FIGHT. DO WHAT YOU HAVE TO.
I SUGGEST YOU MAKE YOUR DECISION QUICKLY.
ALL AROUND US THE PATTERNS OF WAR AND SUFFERING ARE TAKING SHAPE.
AND I FEAR IT'S GOING TO BE MORE THAN ANYONE HERE IS PREPARED FOR.

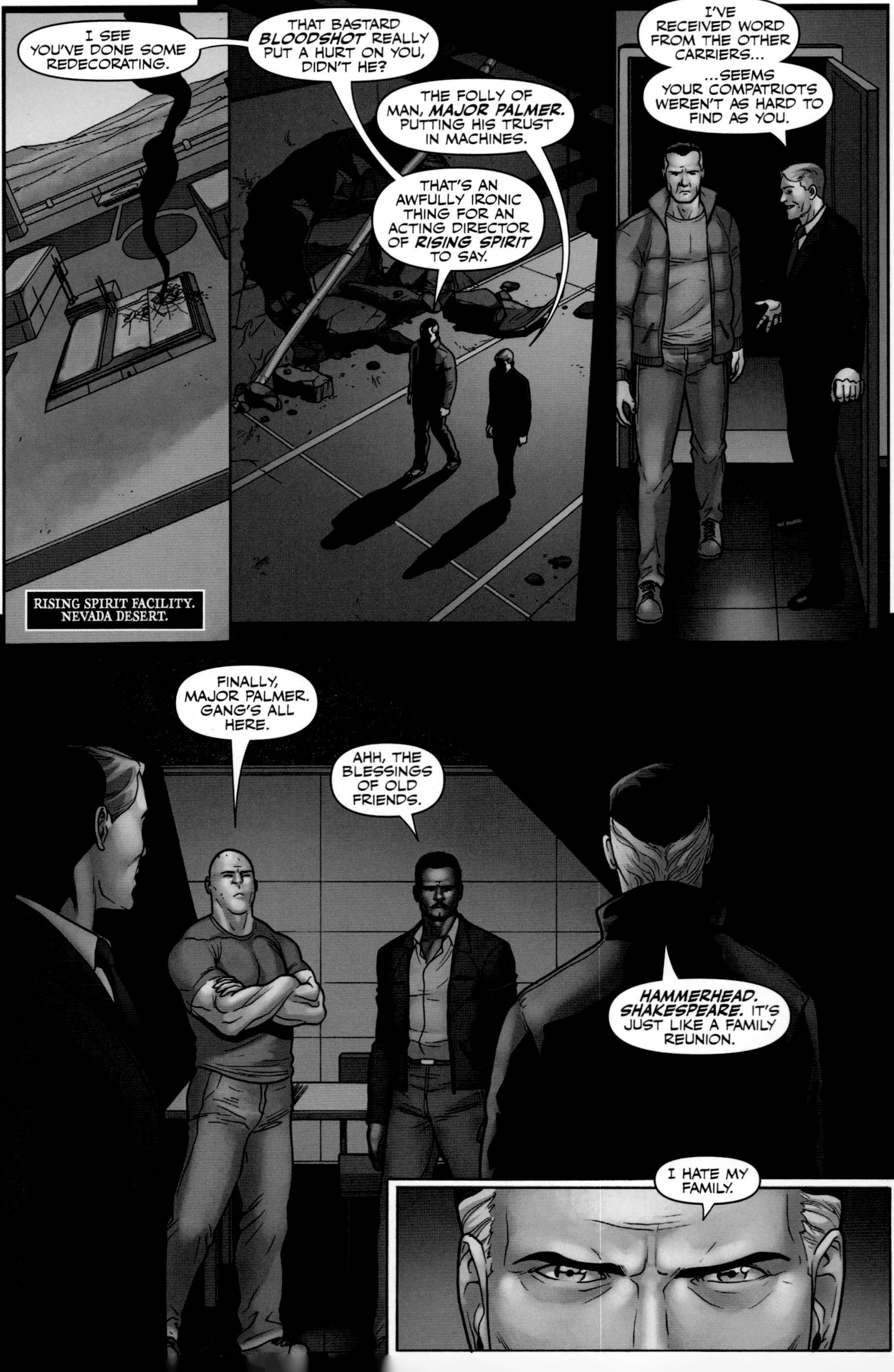

I SEE YOU'VE DONE SOME REDECORATING.
THAT BASTARD BLOODSHOT REALLY PUT A HURT ON YOU, DIDN'T HE?
THE FOLLY OF MAN, MAJOR PALMER. PUTTING HIS TRUST IN MACHINES.
THAT'S AN AWFULLY IRONIC THING FOR AN ACTING DIRECTOR OF RISING SPIRIT TO SAY.
RISING SPIRIT FACILITY. NEVADA DESERT.
I'VE RECEIVED WORD FROM THE OTHER CARRIERS...
...SEEMS YOUR COMPATRIOTS WEREN'T AS HARD TO FIND AS YOU.
FINALLY, MAJOR PALMER. GANG'S ALL HERE.
AHH, THE BLESSINGS OF OLD FRIENDS.
HAMMERHEAD. SHAKESPEARE. IT'S JUST LIKE A FAMILY REUNION.
I HATE MY FAMILY.

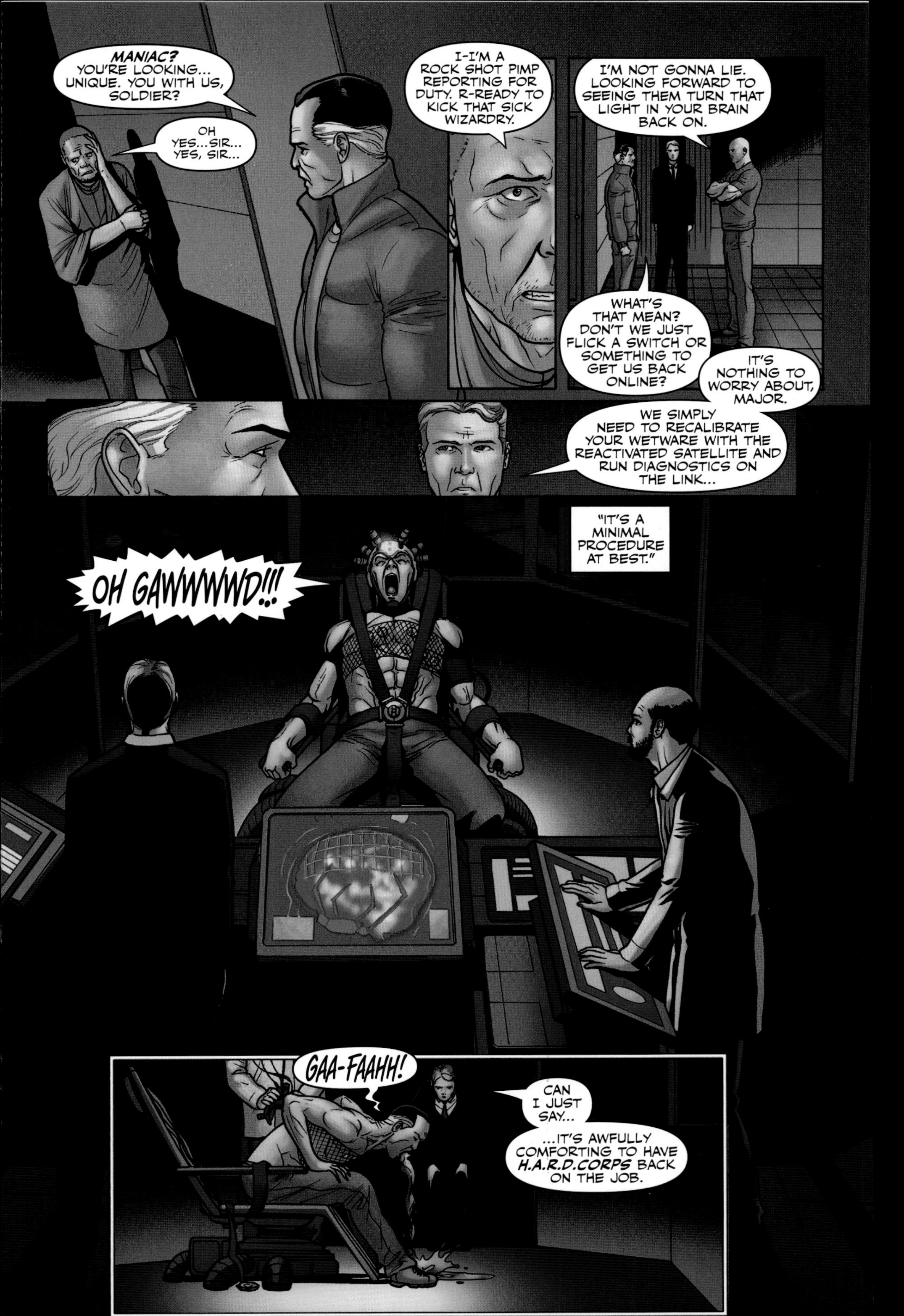
MANIAC? YOU'RE LOOKING... UNIQUE. YOU WITH US, SOLDIER?
OH YES...SIR... YES, SIR...
I-I'M A ROCK SHOT PIMP REPORTING FOR DUTY. R-READY TO KICK THAT SICK WIZARDRY.
I'M NOT GONNA LIE. LOOKING FORWARD TO SEEING THEM TURN THAT LIGHT IN YOUR BRAIN BACK ON.
WHAT'S THAT MEAN? DON'T WE JUST FLICK A SWITCH OR SOMETHING TO GET US BACK ONLINE?
IT'S NOTHING TO WORRY ABOUT, MAJOR.
WE SIMPLY NEED TO RECALIBRATE YOUR WETWARE WITH THE REACTIVATED SATELLITE AND RUN DIAGNOSTICS ON THE LINK...
"IT'S A MINIMAL PROCEDURE AT BEST."
OH GAWWWWD!!!
GAA-FAAHH!
CAN I JUST SAY...
...IT'S AWFULLY COMFORTING TO HAVE H.A.R.D.CORPS BACK ON THE JOB.

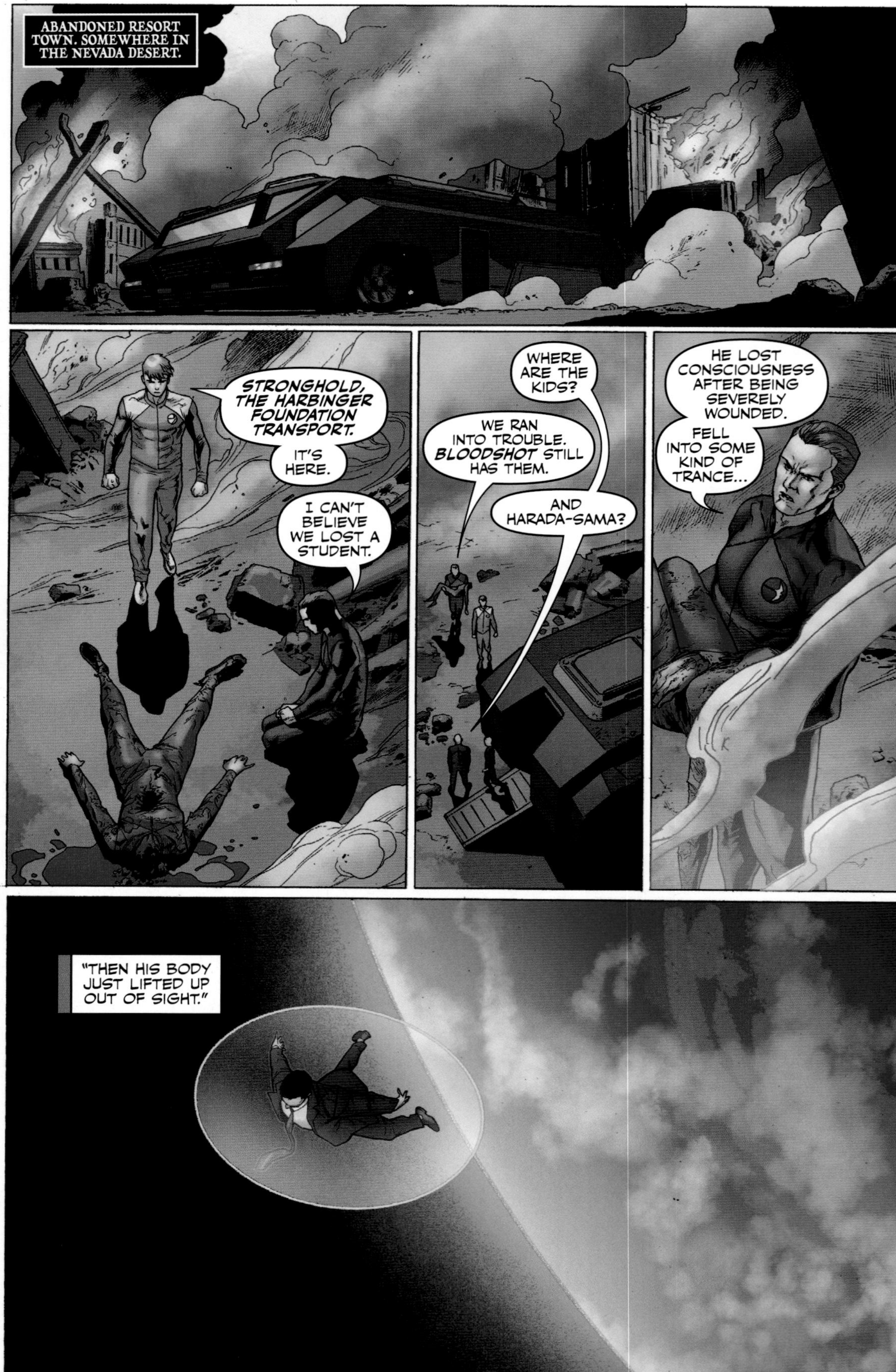
ABANDONED RESORT TOWN. SOMEWHERE IN THE NEVADA DESERT.
STRONGHOLD, THE HARBINGER FOUNDATION TRANSPORT.
IT'S HERE.
I CAN'T BELIEVE WE LOST A STUDENT.
WHERE ARE THE KIDS?
WE RAN INTO TROUBLE. BLOODSHOT STILL HAS THEM.
AND HARADA-SAMA?
HE LOST CONSCIOUSNESS AFTER BEING SEVERELY WOUNDED.
FELL INTO SOME KIND OF TRANCE...
"THEN HIS BODY JUST LIFTED UP OUT OF SIGHT."

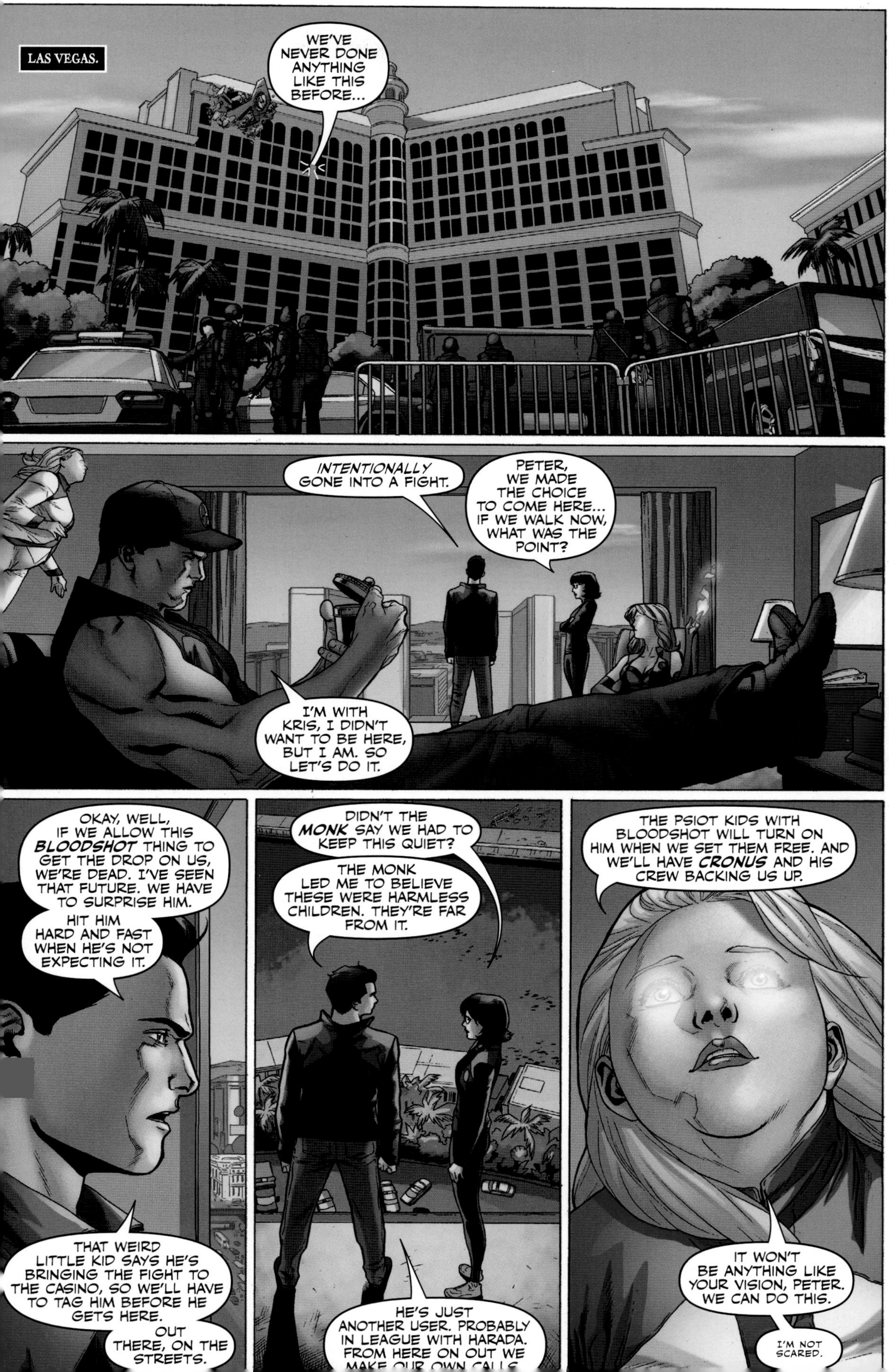

LAS VEGAS.
WE'VE NEVER DONE ANYTHING LIKE THIS BEFORE...
INTENTIONALLY GONE INTO A FIGHT.
PETER, WE MADE THE CHOICE TO COME HERE... IF WE WALK NOW, WHAT WAS THE POINT?
I'M WITH KRIS, I DIDN'T WANT TO BE HERE, BUT I AM. SO LET'S DO IT.
OKAY, WELL, IF WE ALLOW THIS ***BLOODSHOT*** THING TO GET THE DROP ON US, WE'RE DEAD. I'VE SEEN THAT FUTURE. WE HAVE TO SURPRISE HIM.
HIT HIM HARD AND FAST WHEN HE'S NOT EXPECTING IT.
THAT WEIRD LITTLE KID SAYS HE'S BRINGING THE FIGHT TO THE CASINO, SO WE'LL HAVE TO TAG HIM BEFORE HE GETS HERE.
OUT THERE, ON THE STREETS.
DIDN'T THE ***MONK*** SAY WE HAD TO KEEP THIS QUIET?
THE MONK LED ME TO BELIEVE THESE WERE HARMLESS CHILDREN. THEY'RE FAR FROM IT.
HE'S JUST ANOTHER USER. PROBABLY IN LEAGUE WITH HARADA. FROM HERE ON OUT WE
THE PSIOT KIDS WITH BLOODSHOT WILL TURN ON HIM WHEN WE SET THEM FREE. AND WE'LL HAVE ***CRONUS*** AND HIS CREW BACKING US UP.
IT WON'T BE ANYTHING LIKE YOUR VISION, PETER. WE CAN DO THIS.
I'M NOT SCARED.

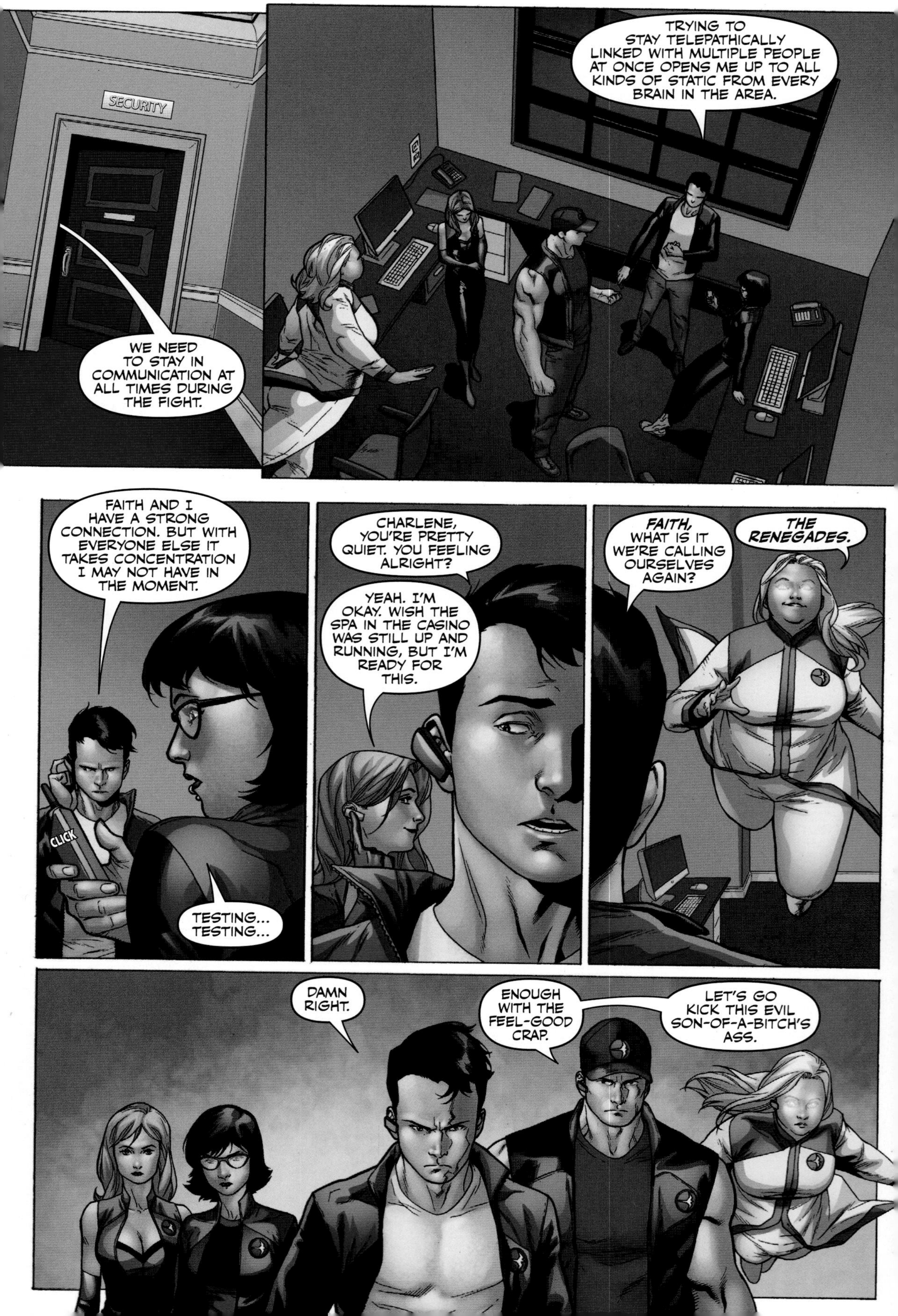
SECURITY
WE NEED TO STAY IN COMMUNICATION AT ALL TIMES DURING THE FIGHT.
TRYING TO STAY TELEPATHICALLY LINKED WITH MULTIPLE PEOPLE AT ONCE OPENS ME UP TO ALL KINDS OF STATIC FROM EVERY BRAIN IN THE AREA.
FAITH AND I HAVE A STRONG CONNECTION. BUT WITH EVERYONE ELSE IT TAKES CONCENTRATION I MAY NOT HAVE IN THE MOMENT.
CLICK
TESTING... TESTING...
CHARLENE, YOU'RE PRETTY QUIET. YOU FEELING ALRIGHT?
YEAH. I'M OKAY. WISH THE SPA IN THE CASINO WAS STILL UP AND RUNNING, BUT I'M READY FOR THIS.
FAITH, WHAT IS IT WE'RE CALLING OURSELVES AGAIN?
THE RENEGADES.
DAMN RIGHT.
ENOUGH WITH THE FEEL-GOOD CRAP.
LET'S GO KICK THIS EVIL SON-OF-A-BITCH'S ASS.

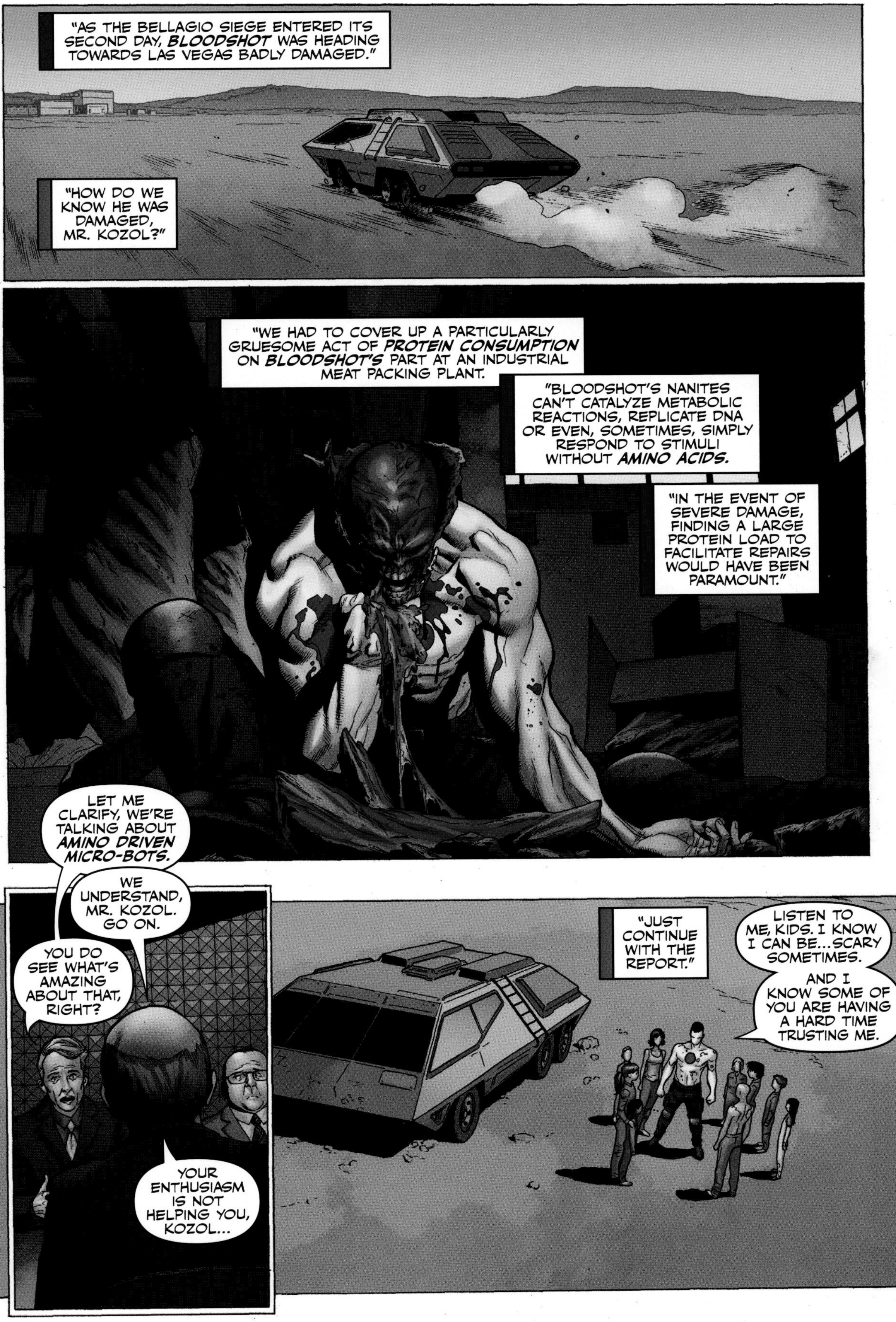
"AS THE BELLAGIO SIEGE ENTERED ITS SECOND DAY, BLOODSHOT WAS HEADING TOWARDS LAS VEGAS BADLY DAMAGED."
"HOW DO WE KNOW HE WAS DAMAGED, MR. KOZOL?"
"WE HAD TO COVER UP A PARTICULARLY GRUESOME ACT OF PROTEIN CONSUMPTION ON BLOODSHOT'S PART AT AN INDUSTRIAL MEAT PACKING PLANT.
"BLOODSHOT'S NANITES CAN'T CATALYZE METABOLIC REACTIONS, REPLICATE DNA OR EVEN, SOMETIMES, SIMPLY RESPOND TO STIMULI WITHOUT AMINO ACIDS.
"IN THE EVENT OF SEVERE DAMAGE, FINDING A LARGE PROTEIN LOAD TO FACILITATE REPAIRS WOULD HAVE BEEN PARAMOUNT."
LET ME CLARIFY, WE'RE TALKING ABOUT AMINO DRIVEN MICRO-BOTS.
WE UNDERSTAND, MR. KOZOL. GO ON.
YOU DO SEE WHAT'S AMAZING ABOUT THAT, RIGHT?
YOUR ENTHUSIASM IS NOT HELPING YOU, KOZOL...
"JUST CONTINUE WITH THE REPORT."
LISTEN TO ME, KIDS. I KNOW I CAN BE...SCARY SOMETIMES.
AND I KNOW SOME OF YOU ARE HAVING A HARD TIME TRUSTING ME.

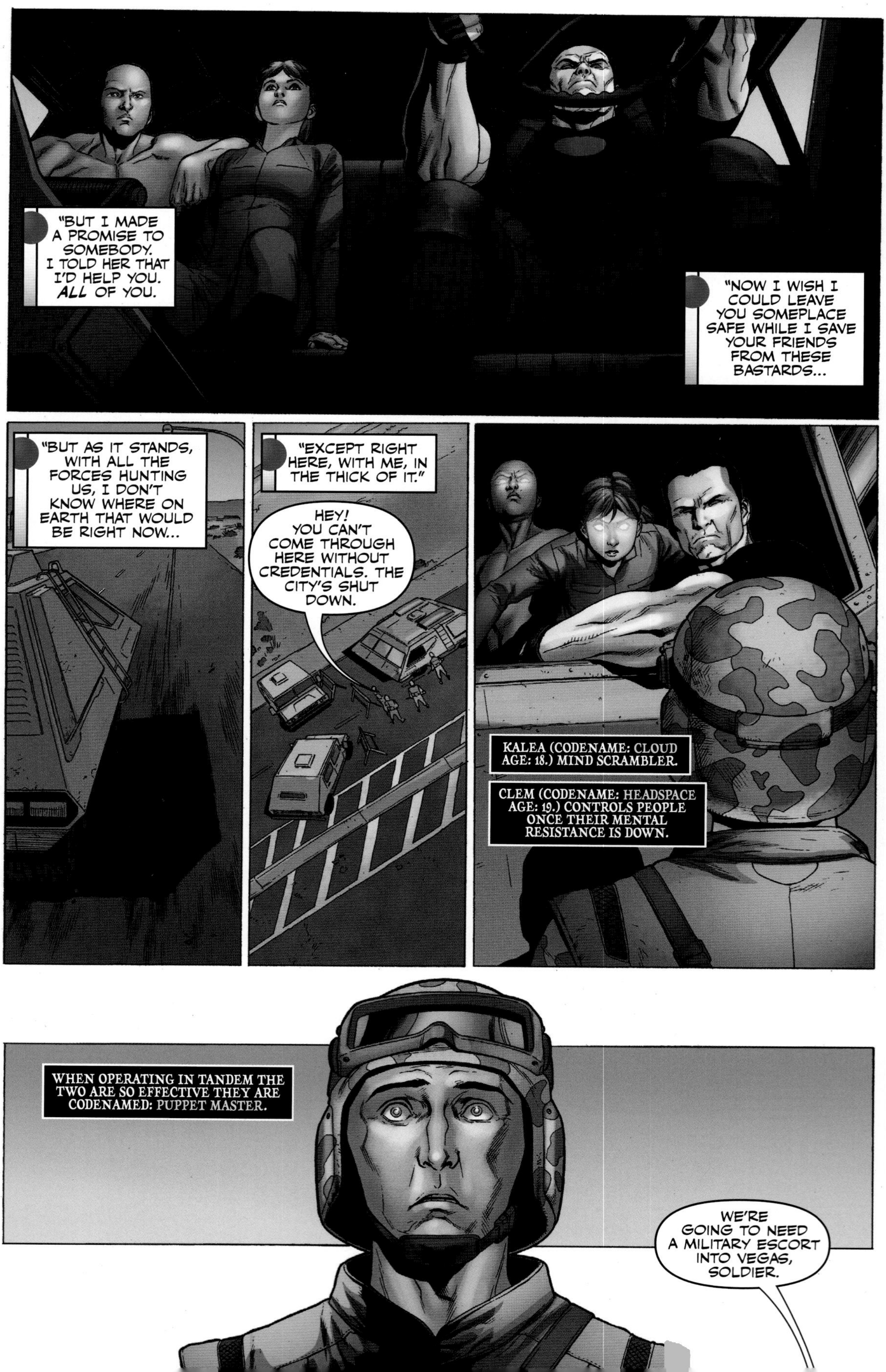
"BUT I MADE A PROMISE TO SOMEBODY. I TOLD HER THAT I'D HELP YOU. ALL OF YOU.
"NOW I WISH I COULD LEAVE YOU SOMEPLACE SAFE WHILE I SAVE YOUR FRIENDS FROM THESE BASTARDS...
"BUT AS IT STANDS, WITH ALL THE FORCES HUNTING US, I DON'T KNOW WHERE ON EARTH THAT WOULD BE RIGHT NOW...
"EXCEPT RIGHT HERE, WITH ME, IN THE THICK OF IT."
HEY! YOU CAN'T COME THROUGH HERE WITHOUT CREDENTIALS. THE CITY'S SHUT DOWN.
KALEA (CODENAME: CLOUD AGE: 18.) MIND SCRAMBLER.
CLEM (CODENAME: HEADSPACE AGE: 19.) CONTROLS PEOPLE ONCE THEIR MENTAL RESISTANCE IS DOWN.
WHEN OPERATING IN TANDEM THE TWO ARE SO EFFECTIVE THEY ARE CODENAMED: PUPPET MASTER.
WE'RE GOING TO NEED A MILITARY ESCORT INTO VEGAS, SOLDIER.

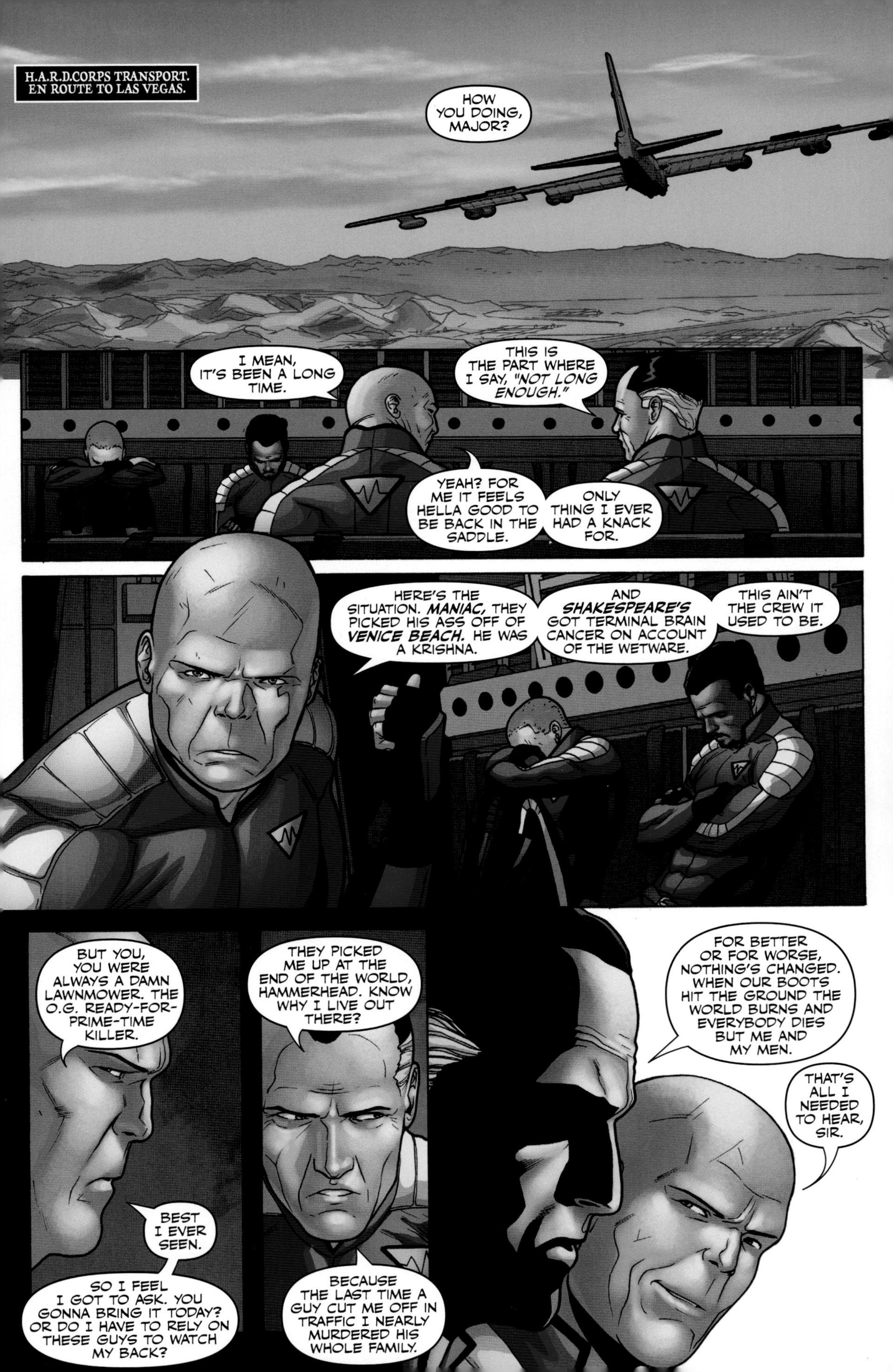
H.A.R.D.CORPS TRANSPORT. EN ROUTE TO LAS VEGAS.
HOW YOU DOING, MAJOR?
I MEAN, IT'S BEEN A LONG TIME.
THIS IS THE PART WHERE I SAY, "NOT LONG ENOUGH."
YEAH? FOR ME IT FEELS HELLA GOOD TO BE BACK IN THE SADDLE.
ONLY THING I EVER HAD A KNACK FOR.
HERE'S THE SITUATION. MANIAC, THEY PICKED HIS ASS OFF OF VENICE BEACH. HE WAS A KRISHNA.
AND SHAKESPEARE'S GOT TERMINAL BRAIN CANCER ON ACCOUNT OF THE WETWARE.
THIS AIN'T THE CREW IT USED TO BE.
BUT YOU, YOU WERE ALWAYS A DAMN LAWNMOWER. THE O.G. READY-FOR-PRIME-TIME KILLER.
BEST I EVER SEEN.
SO I FEEL I GOT TO ASK. YOU GONNA BRING IT TODAY? OR DO I HAVE TO RELY ON THESE GUYS TO WATCH MY BACK?
THEY PICKED ME UP AT THE END OF THE WORLD, HAMMERHEAD. KNOW WHY I LIVE OUT THERE?
BECAUSE THE LAST TIME A GUY CUT ME OFF IN TRAFFIC I NEARLY MURDERED HIS WHOLE FAMILY.
FOR BETTER OR FOR WORSE, NOTHING'S CHANGED. WHEN OUR BOOTS HIT THE GROUND THE WORLD BURNS AND EVERYBODY DIES BUT ME AND MY MEN.
THAT'S ALL I NEEDED TO HEAR, SIR.

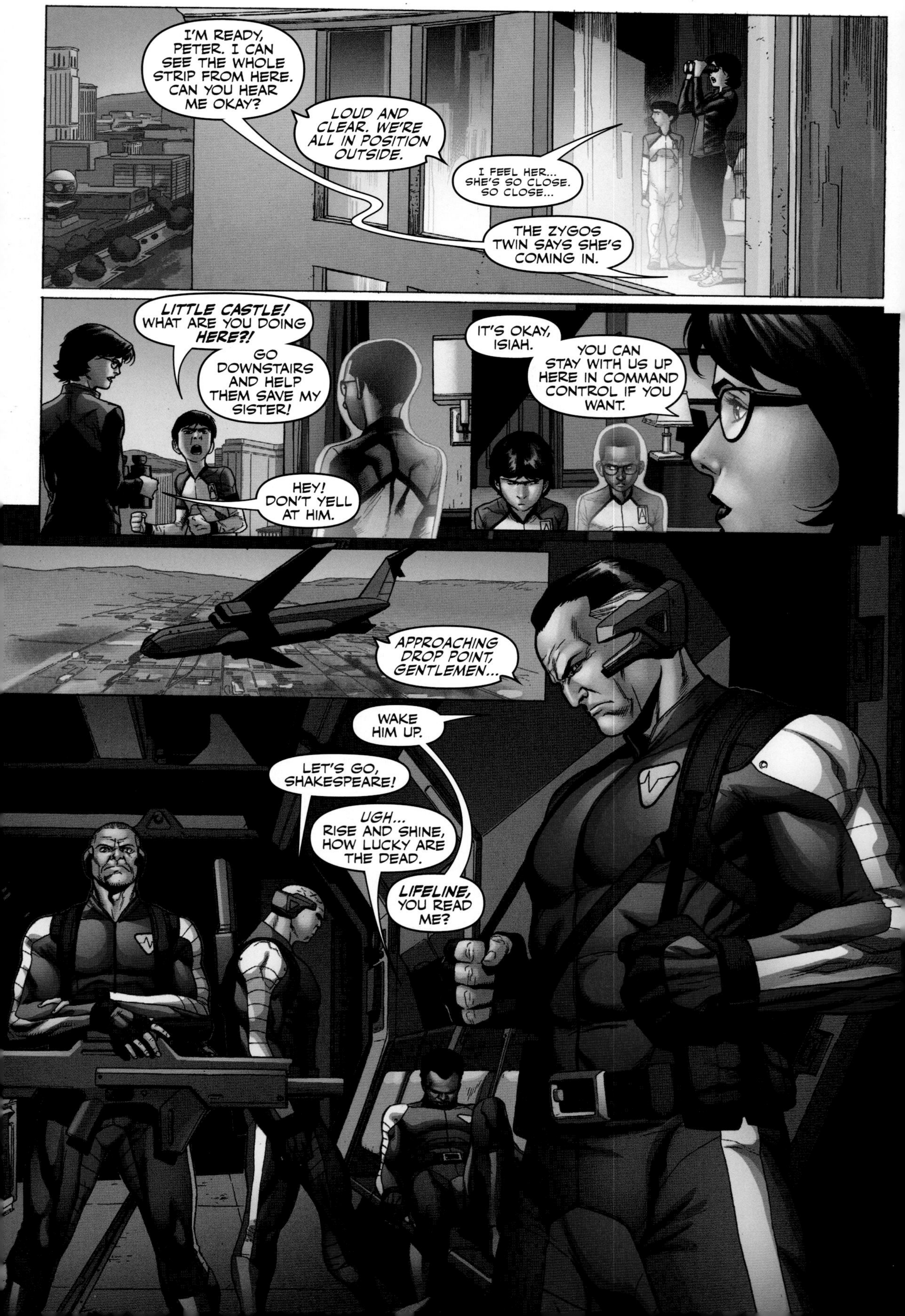
I'M READY, PETER. I CAN SEE THE WHOLE STRIP FROM HERE. CAN YOU HEAR ME OKAY?
LOUD AND CLEAR. WE'RE ALL IN POSITION OUTSIDE.
I FEEL HER... SHE'S SO CLOSE. SO CLOSE...
THE ZYGOS TWIN SAYS SHE'S COMING IN.
LITTLE CASTLE! WHAT ARE YOU DOING HERE?!
GO DOWNSTAIRS AND HELP THEM SAVE MY SISTER!
HEY! DON'T YELL AT HIM.
IT'S OKAY, ISIAH.
YOU CAN STAY WITH US UP HERE IN COMMAND CONTROL IF YOU WANT.
APPROACHING DROP POINT, GENTLEMEN...
WAKE HIM UP.
LET'S GO, SHAKESPEARE!
UGH... RISE AND SHINE, HOW LUCKY ARE THE DEAD.
LIFELINE, YOU READ ME?

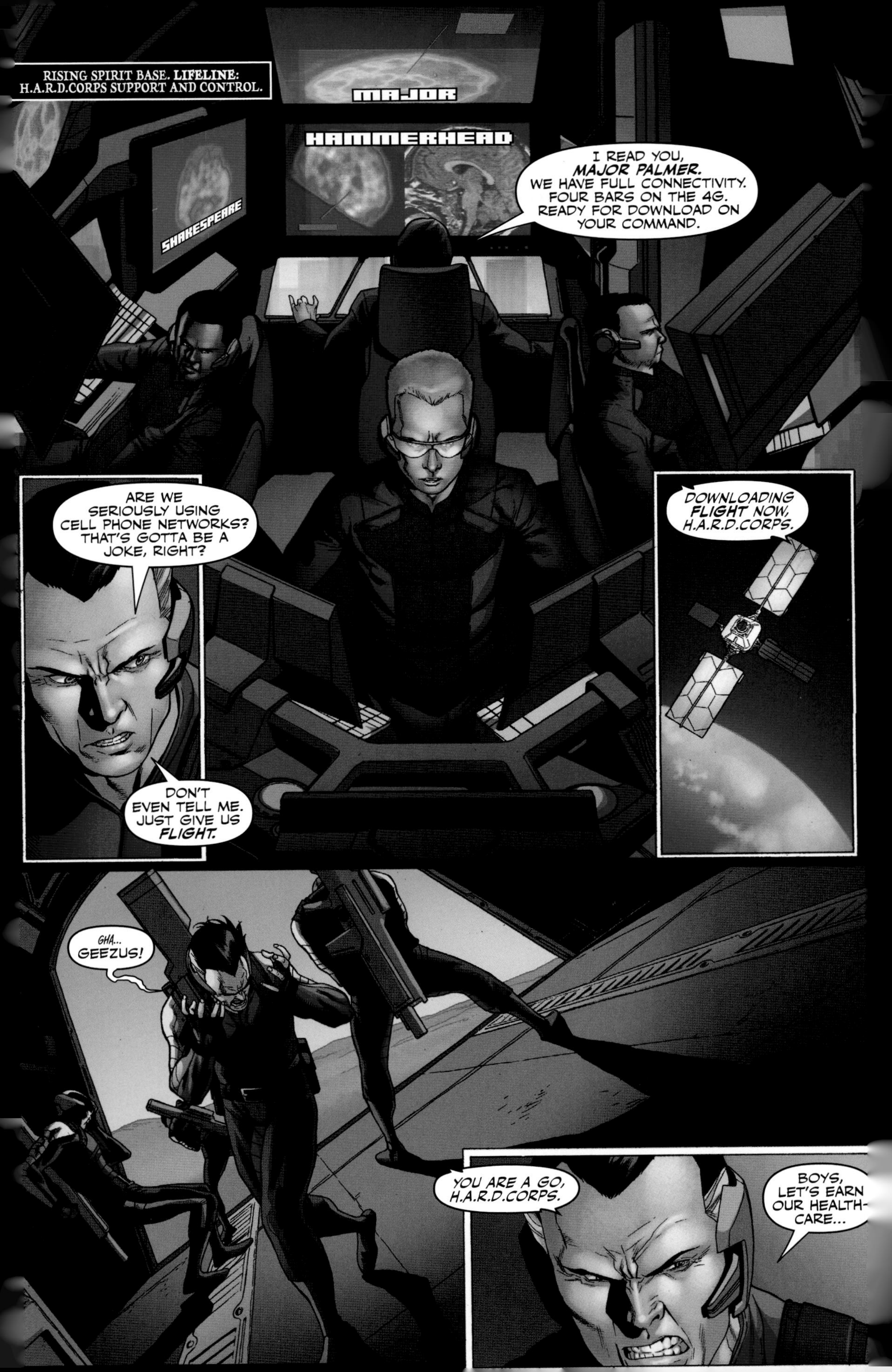

RISING SPIRIT BASE. LIFELINE: H.A.R.D.CORPS SUPPORT AND CONTROL.
MAJOR
HAMMERHEAD
SHAKESPEARE
I READ YOU, MAJOR PALMER. WE HAVE FULL CONNECTIVITY. FOUR BARS ON THE 4G. READY FOR DOWNLOAD ON YOUR COMMAND.
ARE WE SERIOUSLY USING CELL PHONE NETWORKS? THAT'S GOTTA BE A JOKE, RIGHT?
DON'T EVEN TELL ME. JUST GIVE US FLIGHT.
DOWNLOADING FLIGHT NOW, H.A.R.D.CORPS.
GHA... GEEZUS!
YOU ARE A GO, H.A.R.D.CORPS.
BOYS, LET'S EARN OUR HEALTH-CARE...

SHAKESPEARE, FOR OLD TIMES' SAKE, HIT US WITH A CLASSIC.

ONCE MORE UNTO THE BREACH, DEAR FRIENDS, ONCE MORE!

OUR JOB IS TO BACK THE RENEGADES UP AS SOON AS THEY GET BLOODSHOT TO OUR MARKED--

TELIC?

IS SOMETHING WRONG?

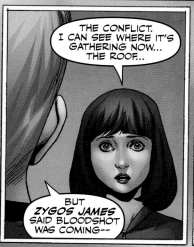

THE CONFLICT. I CAN SEE WHERE IT'S GATHERING NOW... THE ROOF...

BUT *ZYGOS JAMES* SAID BLOODSHOT WAS COMING--

CHRISTIAN... SOMETHING TERRIBLE IS ABOUT TO HAPPEN ABOVE US--

--THE PATTERNS ARE DRIPPING DOWN THE WALLS LIKE BLOOD.

ALL RIGHT. REDEPLOY. THE *RENEGADES* HAVE THE GROUND. WE'LL TAKE THE TOP.

LET'S GO.

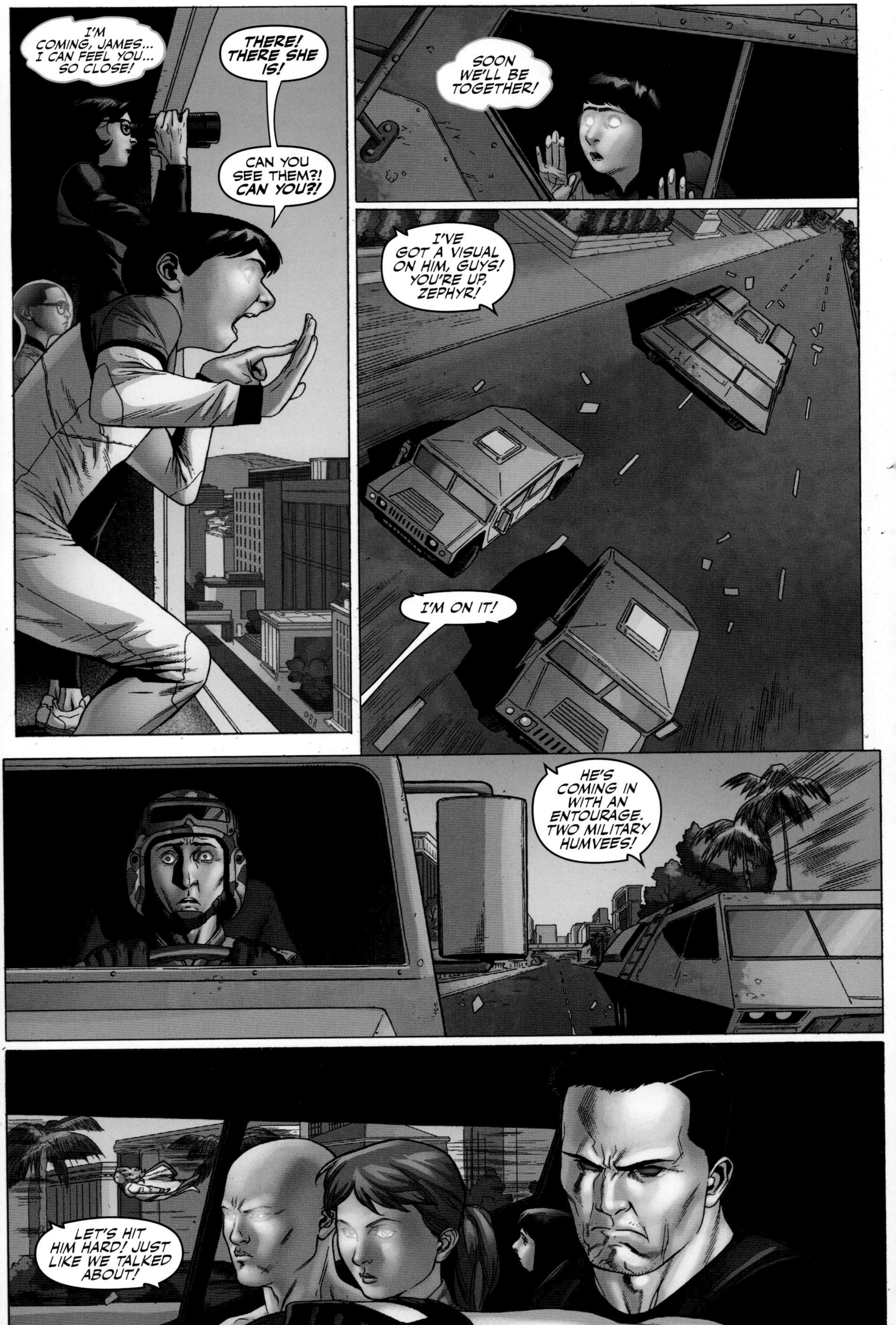
I'M COMING, JAMES... I CAN FEEL YOU... SO CLOSE!
THERE! THERE SHE IS!
CAN YOU SEE THEM?! CAN YOU?!
SOON WE'LL BE TOGETHER!
I'VE GOT A VISUAL ON HIM, GUYS! YOU'RE UP, ZEPHYR!
I'M ON IT!
HE'S COMING IN WITH AN ENTOURAGE. TWO MILITARY HUMVEES!
LET'S HIT HIM HARD! JUST LIKE WE TALKED ABOUT!

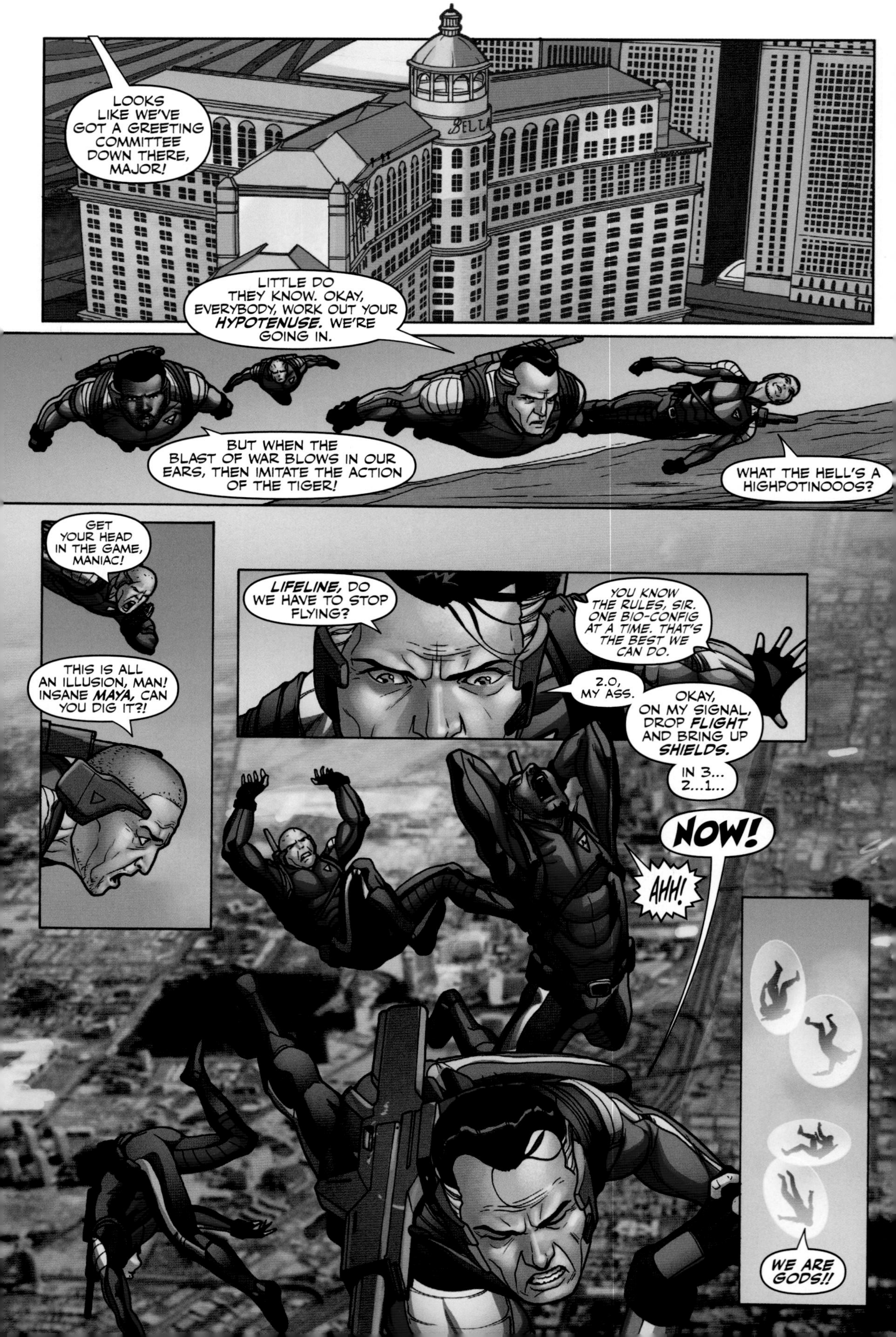
LOOKS LIKE WE'VE GOT A GREETING COMMITTEE DOWN THERE, MAJOR!
LITTLE DO THEY KNOW. OKAY, EVERYBODY, WORK OUT YOUR HYPOTENUSE. WE'RE GOING IN.
BUT WHEN THE BLAST OF WAR BLOWS IN OUR EARS, THEN IMITATE THE ACTION OF THE TIGER!
WHAT THE HELL'S A HIGHPOTINOOOS?
GET YOUR HEAD IN THE GAME, MANIAC!
THIS IS ALL AN ILLUSION, MAN! INSANE MAYA, CAN YOU DIG IT?!
LIFELINE, DO WE HAVE TO STOP FLYING?
YOU KNOW THE RULES, SIR. ONE BIO-CONFIG AT A TIME. THAT'S THE BEST WE CAN DO.
2.0, MY ASS.
OKAY, ON MY SIGNAL, DROP FLIGHT AND BRING UP SHIELDS.
IN 3... 2...1...
NOW!
AHH!
WE ARE GODS!!

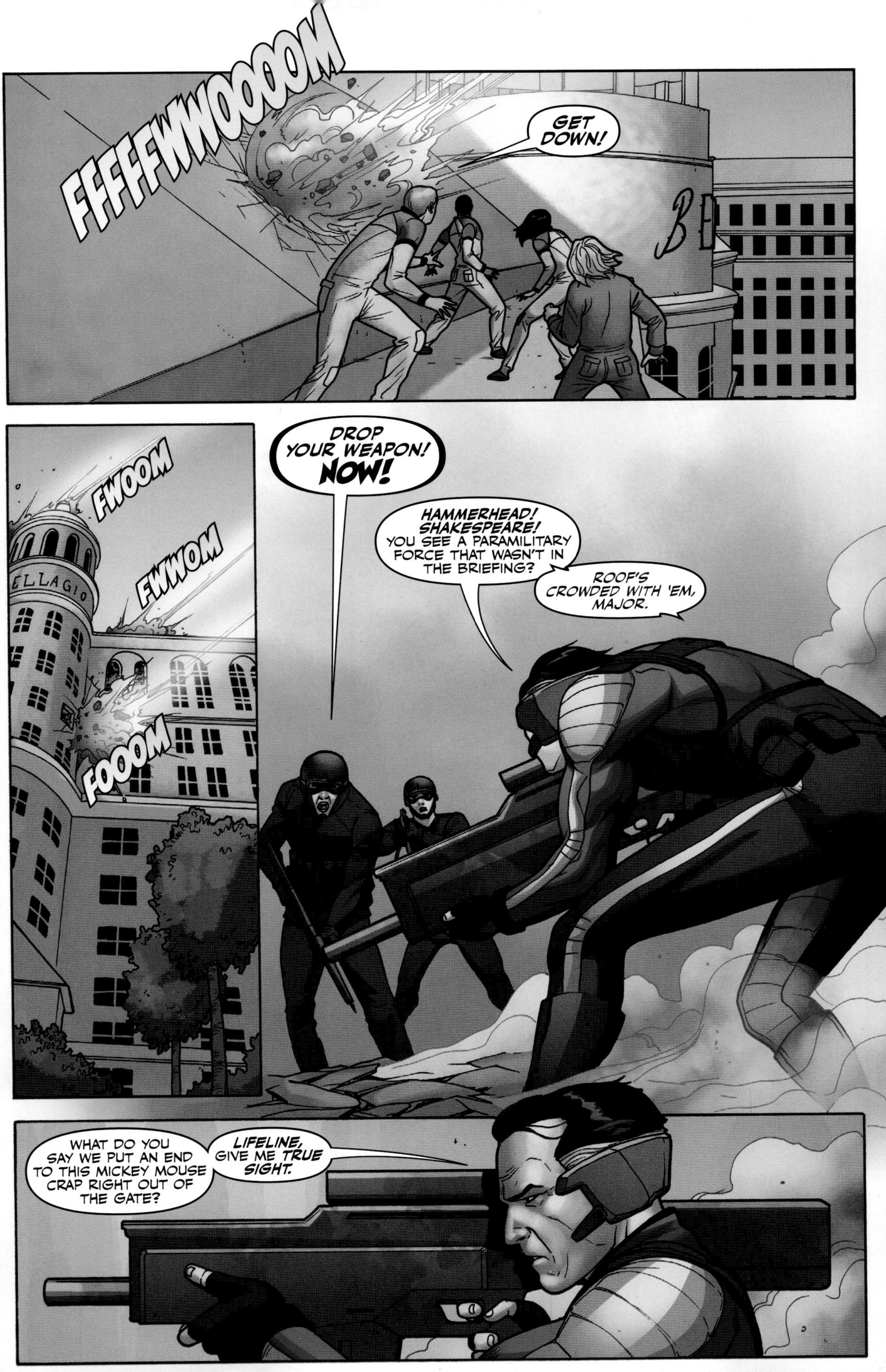
FFFFFWWOOOOM
GET DOWN!
FWOOM
FWWOM
FOOOM
DROP YOUR WEAPON! NOW!
HAMMERHEAD! SHAKESPEARE! YOU SEE A PARAMILITARY FORCE THAT WASN'T IN THE BRIEFING?
ROOF'S CROWDED WITH 'EM, MAJOR.
WHAT DO YOU SAY WE PUT AN END TO THIS MICKEY MOUSE CRAP RIGHT OUT OF THE GATE?
LIFELINE, GIVE ME TRUE SIGHT.

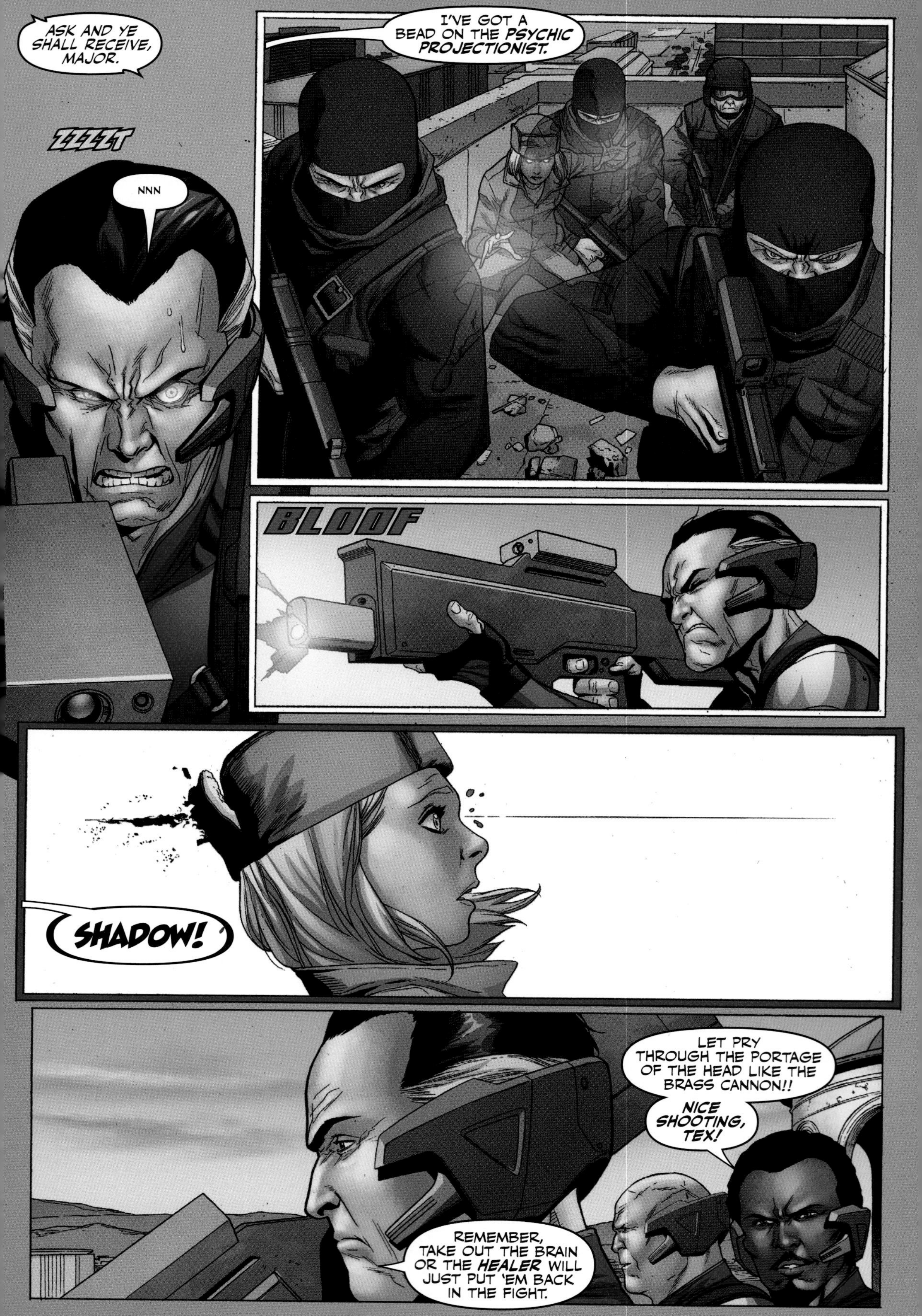
ASK AND YE SHALL RECEIVE, MAJOR.
I'VE GOT A BEAD ON THE PSYCHIC PROJECTIONIST.
ZZZZT
NNN
BLOOF
SHADOW!
LET PRY THROUGH THE PORTAGE OF THE HEAD LIKE THE BRASS CANNON!!
NICE SHOOTING, TEX!
REMEMBER, TAKE OUT THE BRAIN OR THE HEALER WILL JUST PUT 'EM BACK IN THE FIGHT.

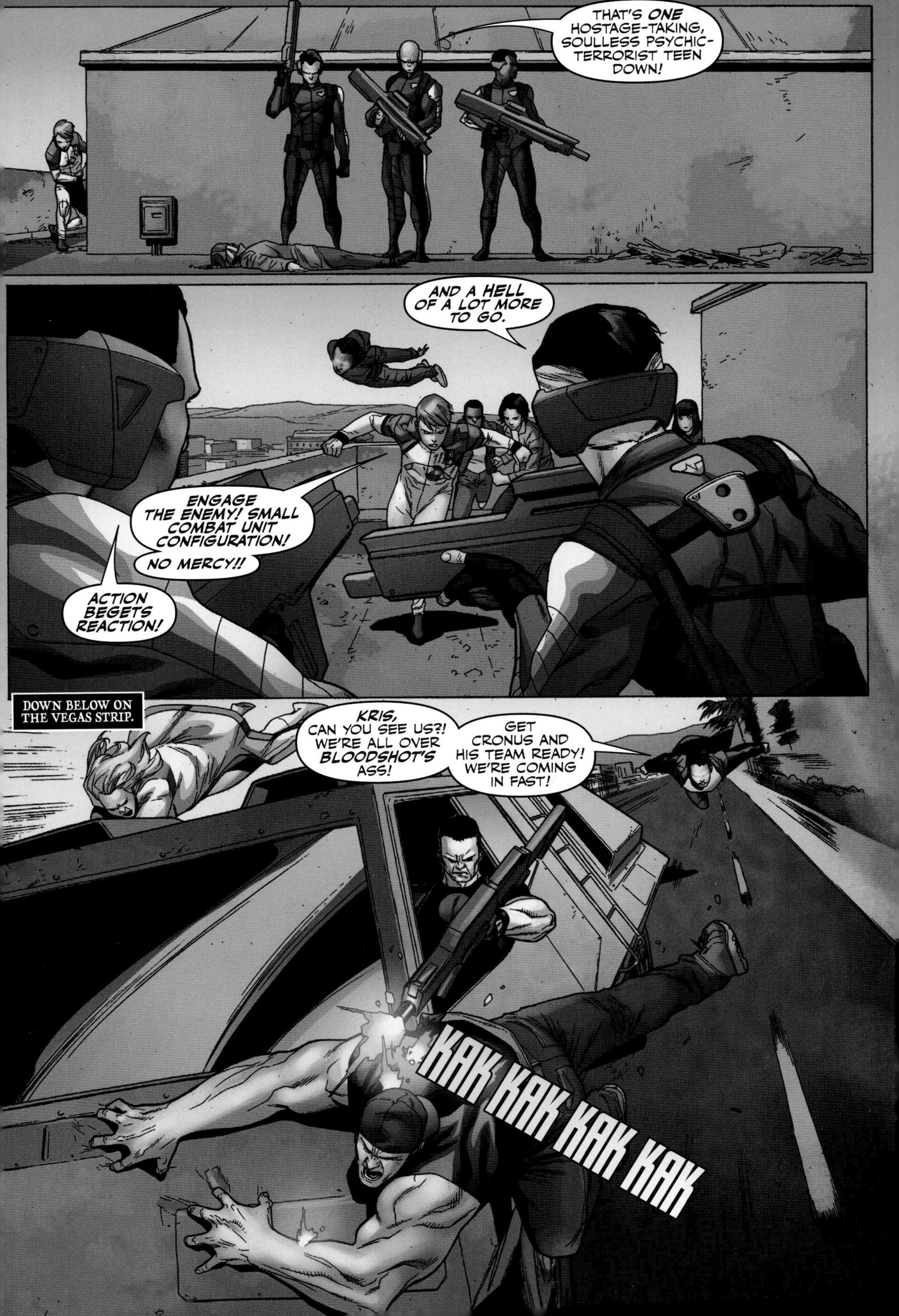
THAT'S ONE HOSTAGE-TAKING, SOULLESS PSYCHIC-TERRORIST TEEN DOWN!
AND A HELL OF A LOT MORE TO GO.
ENGAGE THE ENEMY! SMALL COMBAT UNIT CONFIGURATION!
NO MERCY!!
ACTION BEGETS REACTION!
DOWN BELOW ON THE VEGAS STRIP.
KRIS, CAN YOU SEE US?! WE'RE ALL OVER BLOODSHOT'S ASS!
GET CRONUS AND HIS TEAM READY! WE'RE COMING IN FAST!
KAK KAK KAK KAK

PETER, I THINK THEY'RE BOMBING THE BUILDING?!

WHAT?!

KNOCK! KNOCK!

I HEAR PIGGIES IN THERE!

ISIAH!

BLAM

DON'T BE AFRAID!

THIS IS JUST THE PLAY...THE THING... I HAVE FULL CONTROL OF THE ILLUSION, YOU UNDERSTAND?

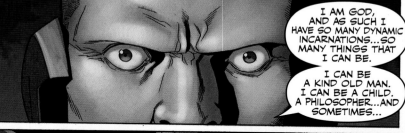

I AM GOD, AND AS SUCH I HAVE SO MANY DYNAMIC INCARNATIONS...SO MANY THINGS THAT I CAN BE.

I CAN BE A KIND OLD MAN. I CAN BE A CHILD. A PHILOSOPHER...AND SOMETIMES...

KRIS? ARE YOU THERE?! SEND IN THE CAVALRY! LIKE, RIGHT NOW! WE'RE IN SERIOUS TROUBLE DOWN HERE!

...I'M A KILLER...

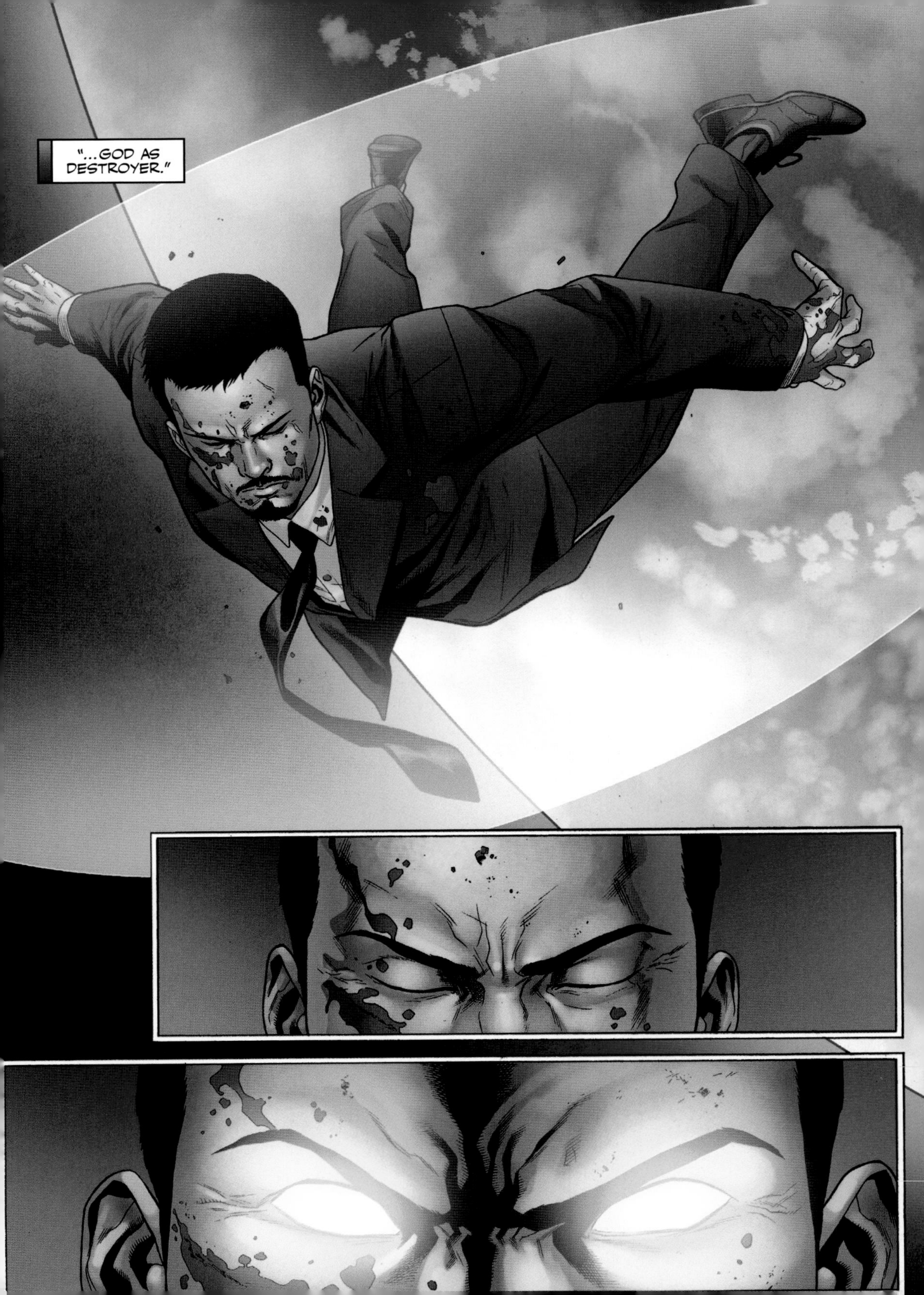
"...GOD AS DESTROYER."

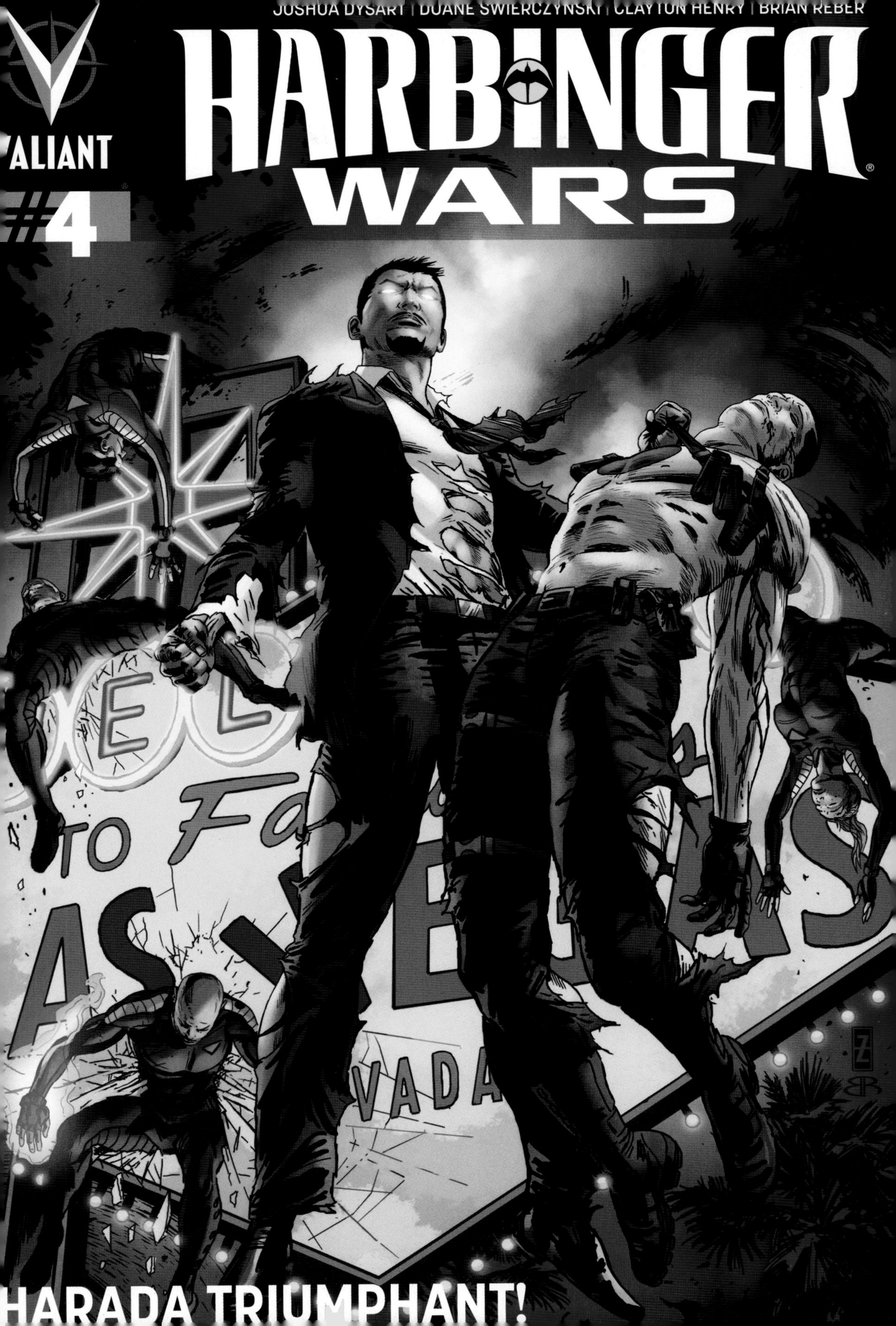

JOSHUA DYSART | DUANE SWIERCZYNSKI | CLAYTON HENRY | BRIAN REBER
VALIANT
HARBINGER WARS
#4
HARADA TRIUMPHANT!

HARBINGER WARS

FINALE

PETER STANCHEK & THE RENEGADES

BLOODSHOT & ESCAPED PSIOTS

HARADA AND THE EGGBREAKERS

H.A.R.D. CORPS

Project Rising Spirit created **Bloodshot** to be the perfect weapon, providing him with an extraordinary array of powers that allow him to accomplish his primary mission - the capture of super-powered children known as **psiots** - with lethal accuracy. Now **Bloodshot** has freed himself from his programming and turned on his masters.

Upon assaulting the **P.R.S.** facility, **Bloodshot** liberated the psiots he helped capture, but the children were separated into two groups. The first, calling itself **Generation Zero**, led by a psiot named **Cronus**, has taken over the Bellagio in Las Vegas. The other has traveled with **Bloodshot** to Vegas - guided by a psiot telepathically linked with her brother at the Bellagio - to reunite with the first.

Bloodshot does not know, however, that **Peter Stanchek** and his gang of **Renegade psiots** await him in Vegas with an ambush of their own. While their battle rages a group of **Project Rising Spirit**'s technologically empowered solider-assassins known as **H.A.R.D.Corps** also arrives in Vegas to eliminate the escaped Psiots. Now a free for all has broken loose in Vegas. As a great man once said, *"In War there are no winners...only survivors."*

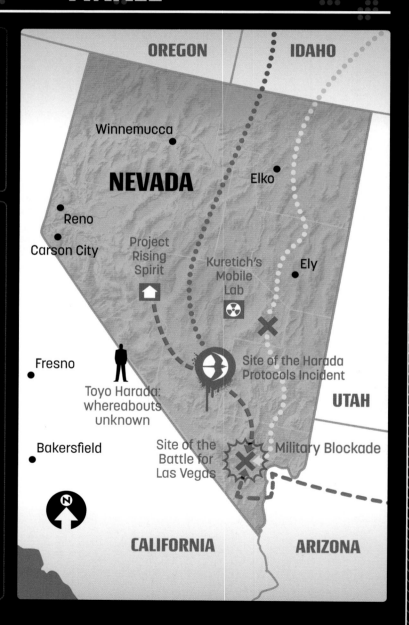

OREGON

IDAHO

Winnemucca

NEVADA

Elko

Reno

Carson City

Project Rising Spirit

Kuretich's Mobile Lab

Ely

Fresno

Site of the Harada Protocols Incident

Toyo Harada: whereabouts unknown

UTAH

Bakersfield

Site of the Battle for Las Vegas

Military Blockade

N

CALIFORNIA

ARIZONA

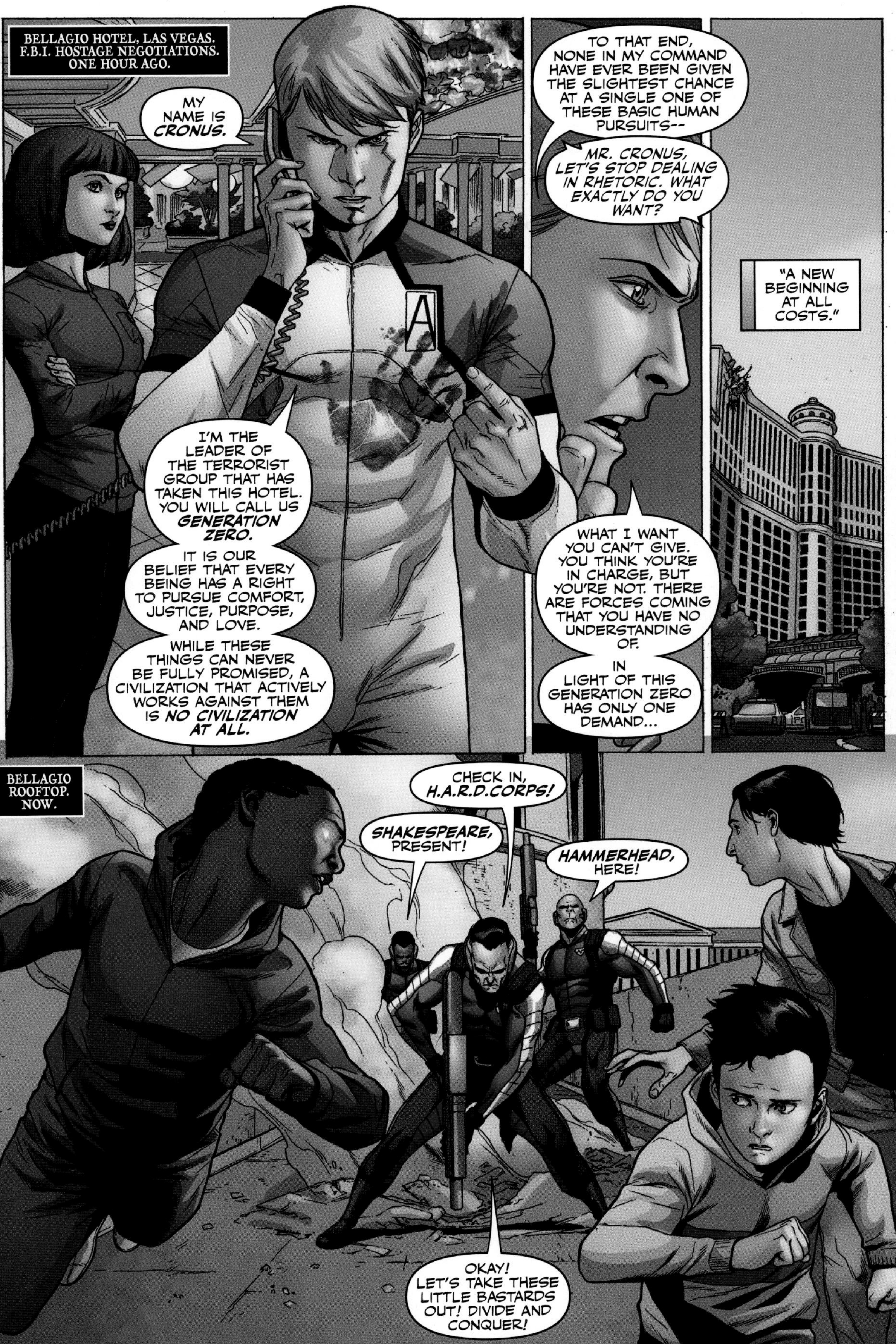
BELLAGIO HOTEL, LAS VEGAS. F.B.I. HOSTAGE NEGOTIATIONS. ONE HOUR AGO.
MY NAME IS CRONUS.
I'M THE LEADER OF THE TERRORIST GROUP THAT HAS TAKEN THIS HOTEL. YOU WILL CALL US GENERATION ZERO.
IT IS OUR BELIEF THAT EVERY BEING HAS A RIGHT TO PURSUE COMFORT, JUSTICE, PURPOSE, AND LOVE.
WHILE THESE THINGS CAN NEVER BE FULLY PROMISED, A CIVILIZATION THAT ACTIVELY WORKS AGAINST THEM IS NO CIVILIZATION AT ALL.
TO THAT END, NONE IN MY COMMAND HAVE EVER BEEN GIVEN THE SLIGHTEST CHANCE AT A SINGLE ONE OF THESE BASIC HUMAN PURSUITS--
MR. CRONUS, LET'S STOP DEALING IN RHETORIC. WHAT EXACTLY DO YOU WANT?
WHAT I WANT YOU CAN'T GIVE. YOU THINK YOU'RE IN CHARGE, BUT YOU'RE NOT. THERE ARE FORCES COMING THAT YOU HAVE NO UNDERSTANDING OF.
IN LIGHT OF THIS GENERATION ZERO HAS ONLY ONE DEMAND...
"A NEW BEGINNING AT ALL COSTS."
BELLAGIO ROOFTOP. NOW.
CHECK IN, H.A.R.D.CORPS!
SHAKESPEARE, PRESENT!
HAMMERHEAD, HERE!
OKAY! LET'S TAKE THESE LITTLE BASTARDS OUT! DIVIDE AND CONQUER!

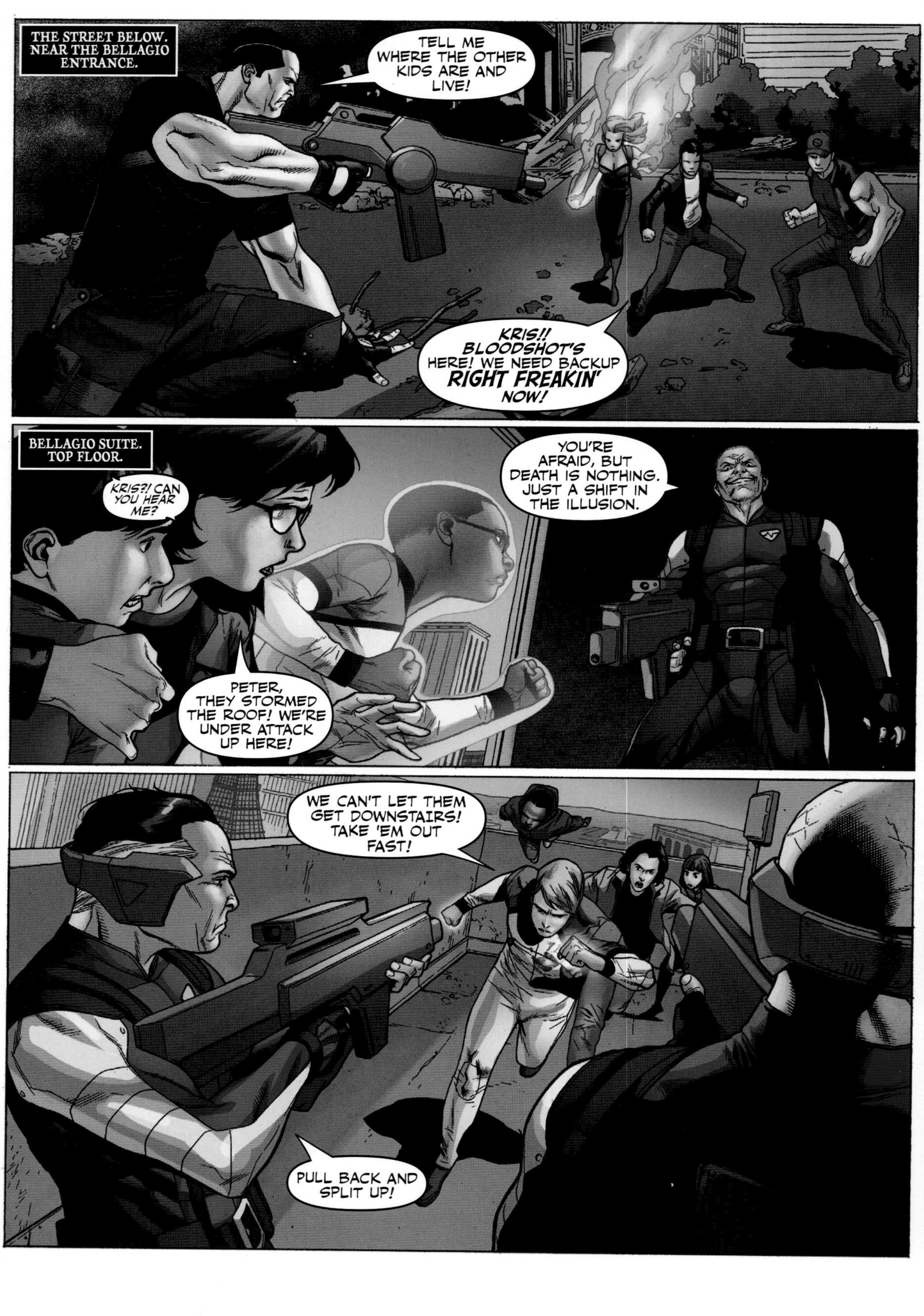
THE STREET BELOW. NEAR THE BELLAGIO ENTRANCE.
TELL ME WHERE THE OTHER KIDS ARE AND LIVE!
KRIS!! BLOODSHOT'S HERE! WE NEED BACKUP RIGHT FREAKIN' NOW!
BELLAGIO SUITE. TOP FLOOR.
KRIS?! CAN YOU HEAR ME?
PETER, THEY STORMED THE ROOF! WE'RE UNDER ATTACK UP HERE!
YOU'RE AFRAID, BUT DEATH IS NOTHING. JUST A SHIFT IN THE ILLUSION.
WE CAN'T LET THEM GET DOWNSTAIRS! TAKE 'EM OUT FAST!
PULL BACK AND SPLIT UP!

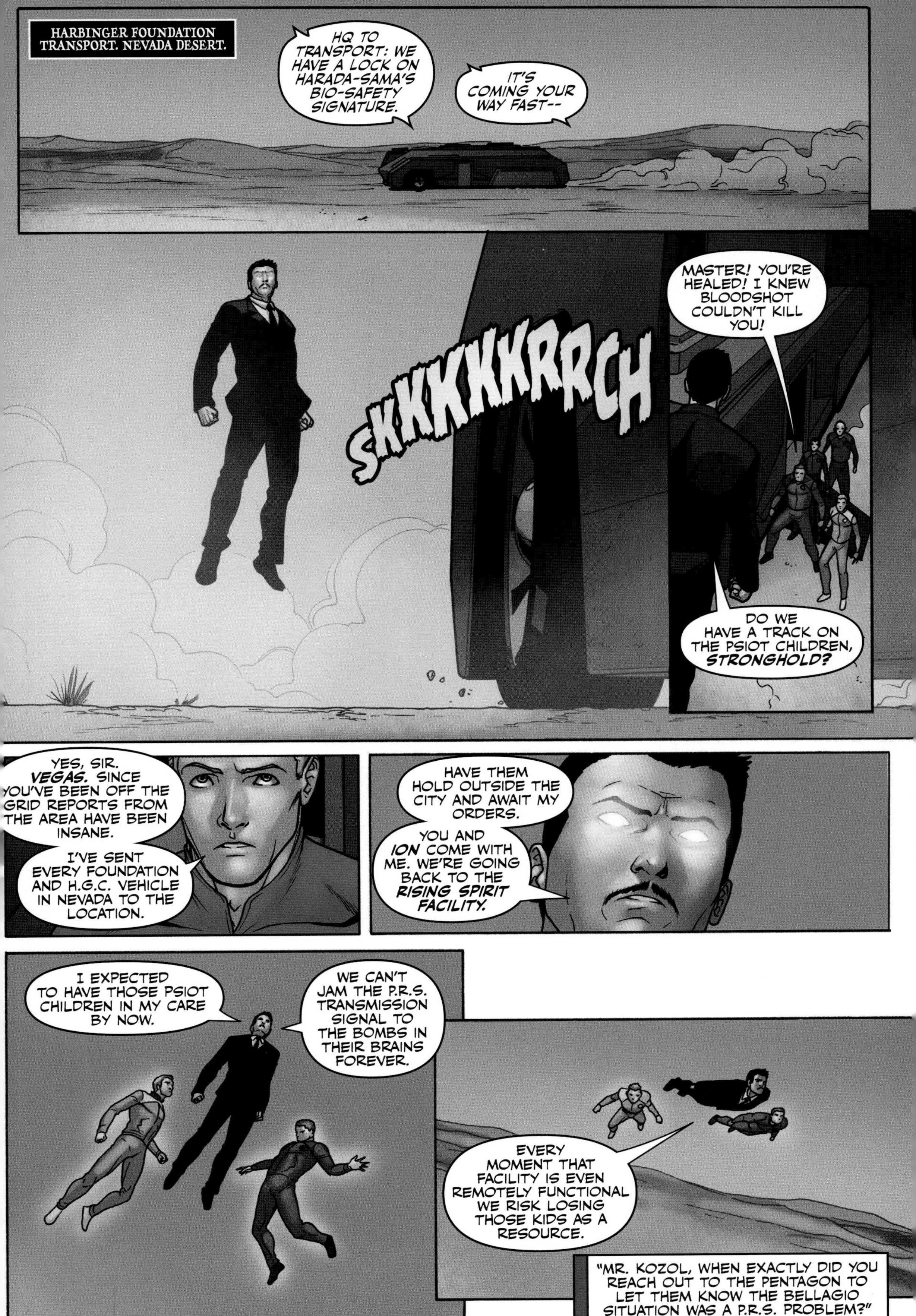
HARBINGER FOUNDATION TRANSPORT. NEVADA DESERT.
HQ TO TRANSPORT: WE HAVE A LOCK ON HARADA-SAMA'S BIO-SAFETY SIGNATURE.
IT'S COMING YOUR WAY FAST--
SKKKKKRRCH
MASTER! YOU'RE HEALED! I KNEW BLOODSHOT COULDN'T KILL YOU!
DO WE HAVE A TRACK ON THE PSIOT CHILDREN, STRONGHOLD?
YES, SIR. VEGAS. SINCE YOU'VE BEEN OFF THE GRID REPORTS FROM THE AREA HAVE BEEN INSANE.
I'VE SENT EVERY FOUNDATION AND H.G.C. VEHICLE IN NEVADA TO THE LOCATION.
HAVE THEM HOLD OUTSIDE THE CITY AND AWAIT MY ORDERS.
YOU AND ION COME WITH ME. WE'RE GOING BACK TO THE RISING SPIRIT FACILITY.
I EXPECTED TO HAVE THOSE PSIOT CHILDREN IN MY CARE BY NOW.
WE CAN'T JAM THE P.R.S. TRANSMISSION SIGNAL TO THE BOMBS IN THEIR BRAINS FOREVER.
EVERY MOMENT THAT FACILITY IS EVEN REMOTELY FUNCTIONAL WE RISK LOSING THOSE KIDS AS A RESOURCE.
"MR. KOZOL, WHEN EXACTLY DID YOU REACH OUT TO THE PENTAGON TO LET THEM KNOW THE BELLAGIO SITUATION WAS A P.R.S. PROBLEM?"

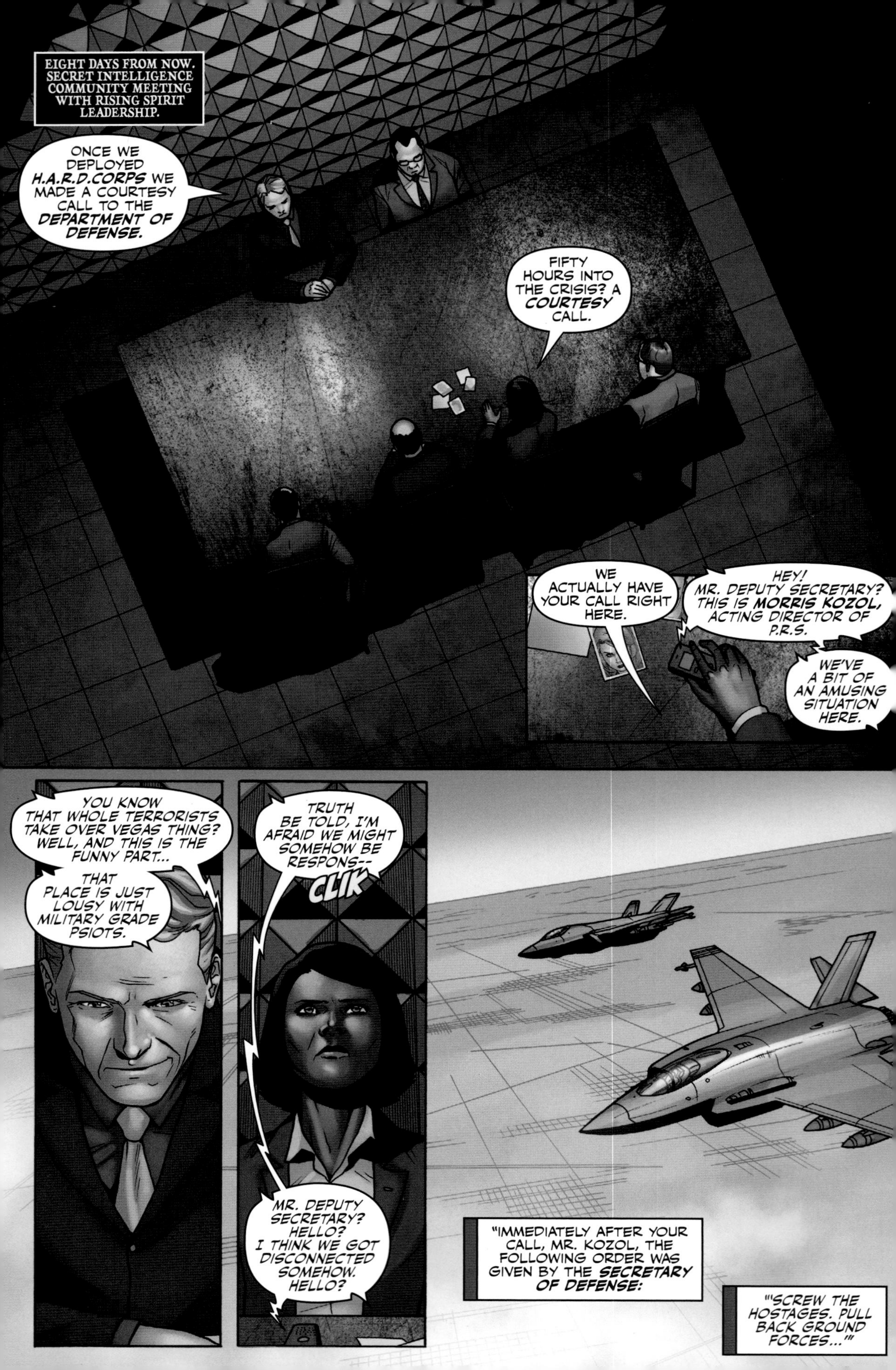

EIGHT DAYS FROM NOW. SECRET INTELLIGENCE COMMUNITY MEETING WITH RISING SPIRIT LEADERSHIP.
ONCE WE DEPLOYED H.A.R.D.CORPS WE MADE A COURTESY CALL TO THE DEPARTMENT OF DEFENSE.
FIFTY HOURS INTO THE CRISIS? A COURTESY CALL.
WE ACTUALLY HAVE YOUR CALL RIGHT HERE.
HEY! MR. DEPUTY SECRETARY? THIS IS MORRIS KOZOL, ACTING DIRECTOR OF P.R.S.
WE'VE A BIT OF AN AMUSING SITUATION HERE.
YOU KNOW THAT WHOLE TERRORISTS TAKE OVER VEGAS THING? WELL, AND THIS IS THE FUNNY PART...
THAT PLACE IS JUST LOUSY WITH MILITARY GRADE PSIOTS.
TRUTH BE TOLD, I'M AFRAID WE MIGHT SOMEHOW BE RESPONS--
CLIK
MR. DEPUTY SECRETARY? HELLO? I THINK WE GOT DISCONNECTED SOMEHOW. HELLO?
"IMMEDIATELY AFTER YOUR CALL, MR. KOZOL, THE FOLLOWING ORDER WAS GIVEN BY THE SECRETARY OF DEFENSE:
"'SCREW THE HOSTAGES. PULL BACK GROUND FORCES...'"

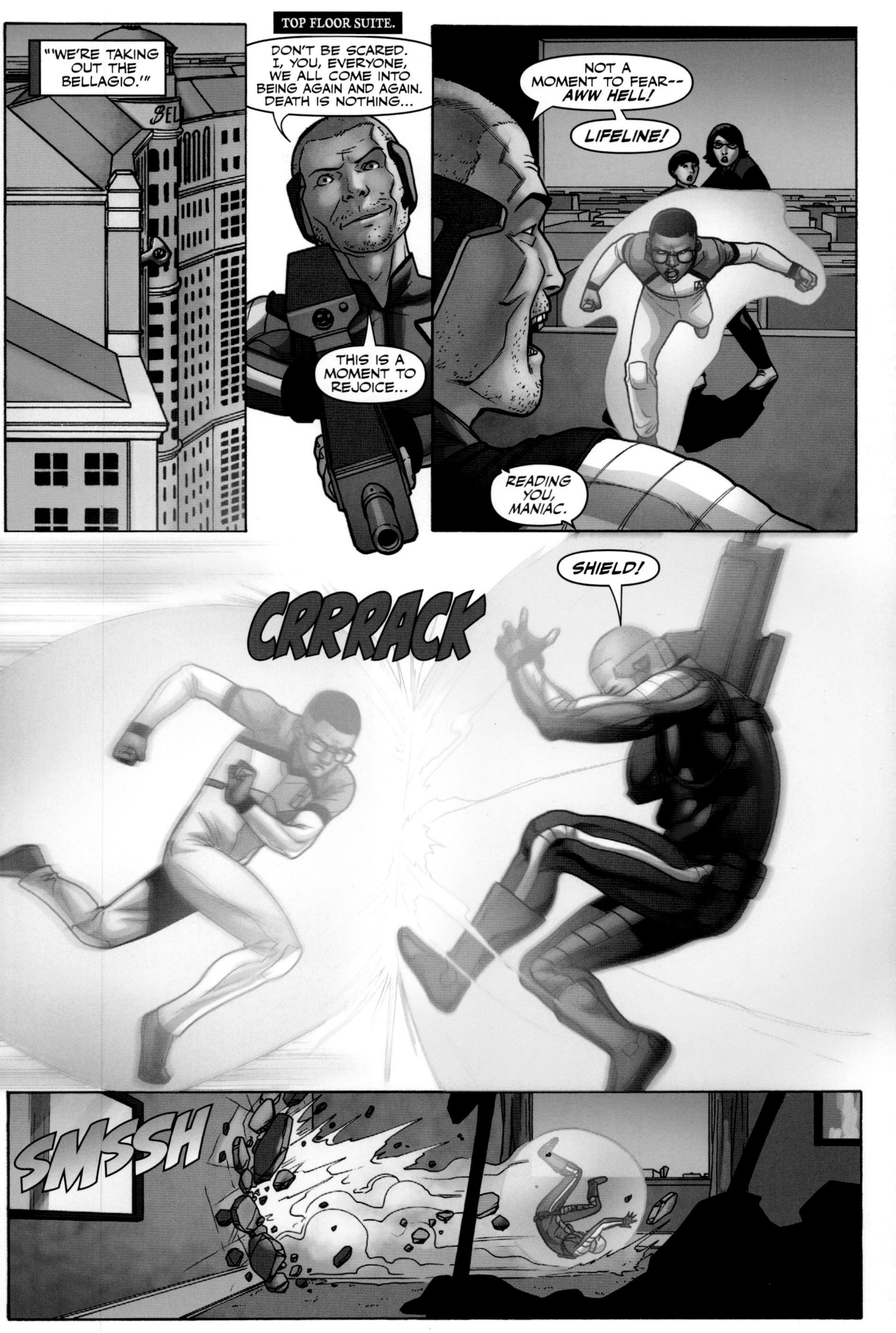
"WE'RE TAKING OUT THE BELLAGIO."
TOP FLOOR SUITE.
DON'T BE SCARED. I, YOU, EVERYONE, WE ALL COME INTO BEING AGAIN AND AGAIN. DEATH IS NOTHING...
THIS IS A MOMENT TO REJOICE...
NOT A MOMENT TO FEAR-- AWW HELL!
LIFELINE!
READING YOU, MANIAC.
SHIELD!
CRRRACK
SMSSH

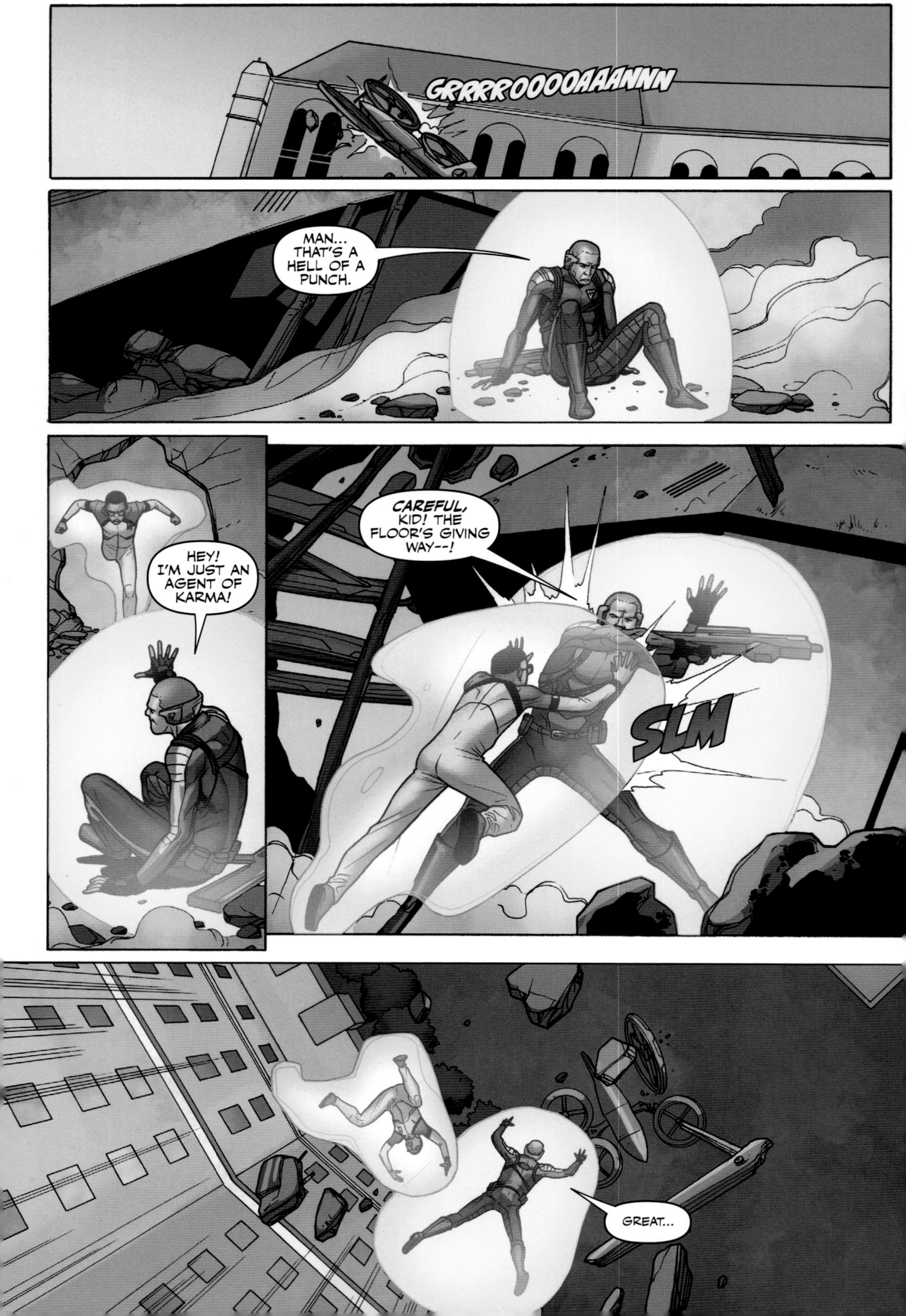
GRRRROOOOAAANNN
MAN... THAT'S A HELL OF A PUNCH.
HEY! I'M JUST AN AGENT OF KARMA!
CAREFUL, KID! THE FLOOR'S GIVING WAY--!
SLM
GREAT...

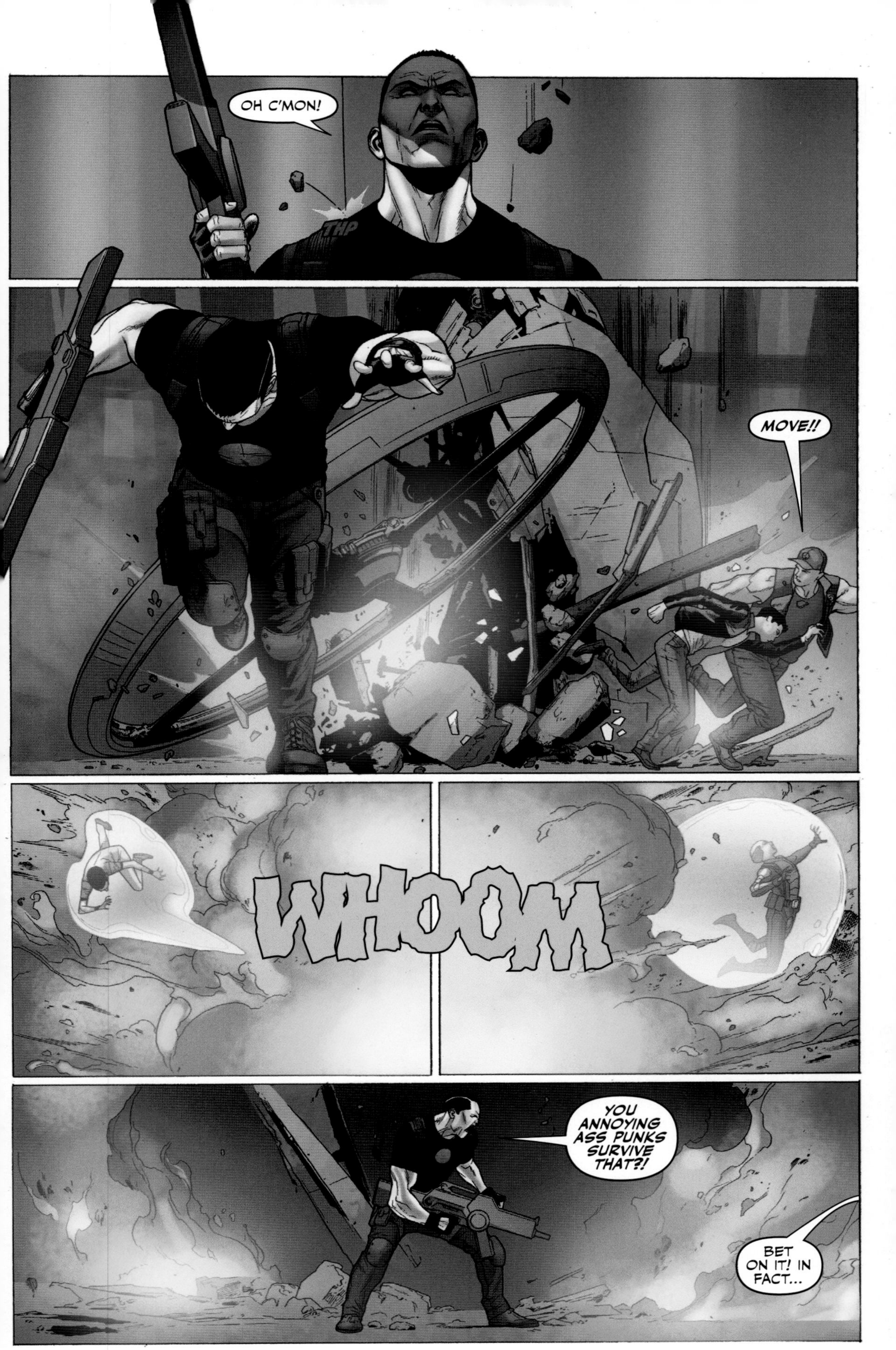
OH C'MON!
THP
MOVE!!
WHOOM
YOU ANNOYING ASS PUNKS SURVIVE THAT?!
BET ON IT! IN FACT...

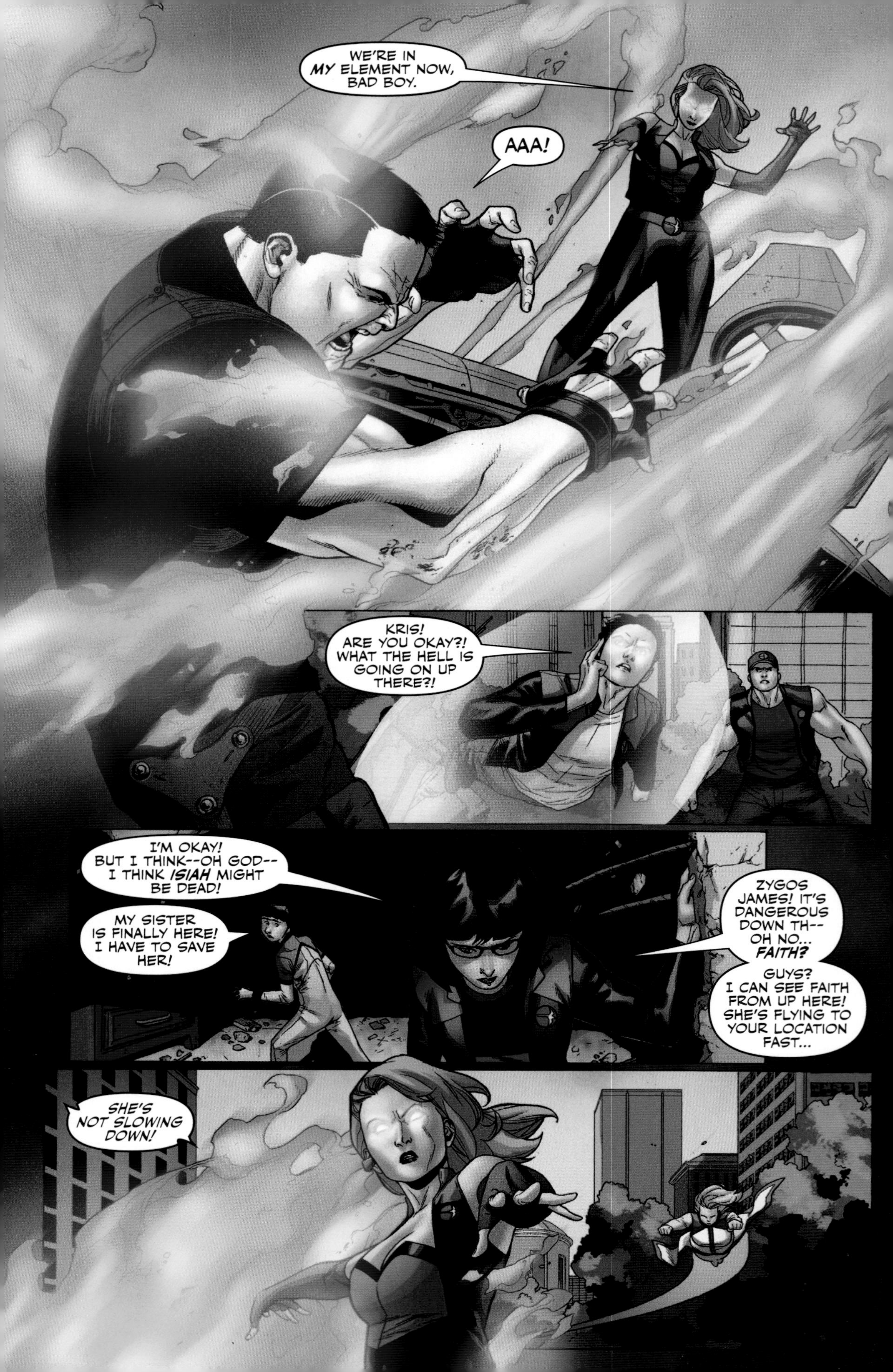
WE'RE IN MY ELEMENT NOW, BAD BOY.
AAA!
KRIS! ARE YOU OKAY?! WHAT THE HELL IS GOING ON UP THERE?!
I'M OKAY! BUT I THINK--OH GOD-- I THINK ISIAH MIGHT BE DEAD!
MY SISTER IS FINALLY HERE! I HAVE TO SAVE HER!
ZYGOS JAMES! IT'S DANGEROUS DOWN TH-- OH NO... FAITH?
GUYS? I CAN SEE FAITH FROM UP HERE! SHE'S FLYING TO YOUR LOCATION FAST...
SHE'S NOT SLOWING DOWN!

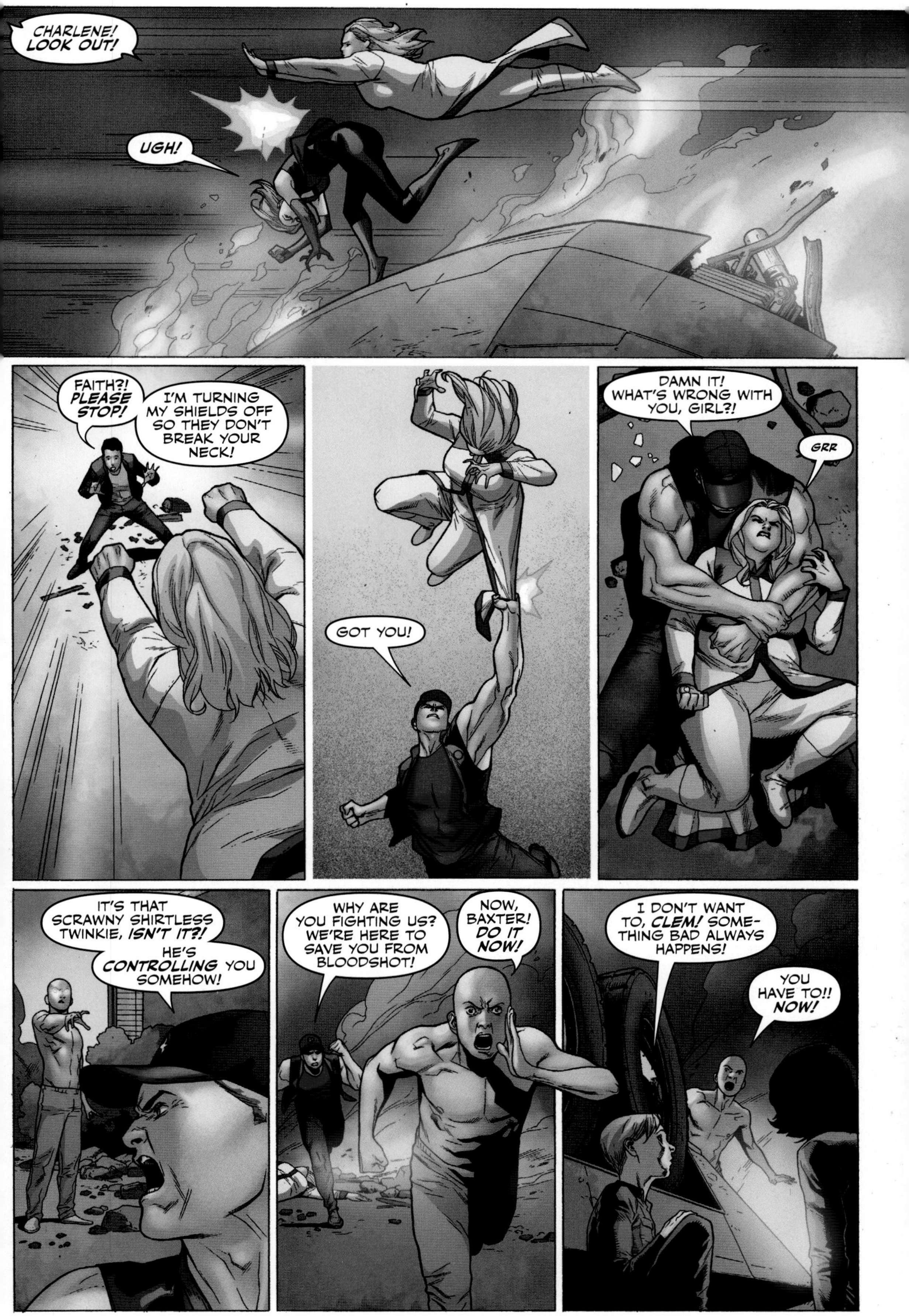
CHARLENE! LOOK OUT!
UGH!
FAITH?! PLEASE STOP!
I'M TURNING MY SHIELDS OFF SO THEY DON'T BREAK YOUR NECK!
GOT YOU!
DAMN IT! WHAT'S WRONG WITH YOU, GIRL?!
GRR
IT'S THAT SCRAWNY SHIRTLESS TWINKIE, ISN'T IT?!
HE'S CONTROLLING YOU SOMEHOW!
WHY ARE YOU FIGHTING US? WE'RE HERE TO SAVE YOU FROM BLOODSHOT!
NOW, BAXTER! DO IT NOW!
I DON'T WANT TO, CLEM! SOMETHING BAD ALWAYS HAPPENS!
YOU HAVE TO!! NOW!

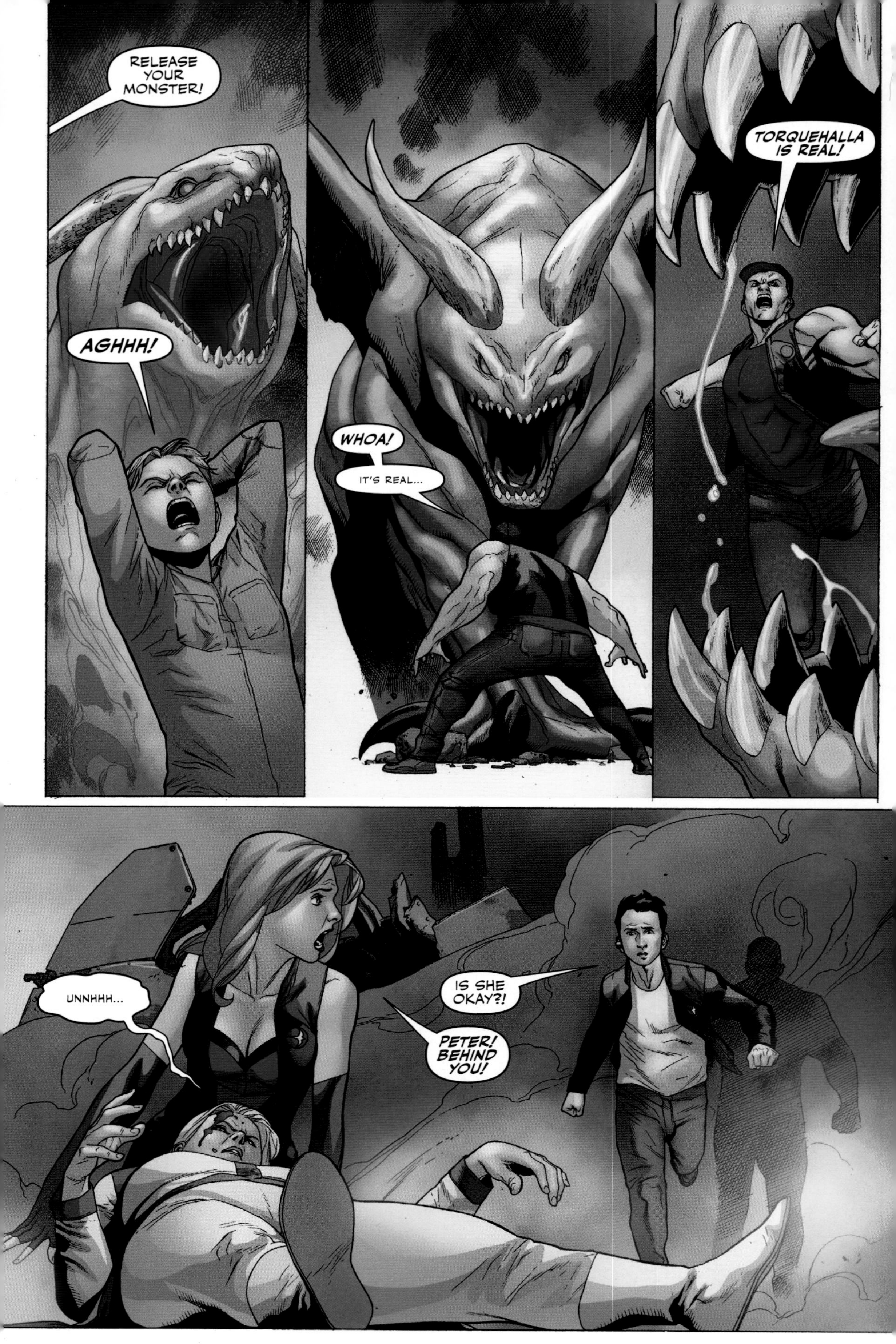
RELEASE YOUR MONSTER!
AGHHH!
WHOA!
IT'S REAL...
TORQUEHALLA IS REAL!
UNNHHH...
IS SHE OKAY?!
PETER! BEHIND YOU!

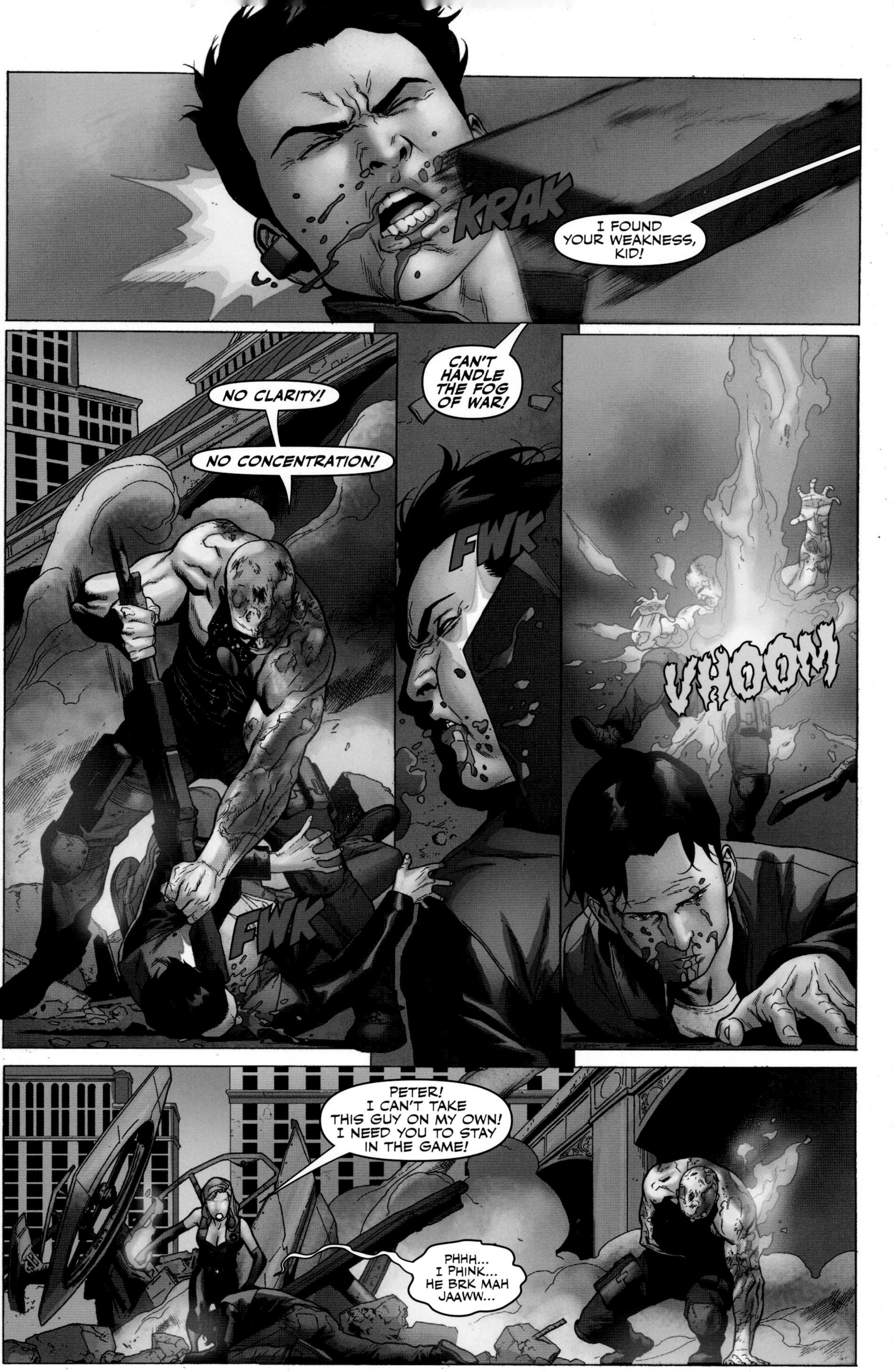
KRAK
I FOUND YOUR WEAKNESS, KID!
NO CLARITY!
NO CONCENTRATION!
FWK
CAN'T HANDLE THE FOG OF WAR!
FWK
VHOOM
PETER! I CAN'T TAKE THIS GUY ON MY OWN! I NEED YOU TO STAY IN THE GAME!
PHHH... I PHINK... HE BRK MAH JAAWW...

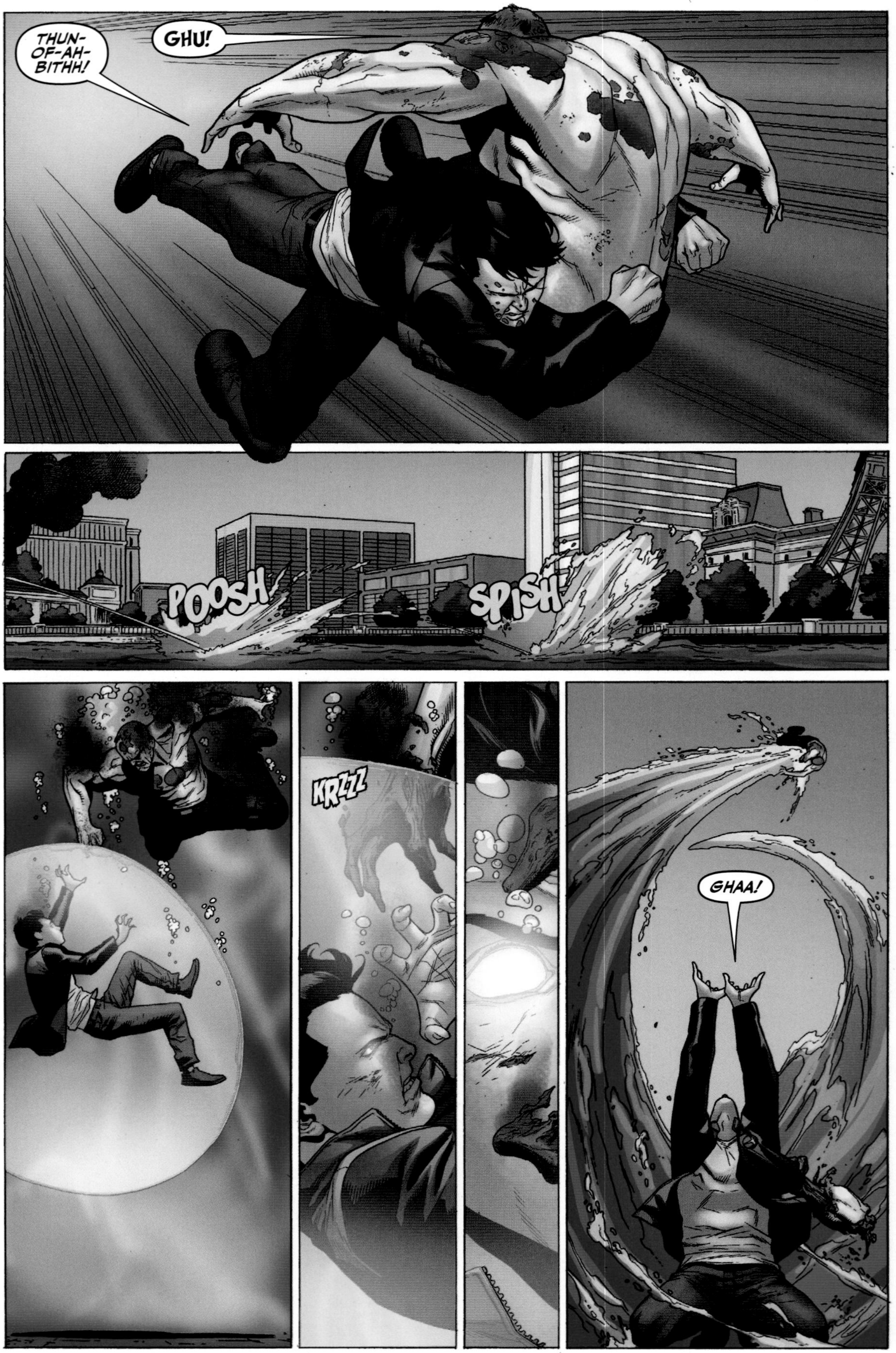
THUN-OF-AH-BITHH!
GHU!
POOSH
SPISH
KRZZZ
GHAA!

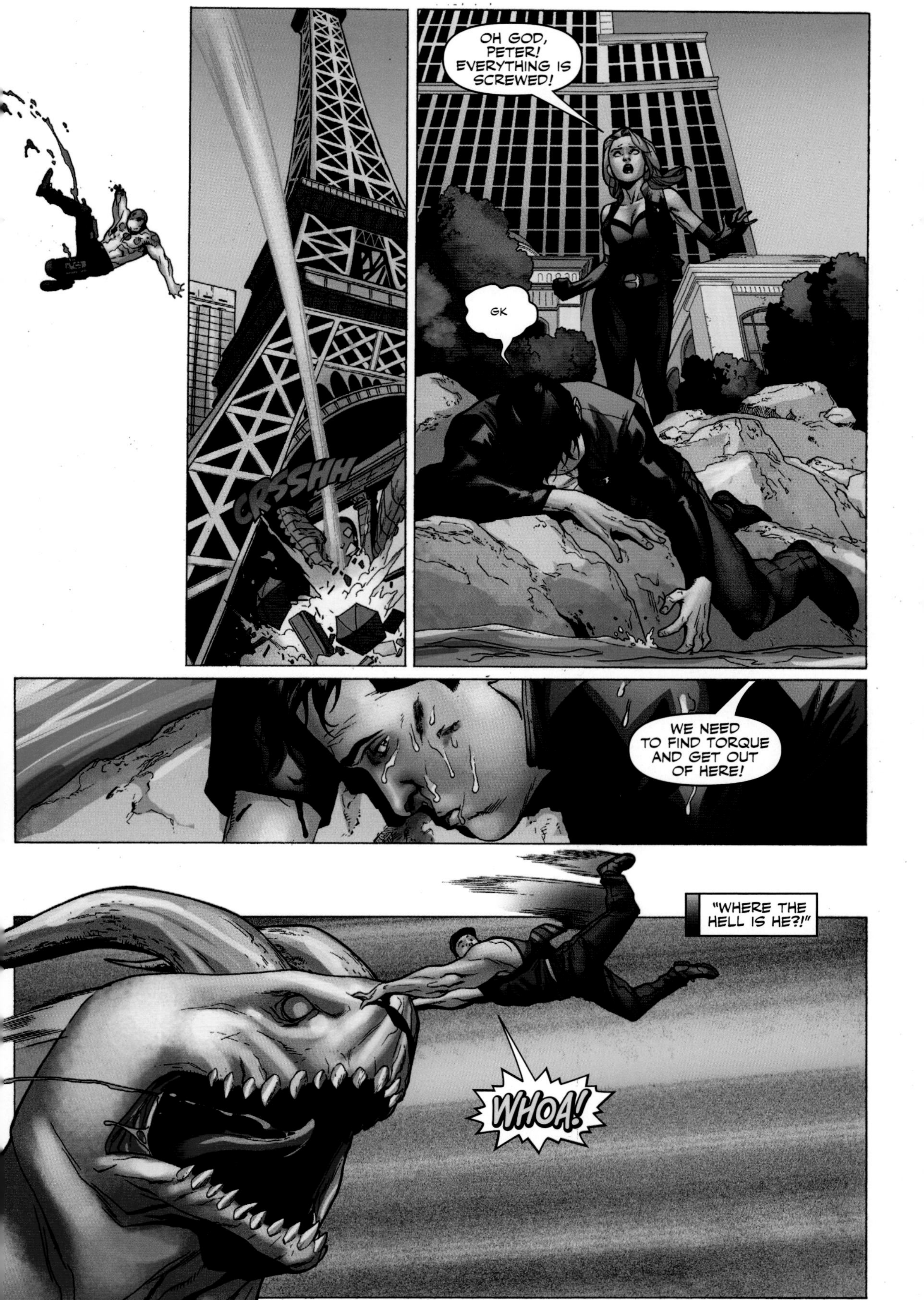
CRSSHH
OH GOD, PETER! EVERYTHING IS SCREWED!
GK
WE NEED TO FIND TORQUE AND GET OUT OF HERE!
"WHERE THE HELL IS HE?!"
WHOA!

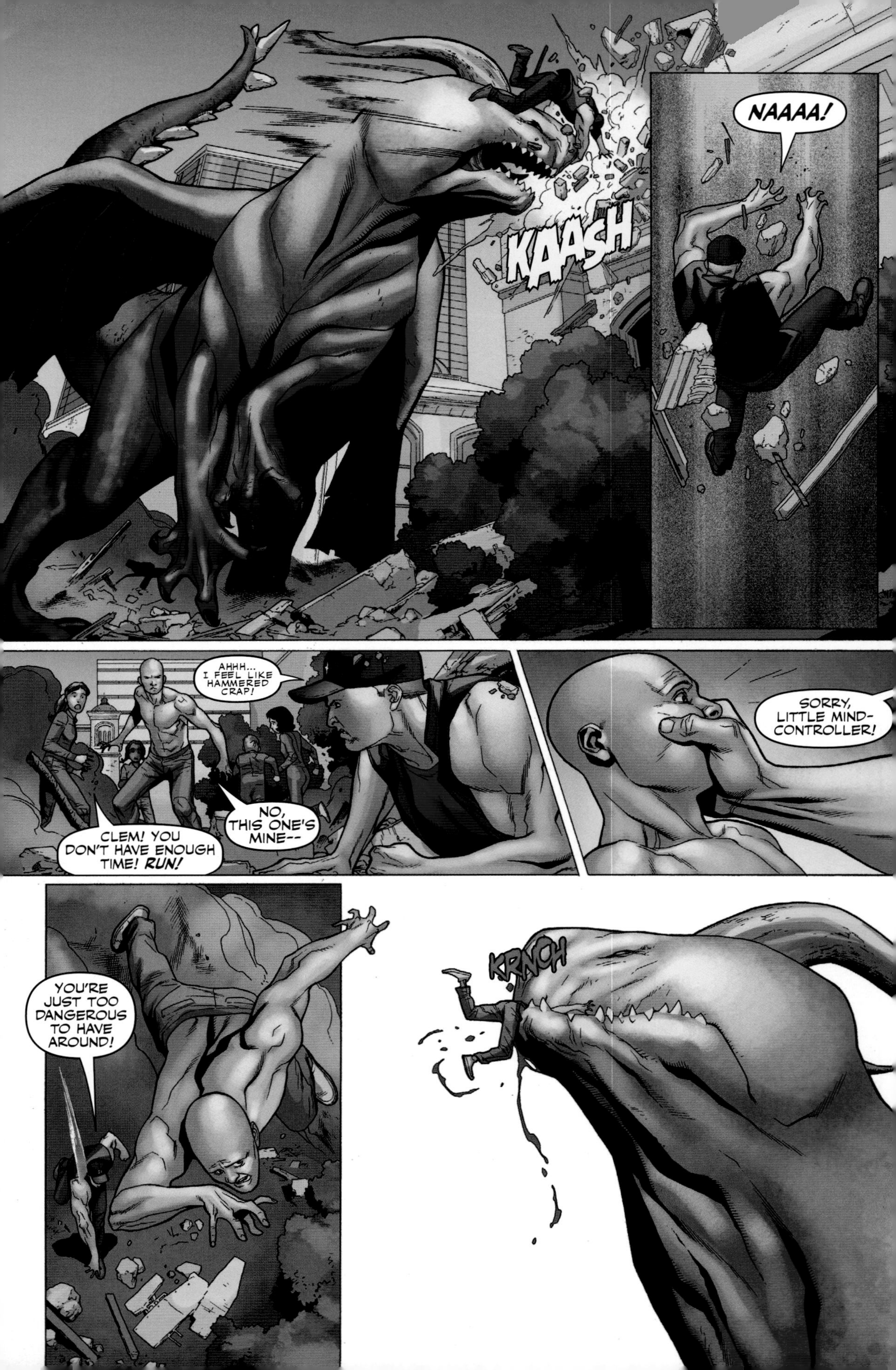
NAAAA!
KAASH
AHHH... I FEEL LIKE HAMMERED CRAP!
NO, THIS ONE'S MINE--
CLEM! YOU DON'T HAVE ENOUGH TIME! RUN!
SORRY, LITTLE MIND-CONTROLLER!
YOU'RE JUST TOO DANGEROUS TO HAVE AROUND!
KRNCH

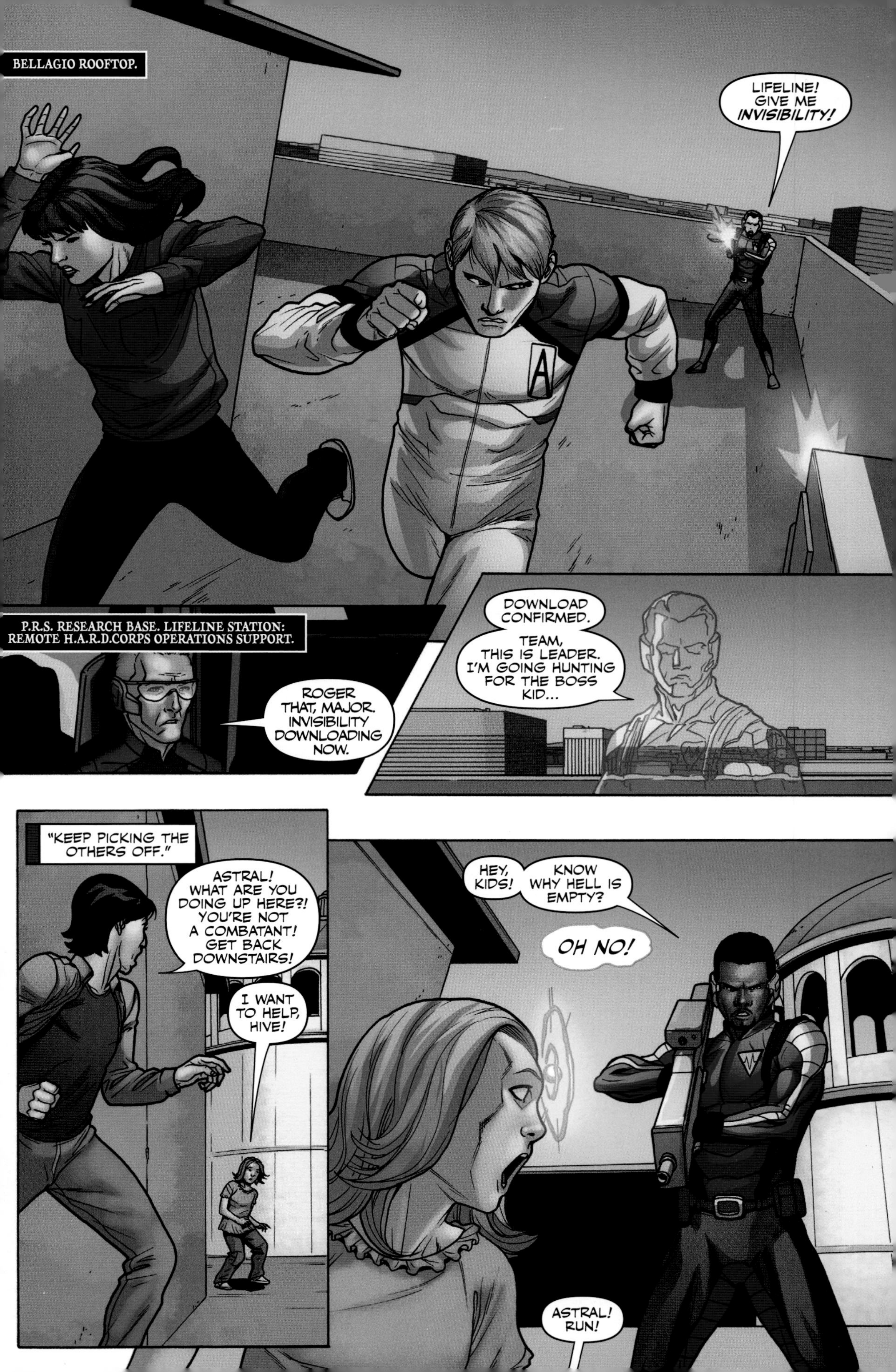

BELLAGIO ROOFTOP.
LIFELINE! GIVE ME INVISIBILITY!
P.R.S. RESEARCH BASE. LIFELINE STATION: REMOTE H.A.R.D.CORPS OPERATIONS SUPPORT.
ROGER THAT, MAJOR. INVISIBILITY DOWNLOADING NOW.
DOWNLOAD CONFIRMED.
TEAM, THIS IS LEADER. I'M GOING HUNTING FOR THE BOSS KID...
"KEEP PICKING THE OTHERS OFF."
ASTRAL! WHAT ARE YOU DOING UP HERE?! YOU'RE NOT A COMBATANT! GET BACK DOWNSTAIRS!
I WANT TO HELP, HIVE!
HEY, KIDS!
KNOW WHY HELL IS EMPTY?
OH NO!
ASTRAL! RUN!

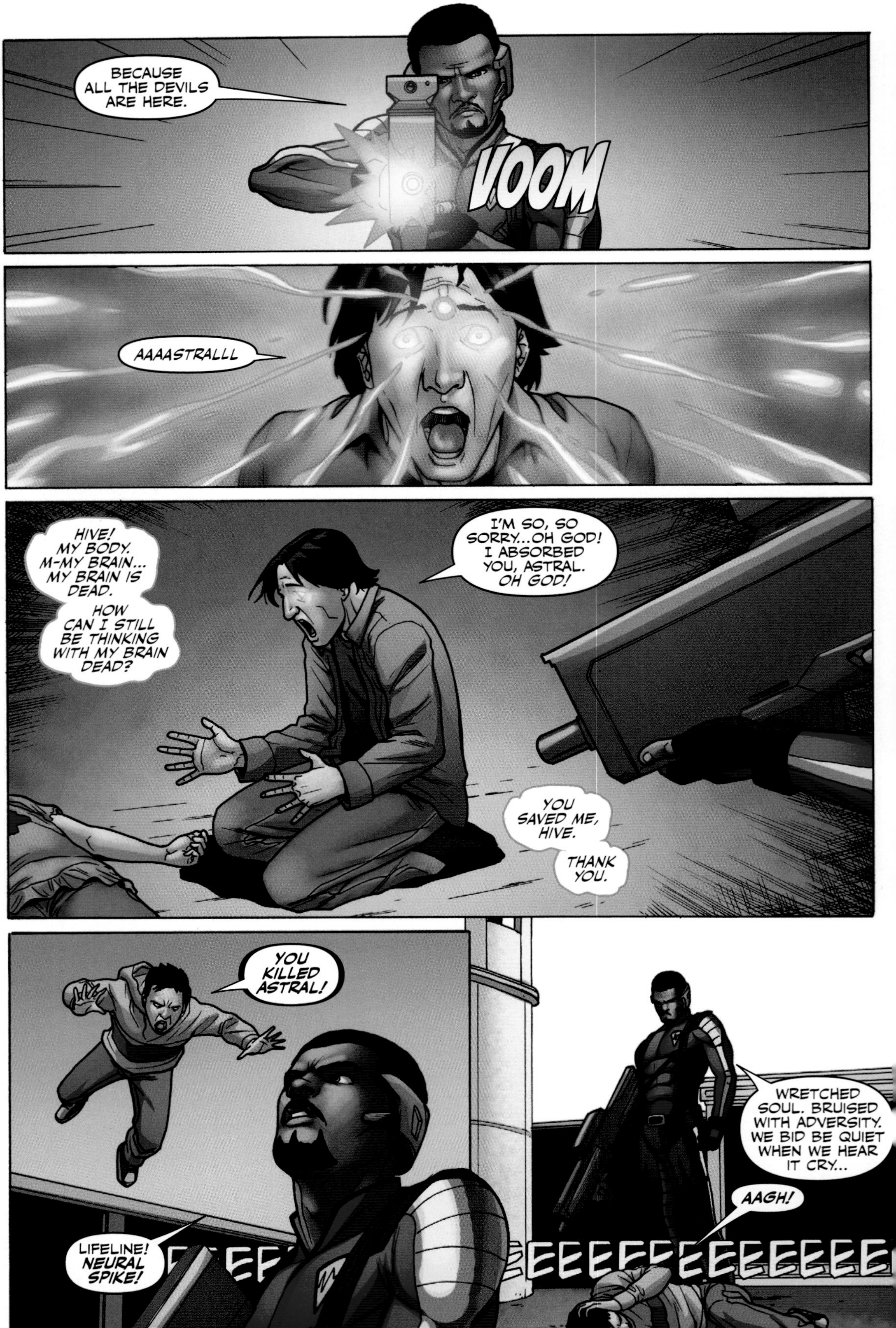
BECAUSE ALL THE DEVILS ARE HERE.
VOOM
AAAASTRALLL
HIVE! MY BODY. M-MY BRAIN... MY BRAIN IS DEAD.
HOW CAN I STILL BE THINKING WITH MY BRAIN DEAD?
I'M SO, SO SORRY...OH GOD! I ABSORBED YOU, ASTRAL. OH GOD!
YOU SAVED ME, HIVE.
THANK YOU.
YOU KILLED ASTRAL!
LIFELINE! NEURAL SPIKE!
WRETCHED SOUL. BRUISED WITH ADVERSITY. WE BID BE QUIET WHEN WE HEAR IT CRY...
AAGH!
EEEEEEEEEEEE

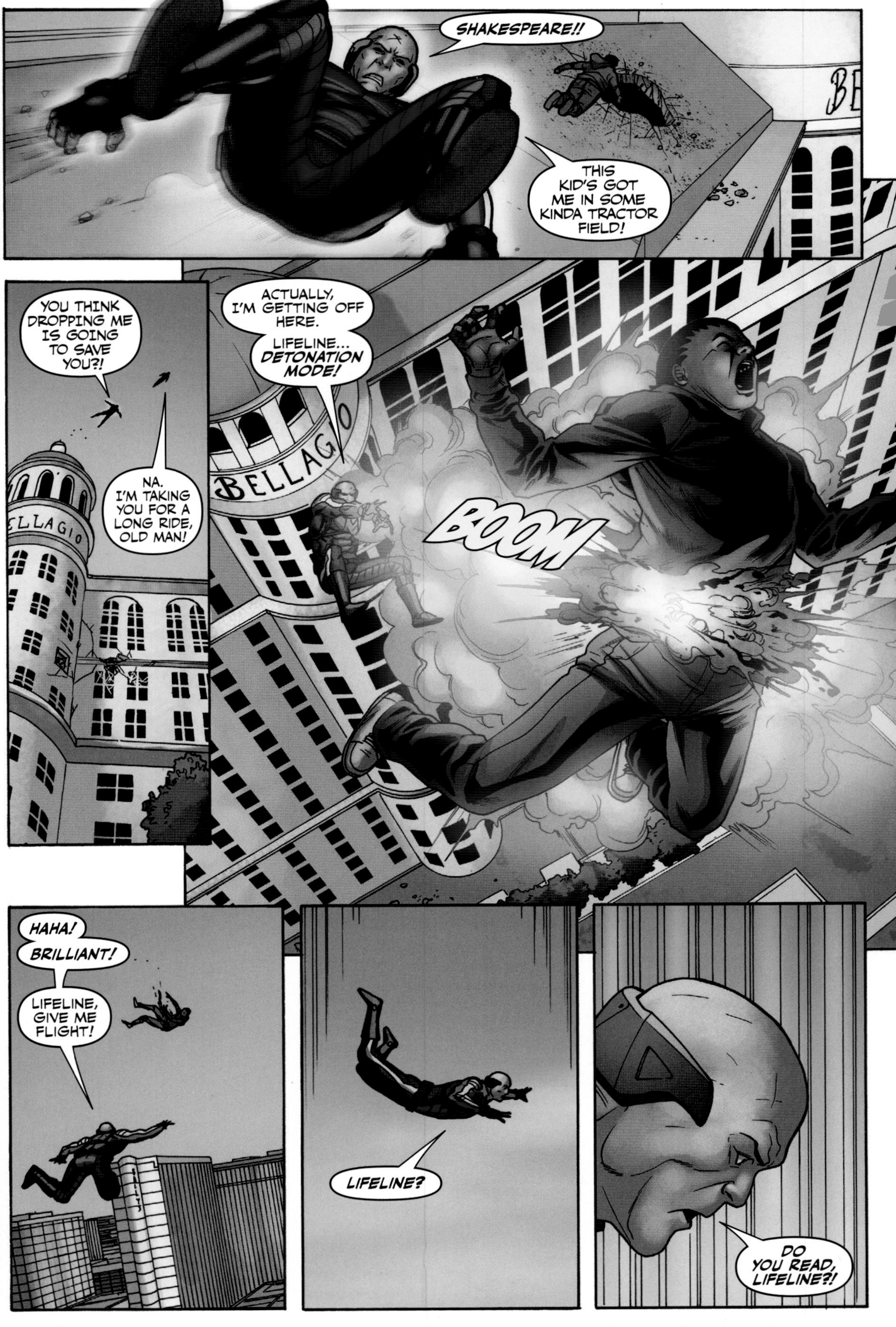
SHAKESPEARE!!
THIS KID'S GOT ME IN SOME KINDA TRACTOR FIELD!
YOU THINK DROPPING ME IS GOING TO SAVE YOU?!
NA. I'M TAKING YOU FOR A LONG RIDE, OLD MAN!
ACTUALLY, I'M GETTING OFF HERE.
LIFELINE... DETONATION MODE!
BELLAGIO
BOOM
HAHA!
BRILLIANT!
LIFELINE, GIVE ME FLIGHT!
LIFELINE?
DO YOU READ, LIFELINE?!

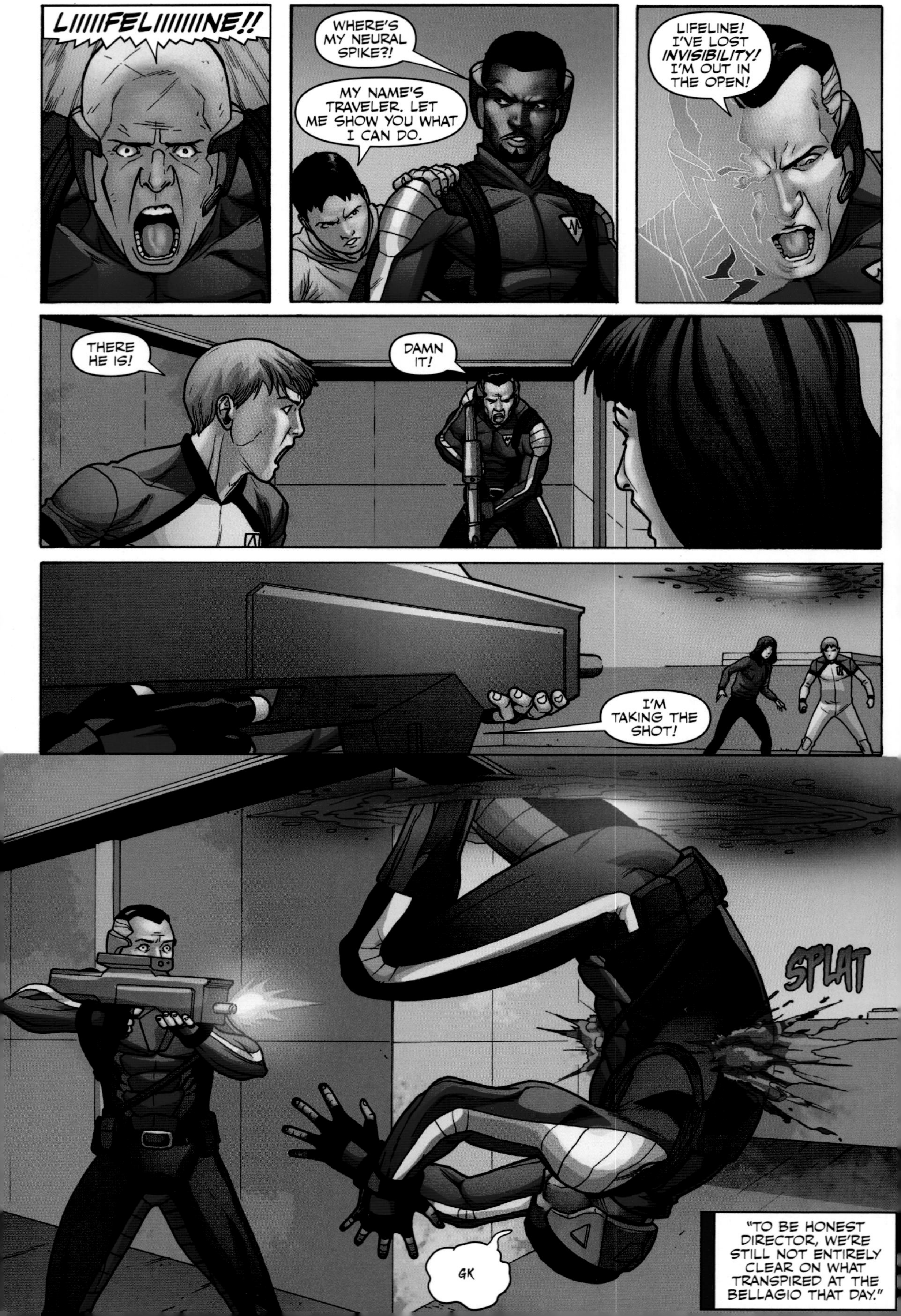
LIIIIIFELIIIIIIINE!!
WHERE'S MY NEURAL SPIKE?!
MY NAME'S TRAVELER. LET ME SHOW YOU WHAT I CAN DO.
LIFELINE! I'VE LOST *INVISIBILITY!* I'M OUT IN THE OPEN!
THERE HE IS!
DAMN IT!
I'M TAKING THE SHOT!
SPLAT
GK
"TO BE HONEST DIRECTOR, WE'RE STILL NOT ENTIRELY CLEAR ON WHAT TRANSPIRED AT THE BELLAGIO THAT DAY."

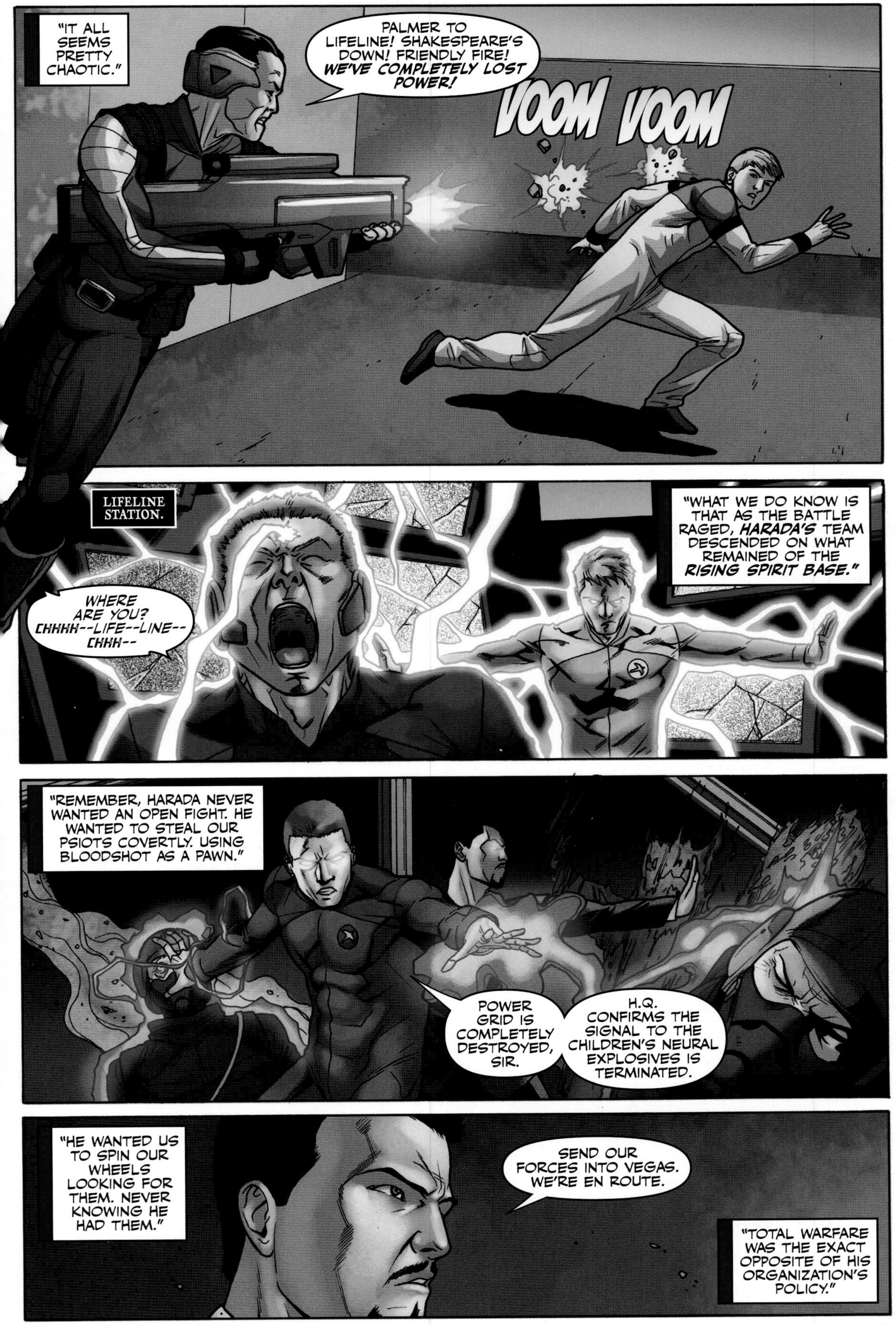
"IT ALL SEEMS PRETTY CHAOTIC."
PALMER TO LIFELINE! SHAKESPEARE'S DOWN! FRIENDLY FIRE! WE'VE COMPLETELY LOST POWER!
VOOM VOOM
LIFELINE STATION.
"WHAT WE DO KNOW IS THAT AS THE BATTLE RAGED, HARADA'S TEAM DESCENDED ON WHAT REMAINED OF THE RISING SPIRIT BASE."
WHERE ARE YOU? CHHHH--LIFE--LINE-- CHHH--
"REMEMBER, HARADA NEVER WANTED AN OPEN FIGHT. HE WANTED TO STEAL OUR PSIOTS COVERTLY. USING BLOODSHOT AS A PAWN."
POWER GRID IS COMPLETELY DESTROYED, SIR.
H.Q. CONFIRMS THE SIGNAL TO THE CHILDREN'S NEURAL EXPLOSIVES IS TERMINATED.
"HE WANTED US TO SPIN OUR WHEELS LOOKING FOR THEM. NEVER KNOWING HE HAD THEM."
SEND OUR FORCES INTO VEGAS. WE'RE EN ROUTE.
"TOTAL WARFARE WAS THE EXACT OPPOSITE OF HIS ORGANIZATION'S POLICY."

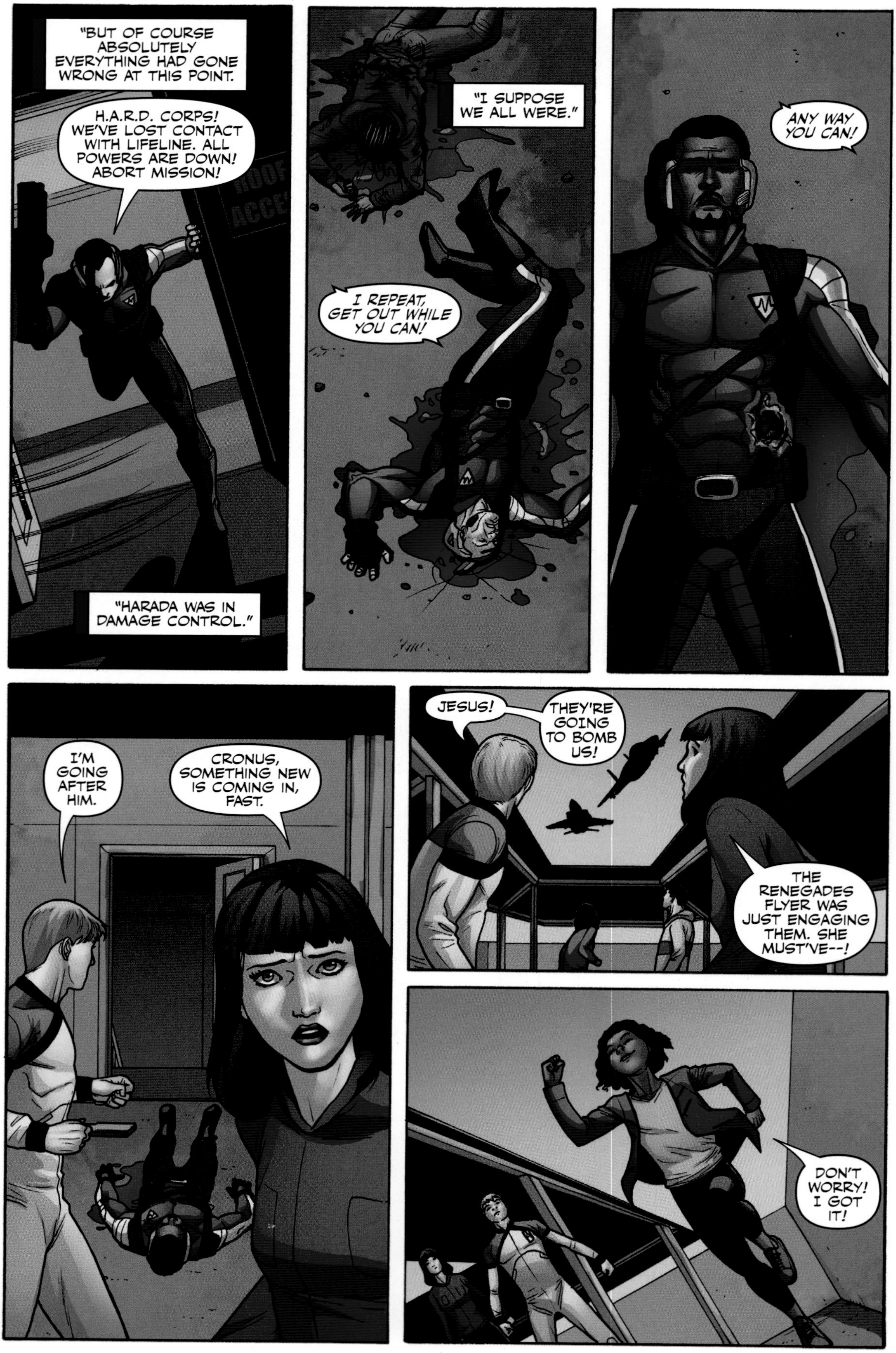
"BUT OF COURSE ABSOLUTELY EVERYTHING HAD GONE WRONG AT THIS POINT.
H.A.R.D. CORPS! WE'VE LOST CONTACT WITH LIFELINE. ALL POWERS ARE DOWN! ABORT MISSION!
ROOF ACCES
"HARADA WAS IN DAMAGE CONTROL."
"I SUPPOSE WE ALL WERE."
I REPEAT, GET OUT WHILE YOU CAN!
ANY WAY YOU CAN!
I'M GOING AFTER HIM.
CRONUS, SOMETHING NEW IS COMING IN, FAST.
JESUS!
THEY'RE GOING TO BOMB US!
THE RENEGADES FLYER WAS JUST ENGAGING THEM. SHE MUST'VE--!
DON'T WORRY! I GOT IT!

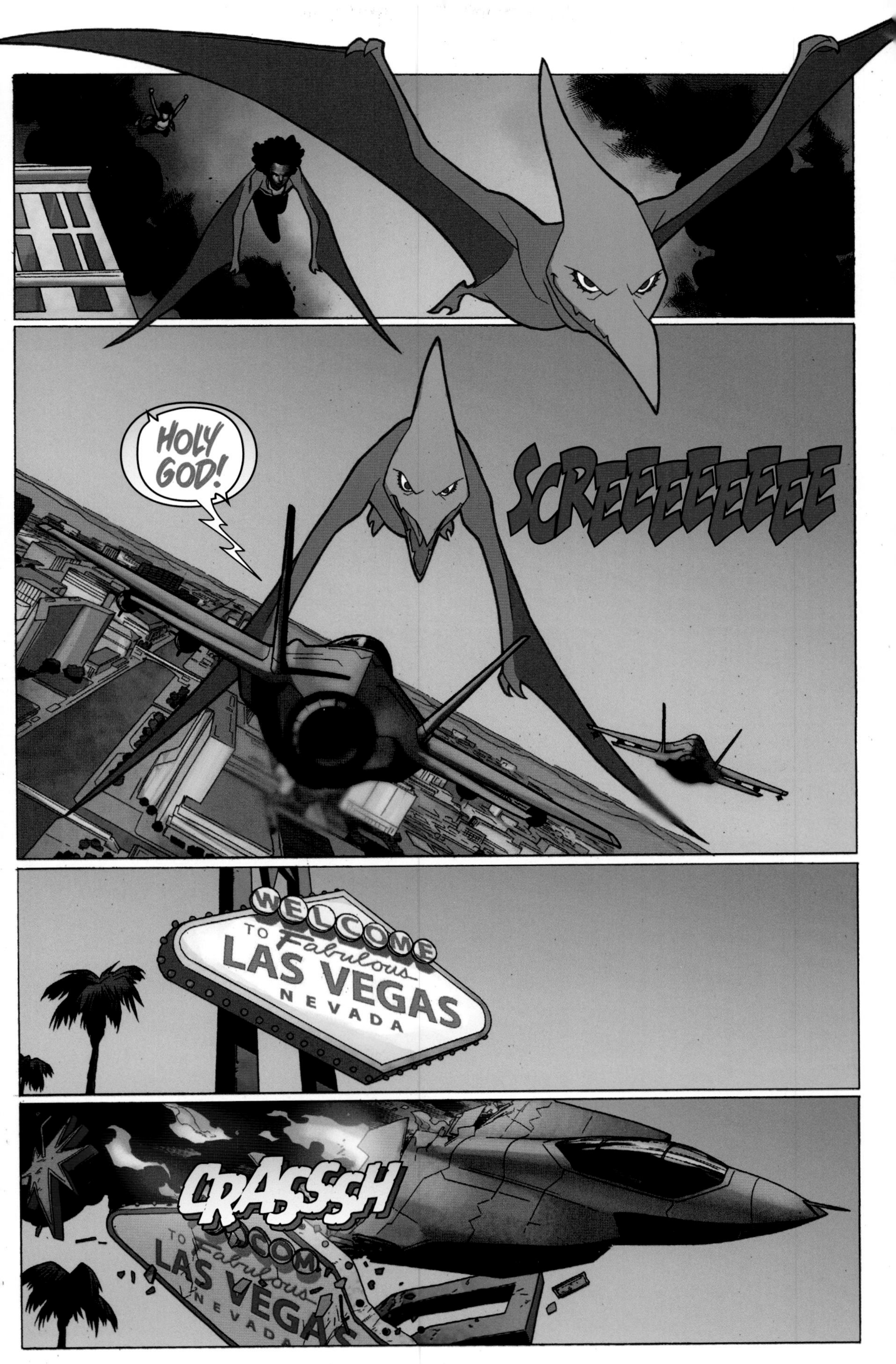
HOLY GOD!
SCREEEEEEEEE
WELCOME TO Fabulous LAS VEGAS NEVADA
CRASSSH

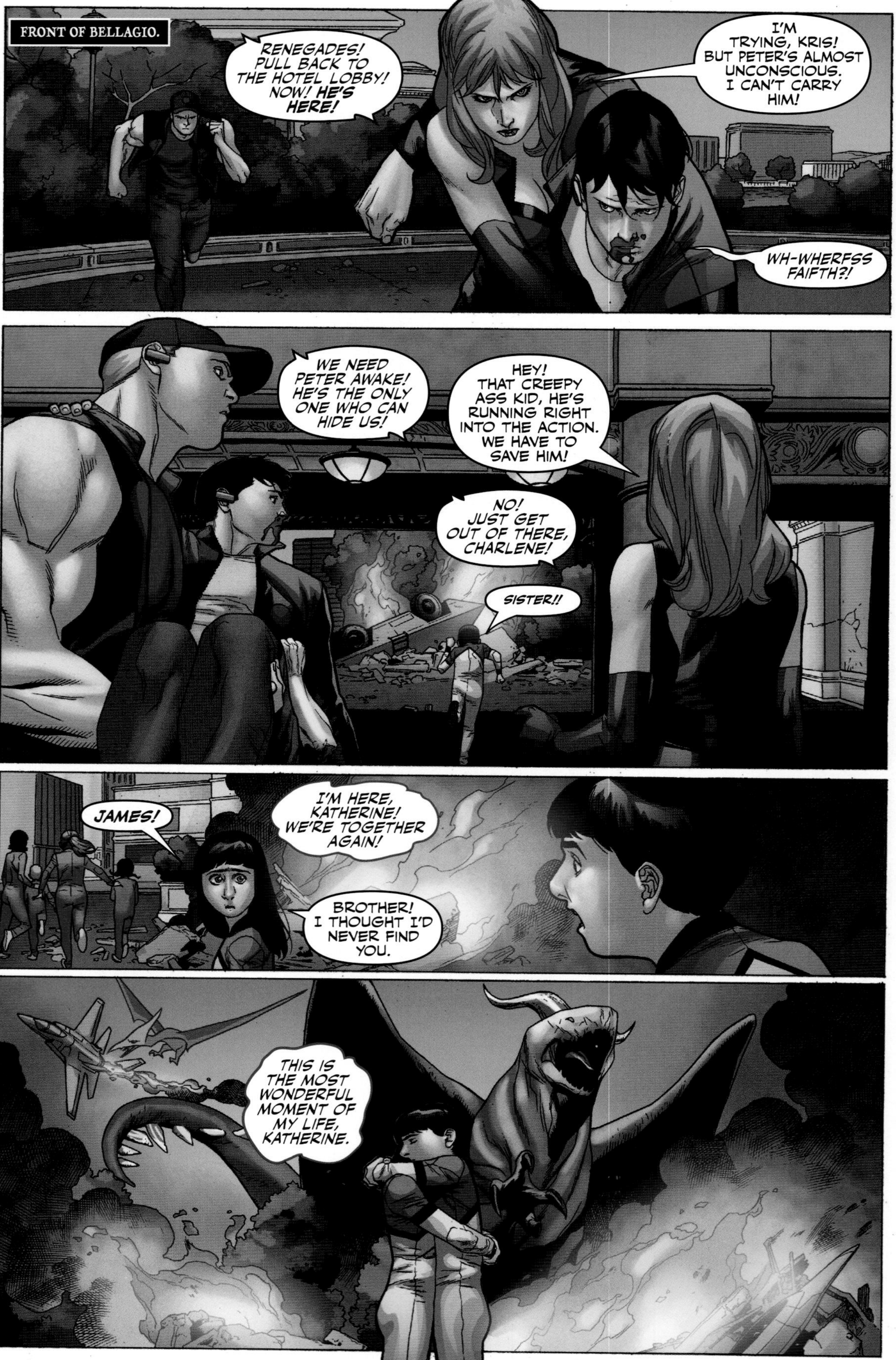
FRONT OF BELLAGIO.
RENEGADES! PULL BACK TO THE HOTEL LOBBY! NOW! HE'S HERE!
I'M TRYING, KRIS! BUT PETER'S ALMOST UNCONSCIOUS. I CAN'T CARRY HIM!
WH-WHERFSS FAIFTH?!
WE NEED PETER AWAKE! HE'S THE ONLY ONE WHO CAN HIDE US!
HEY! THAT CREEPY ASS KID, HE'S RUNNING RIGHT INTO THE ACTION. WE HAVE TO SAVE HIM!
NO! JUST GET OUT OF THERE, CHARLENE!
SISTER!!
JAMES!
I'M HERE, KATHERINE! WE'RE TOGETHER AGAIN!
BROTHER! I THOUGHT I'D NEVER FIND YOU.
THIS IS THE MOST WONDERFUL MOMENT OF MY LIFE, KATHERINE.

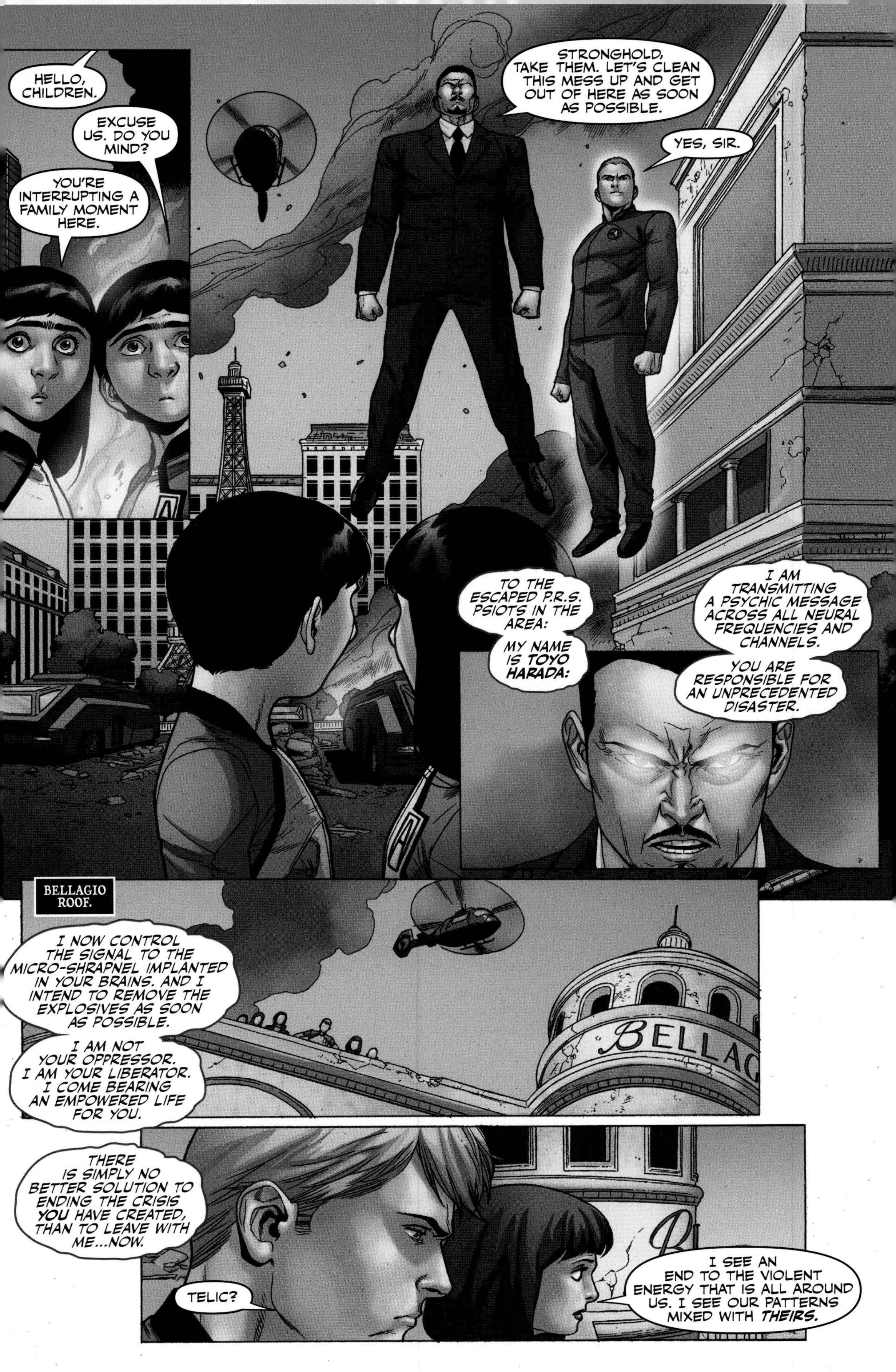
HELLO, CHILDREN.
EXCUSE US. DO YOU MIND?
YOU'RE INTERRUPTING A FAMILY MOMENT HERE.
STRONGHOLD, TAKE THEM. LET'S CLEAN THIS MESS UP AND GET OUT OF HERE AS SOON AS POSSIBLE.
YES, SIR.
TO THE ESCAPED P.R.S. PSIOTS IN THE AREA:
MY NAME IS TOYO HARADA:
I AM TRANSMITTING A PSYCHIC MESSAGE ACROSS ALL NEURAL FREQUENCIES AND CHANNELS.
YOU ARE RESPONSIBLE FOR AN UNPRECEDENTED DISASTER.
BELLAGIO ROOF.
I NOW CONTROL THE SIGNAL TO THE MICRO-SHRAPNEL IMPLANTED IN YOUR BRAINS. AND I INTEND TO REMOVE THE EXPLOSIVES AS SOON AS POSSIBLE.
I AM NOT YOUR OPPRESSOR. I AM YOUR LIBERATOR. I COME BEARING AN EMPOWERED LIFE FOR YOU.
BELLAGIO
THERE IS SIMPLY NO BETTER SOLUTION TO ENDING THE CRISIS YOU HAVE CREATED, THAN TO LEAVE WITH ME...NOW.
TELIC?
I SEE AN END TO THE VIOLENT ENERGY THAT IS ALL AROUND US. I SEE OUR PATTERNS MIXED WITH THEIRS.

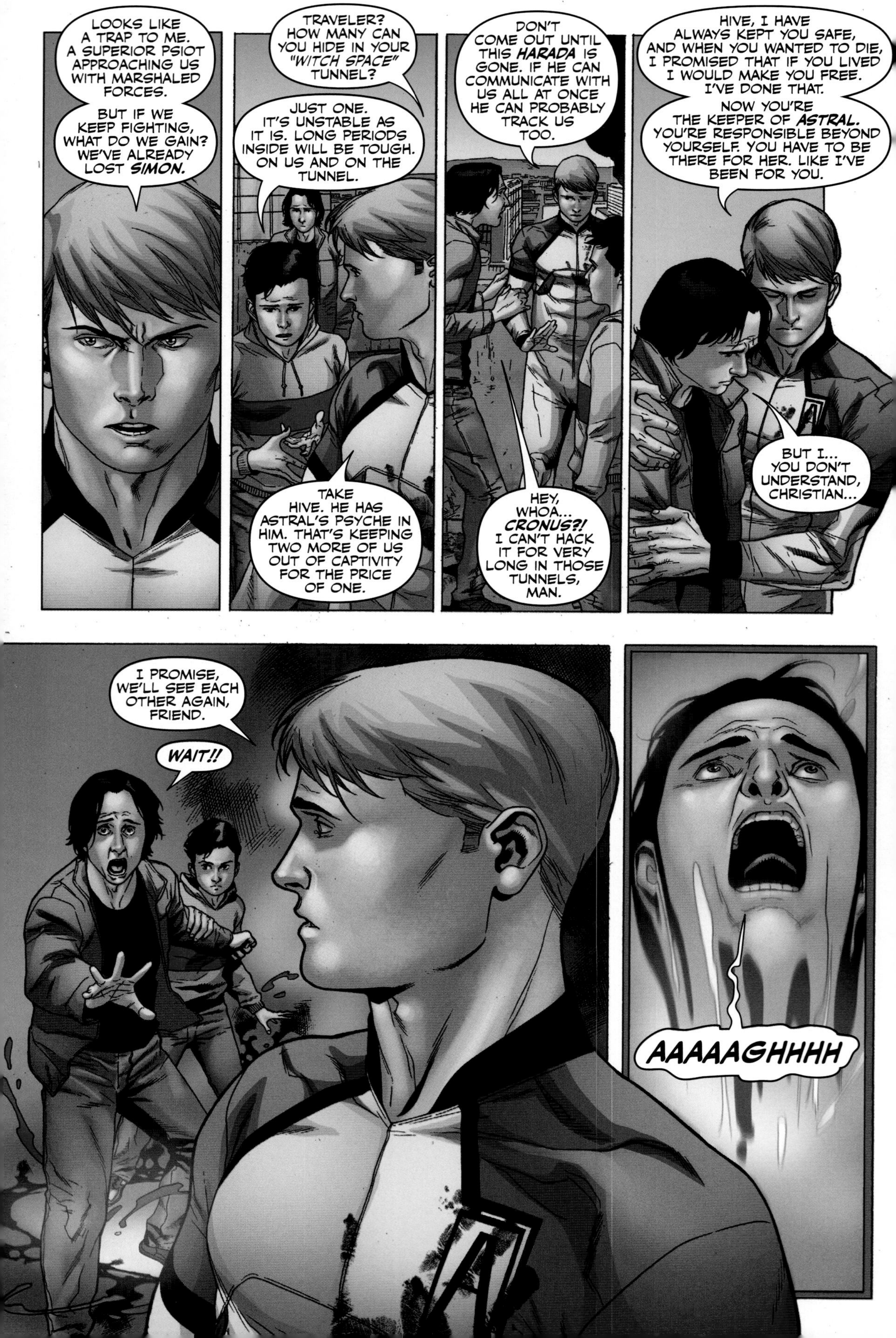
LOOKS LIKE A TRAP TO ME. A SUPERIOR PSIOT APPROACHING US WITH MARSHALED FORCES.
BUT IF WE KEEP FIGHTING, WHAT DO WE GAIN? WE'VE ALREADY LOST SIMON.
TRAVELER? HOW MANY CAN YOU HIDE IN YOUR "WITCH SPACE" TUNNEL?
JUST ONE. IT'S UNSTABLE AS IT IS. LONG PERIODS INSIDE WILL BE TOUGH. ON US AND ON THE TUNNEL.
TAKE HIVE. HE HAS ASTRAL'S PSYCHE IN HIM. THAT'S KEEPING TWO MORE OF US OUT OF CAPTIVITY FOR THE PRICE OF ONE.
DON'T COME OUT UNTIL THIS HARADA IS GONE. IF HE CAN COMMUNICATE WITH US ALL AT ONCE HE CAN PROBABLY TRACK US TOO.
HEY, WHOA... CRONUS?! I CAN'T HACK IT FOR VERY LONG IN THOSE TUNNELS, MAN.
HIVE, I HAVE ALWAYS KEPT YOU SAFE, AND WHEN YOU WANTED TO DIE, I PROMISED THAT IF YOU LIVED I WOULD MAKE YOU FREE. I'VE DONE THAT.
NOW YOU'RE THE KEEPER OF ASTRAL. YOU'RE RESPONSIBLE BEYOND YOURSELF. YOU HAVE TO BE THERE FOR HER. LIKE I'VE BEEN FOR YOU.
BUT I... YOU DON'T UNDERSTAND, CHRISTIAN...
I PROMISE, WE'LL SEE EACH OTHER AGAIN, FRIEND.
WAIT!!
AAAAAGHHHH

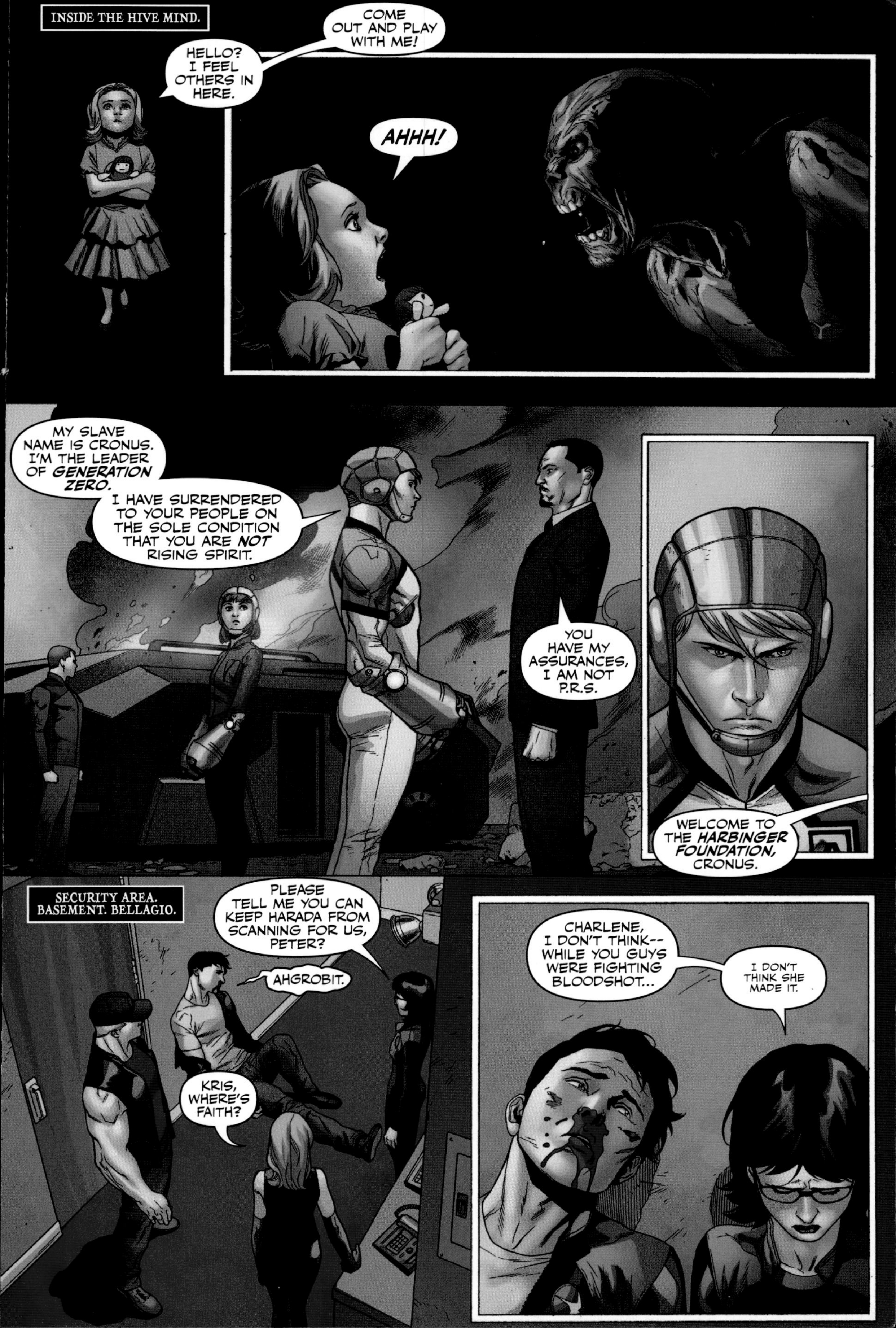
INSIDE THE HIVE MIND.
HELLO? I FEEL OTHERS IN HERE.
COME OUT AND PLAY WITH ME!
AHHH!
MY SLAVE NAME IS CRONUS. I'M THE LEADER OF GENERATION ZERO.
I HAVE SURRENDERED TO YOUR PEOPLE ON THE SOLE CONDITION THAT YOU ARE NOT RISING SPIRIT.
YOU HAVE MY ASSURANCES, I AM NOT P.R.S.
WELCOME TO THE HARBINGER FOUNDATION, CRONUS.
SECURITY AREA. BASEMENT. BELLAGIO.
PLEASE TELL ME YOU CAN KEEP HARADA FROM SCANNING FOR US, PETER?
AHGROBIT.
KRIS, WHERE'S FAITH?
CHARLENE, I DON'T THINK-- WHILE YOU GUYS WERE FIGHTING BLOODSHOT...
I DON'T THINK SHE MADE IT.

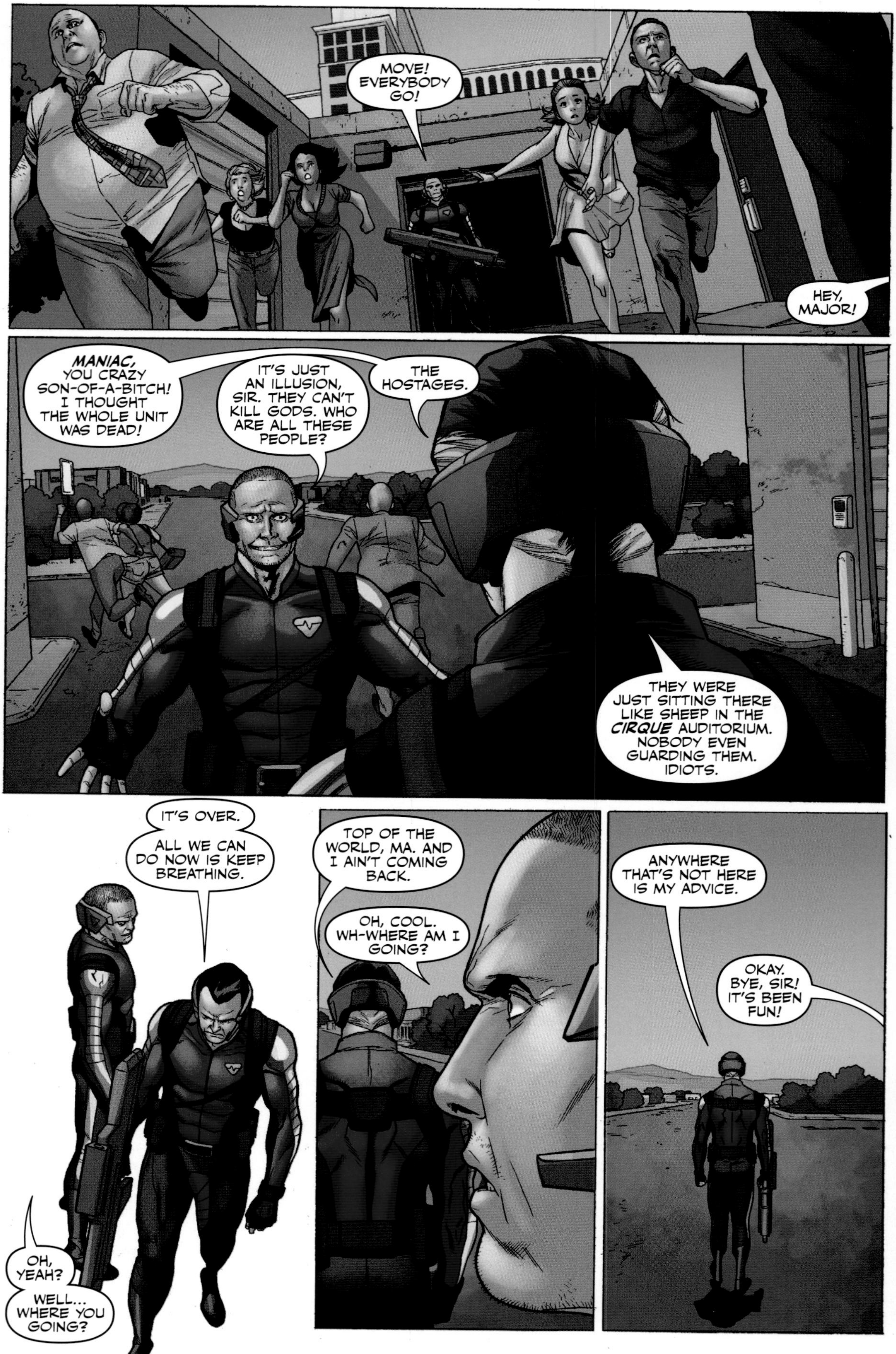
MOVE! EVERYBODY GO!
HEY, MAJOR!
MANIAC, YOU CRAZY SON-OF-A-BITCH! I THOUGHT THE WHOLE UNIT WAS DEAD!
IT'S JUST AN ILLUSION, SIR. THEY CAN'T KILL GODS. WHO ARE ALL THESE PEOPLE?
THE HOSTAGES.
THEY WERE JUST SITTING THERE LIKE SHEEP IN THE CIRQUE AUDITORIUM. NOBODY EVEN GUARDING THEM. IDIOTS.
IT'S OVER.
ALL WE CAN DO NOW IS KEEP BREATHING.
OH, YEAH? WELL... WHERE YOU GOING?
TOP OF THE WORLD, MA. AND I AIN'T COMING BACK.
OH, COOL. WH-WHERE AM I GOING?
ANYWHERE THAT'S NOT HERE IS MY ADVICE.
OKAY. BYE, SIR! IT'S BEEN FUN!

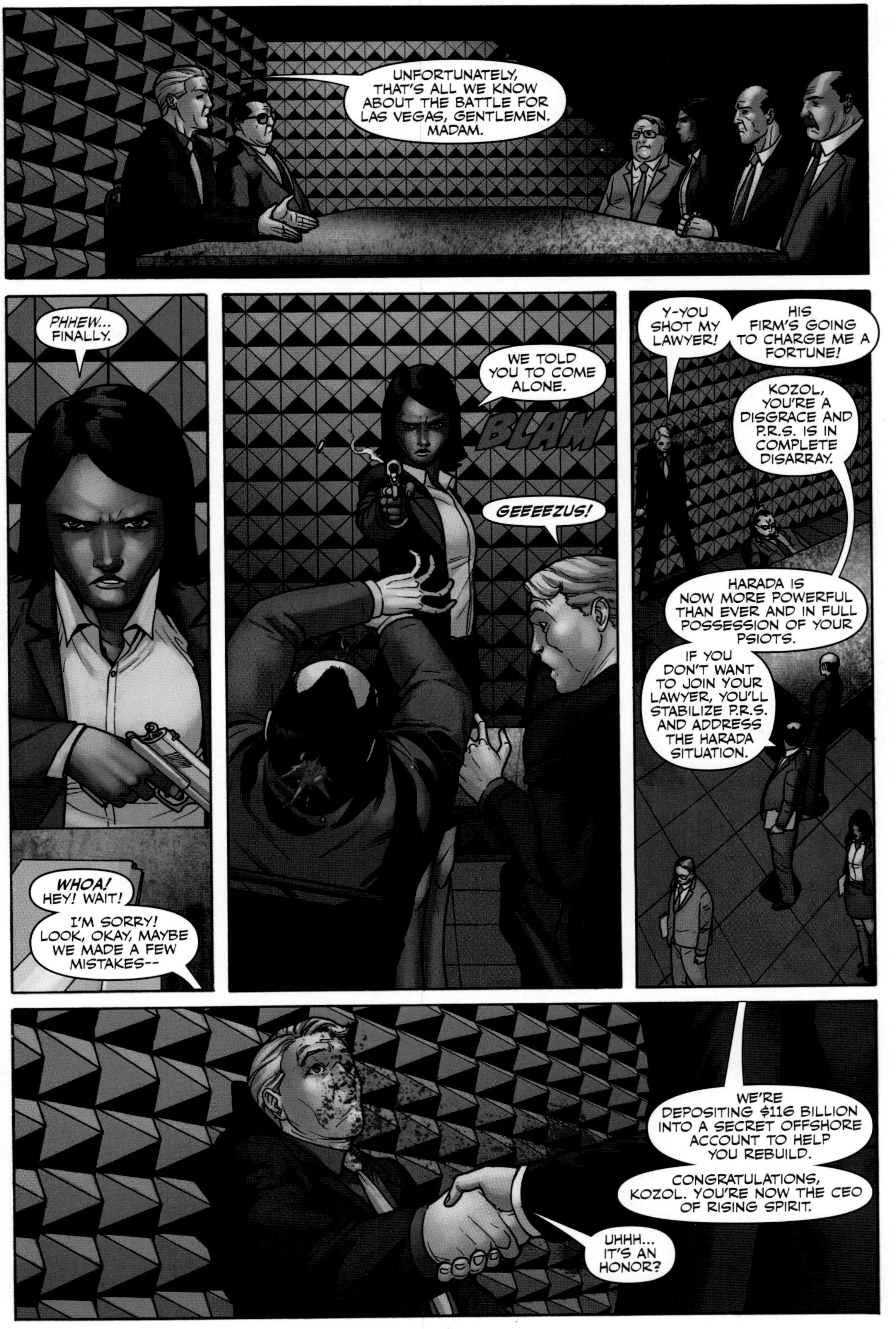
UNFORTUNATELY, THAT'S ALL WE KNOW ABOUT THE BATTLE FOR LAS VEGAS, GENTLEMEN. MADAM.
PHHEW... FINALLY.
WHOA! HEY! WAIT!
I'M SORRY! LOOK, OKAY, MAYBE WE MADE A FEW MISTAKES--
WE TOLD YOU TO COME ALONE.
BLAM
GEEEEZUS!
Y-YOU SHOT MY LAWYER!
HIS FIRM'S GOING TO CHARGE ME A FORTUNE!
KOZOL, YOU'RE A DISGRACE AND P.R.S. IS IN COMPLETE DISARRAY.
HARADA IS NOW MORE POWERFUL THAN EVER AND IN FULL POSSESSION OF YOUR PSIOTS.
IF YOU DON'T WANT TO JOIN YOUR LAWYER, YOU'LL STABILIZE P.R.S. AND ADDRESS THE HARADA SITUATION.
WE'RE DEPOSITING $116 BILLION INTO A SECRET OFFSHORE ACCOUNT TO HELP YOU REBUILD.
CONGRATULATIONS, KOZOL. YOU'RE NOW THE CEO OF RISING SPIRIT.
UHHH... IT'S AN HONOR?

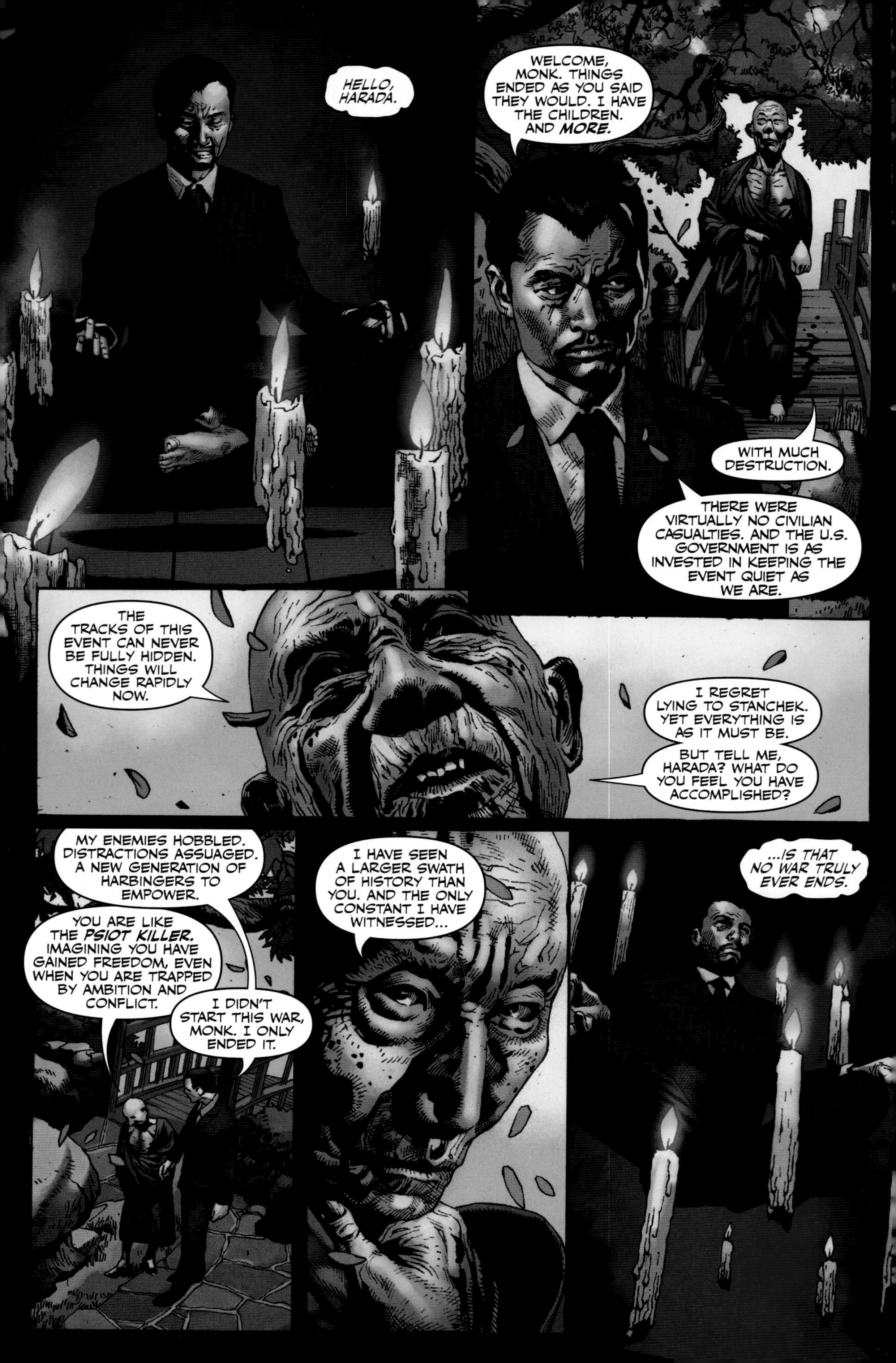
HELLO, HARADA.
WELCOME, MONK. THINGS ENDED AS YOU SAID THEY WOULD. I HAVE THE CHILDREN. AND MORE.
WITH MUCH DESTRUCTION.
THERE WERE VIRTUALLY NO CIVILIAN CASUALTIES. AND THE U.S. GOVERNMENT IS AS INVESTED IN KEEPING THE EVENT QUIET AS WE ARE.
THE TRACKS OF THIS EVENT CAN NEVER BE FULLY HIDDEN. THINGS WILL CHANGE RAPIDLY NOW.
I REGRET LYING TO STANCHEK. YET EVERYTHING IS AS IT MUST BE.
BUT TELL ME, HARADA? WHAT DO YOU FEEL YOU HAVE ACCOMPLISHED?
MY ENEMIES HOBBLED. DISTRACTIONS ASSUAGED. A NEW GENERATION OF HARBINGERS TO EMPOWER.
YOU ARE LIKE THE PSIOT KILLER. IMAGINING YOU HAVE GAINED FREEDOM, EVEN WHEN YOU ARE TRAPPED BY AMBITION AND CONFLICT.
I DIDN'T START THIS WAR, MONK. I ONLY ENDED IT.
I HAVE SEEN A LARGER SWATH OF HISTORY THAN YOU. AND THE ONLY CONSTANT I HAVE WITNESSED...
...IS THAT NO WAR TRULY EVER ENDS.

GALLERY

HARBINGER WARS #1 VARIANT
Cover by CLAYTON CRAIN

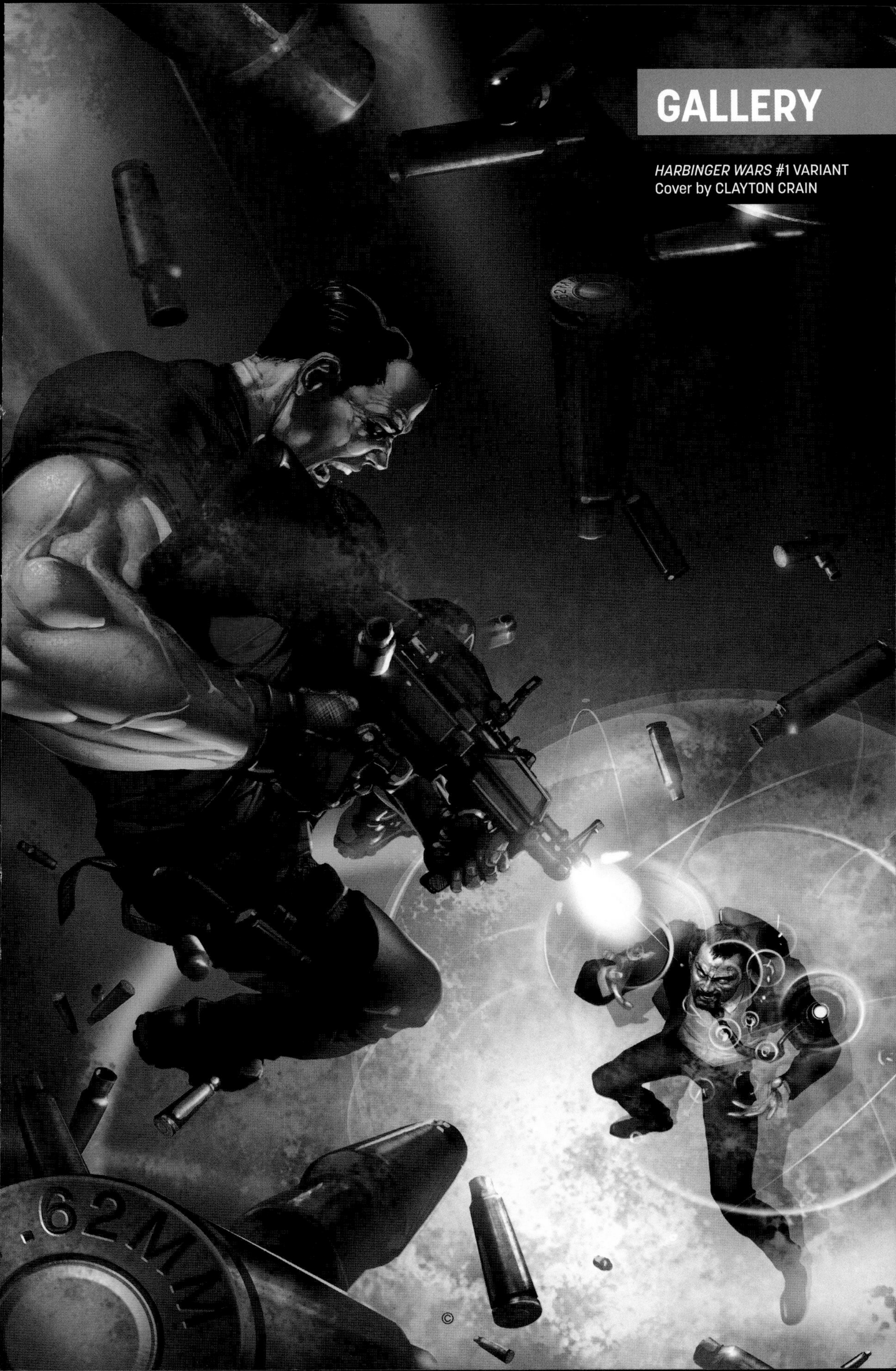
.62MM

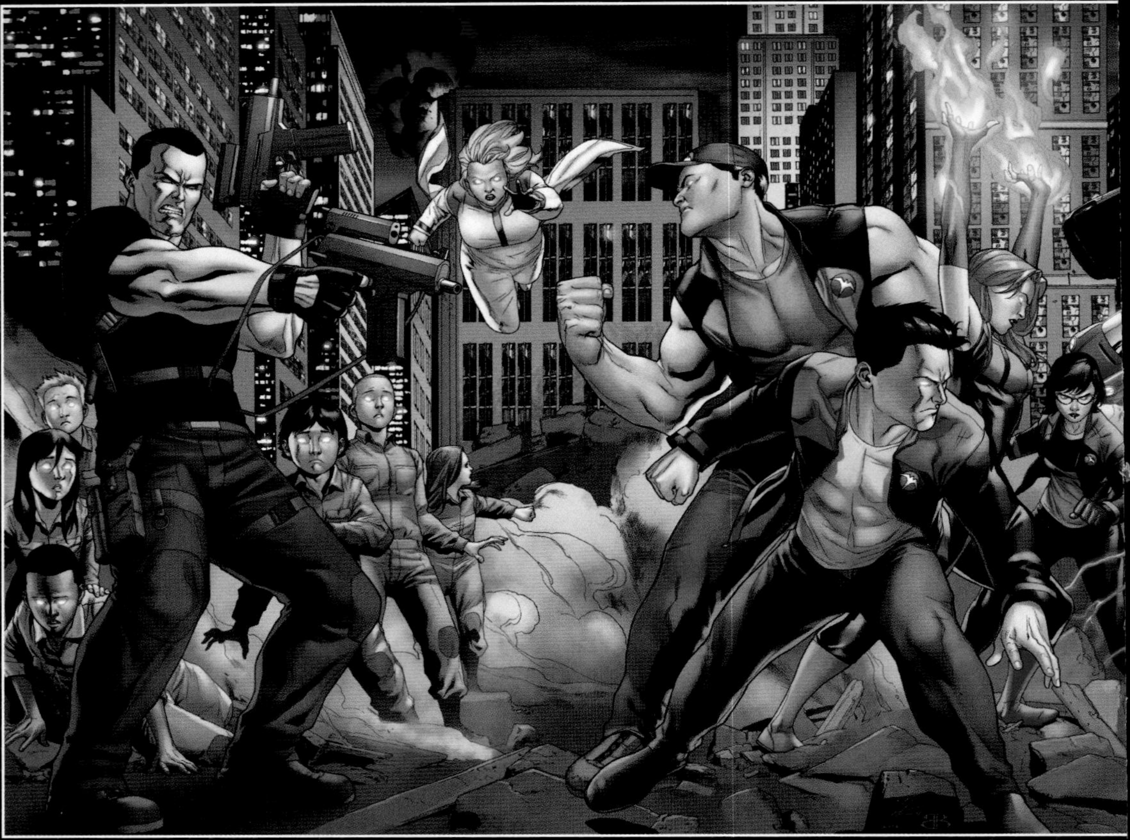

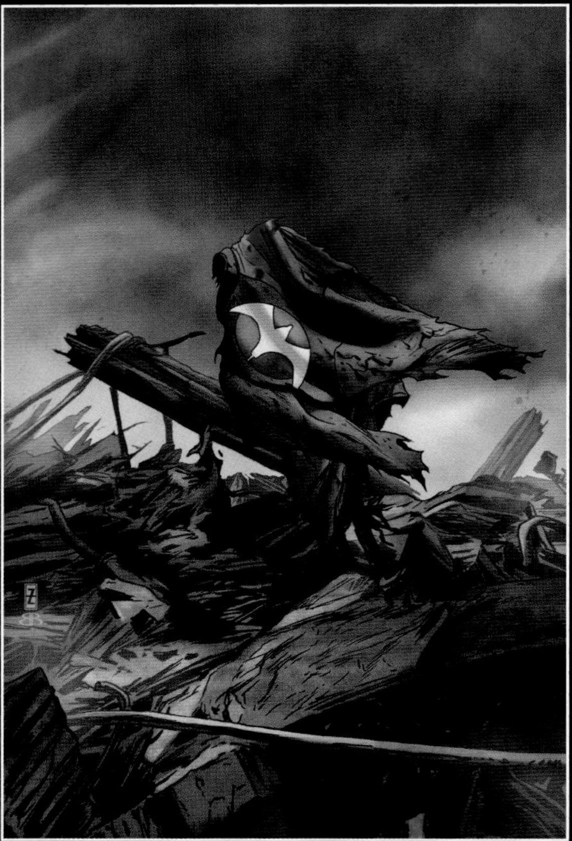

HARBINGER WARS #1
PULLBOX VARIANT
Cover by PATRICK ZIRCHER

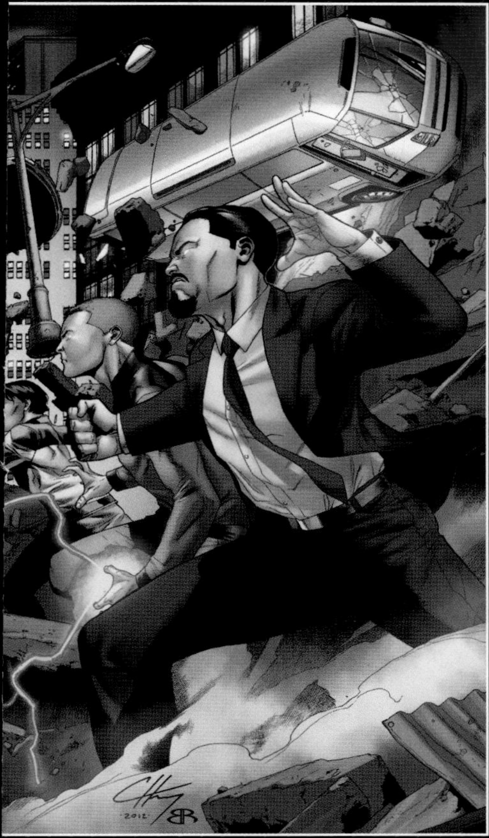

BLOODSHOT #10, *HARBINGER* #11,
HARBINGER WARS #1
INTERLOCKING PULLBOX VARIANT
Covers by CLAYTON HENRY

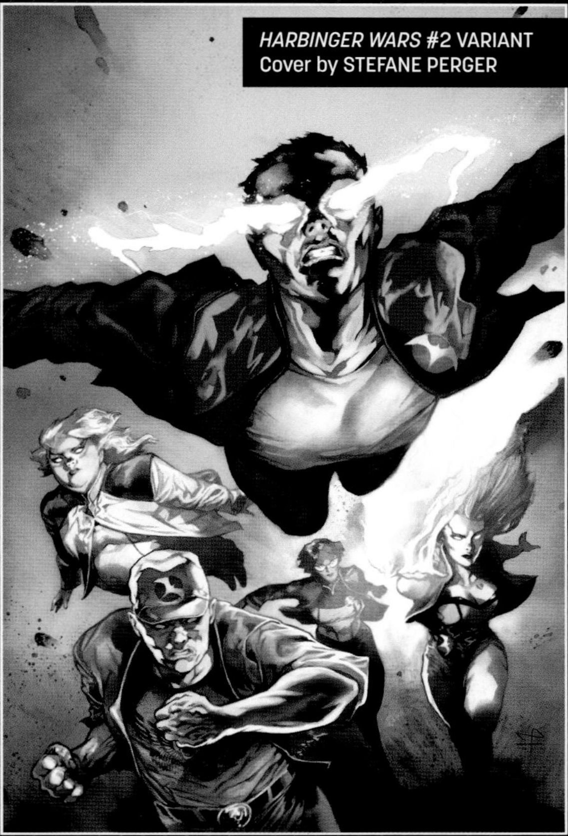

HARBINGER WARS #2 VARIANT
Cover by STEFANE PERGER

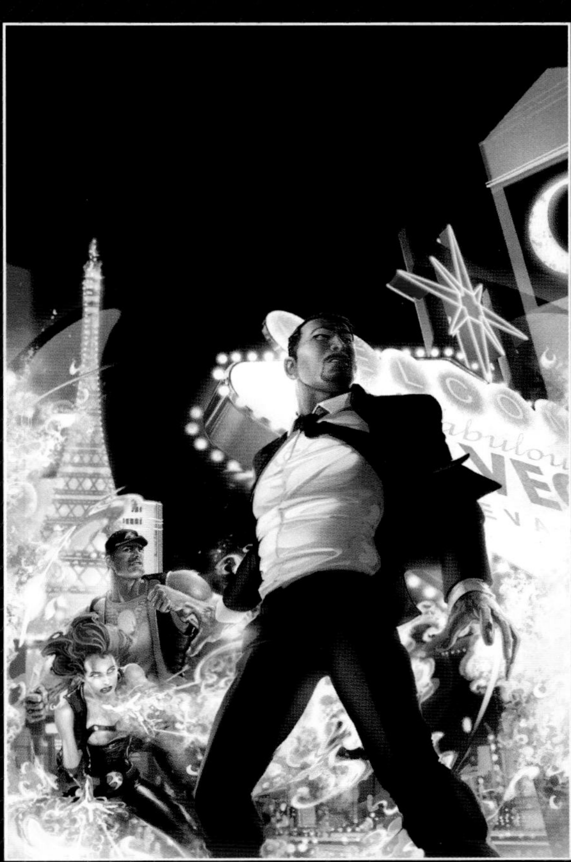

HARBINGER WARS #2 VARIANT
Cover by CLAYTON CRAIN

HARBINGER WARS #2 VARIANT
Cover by LEWIS LAROSA

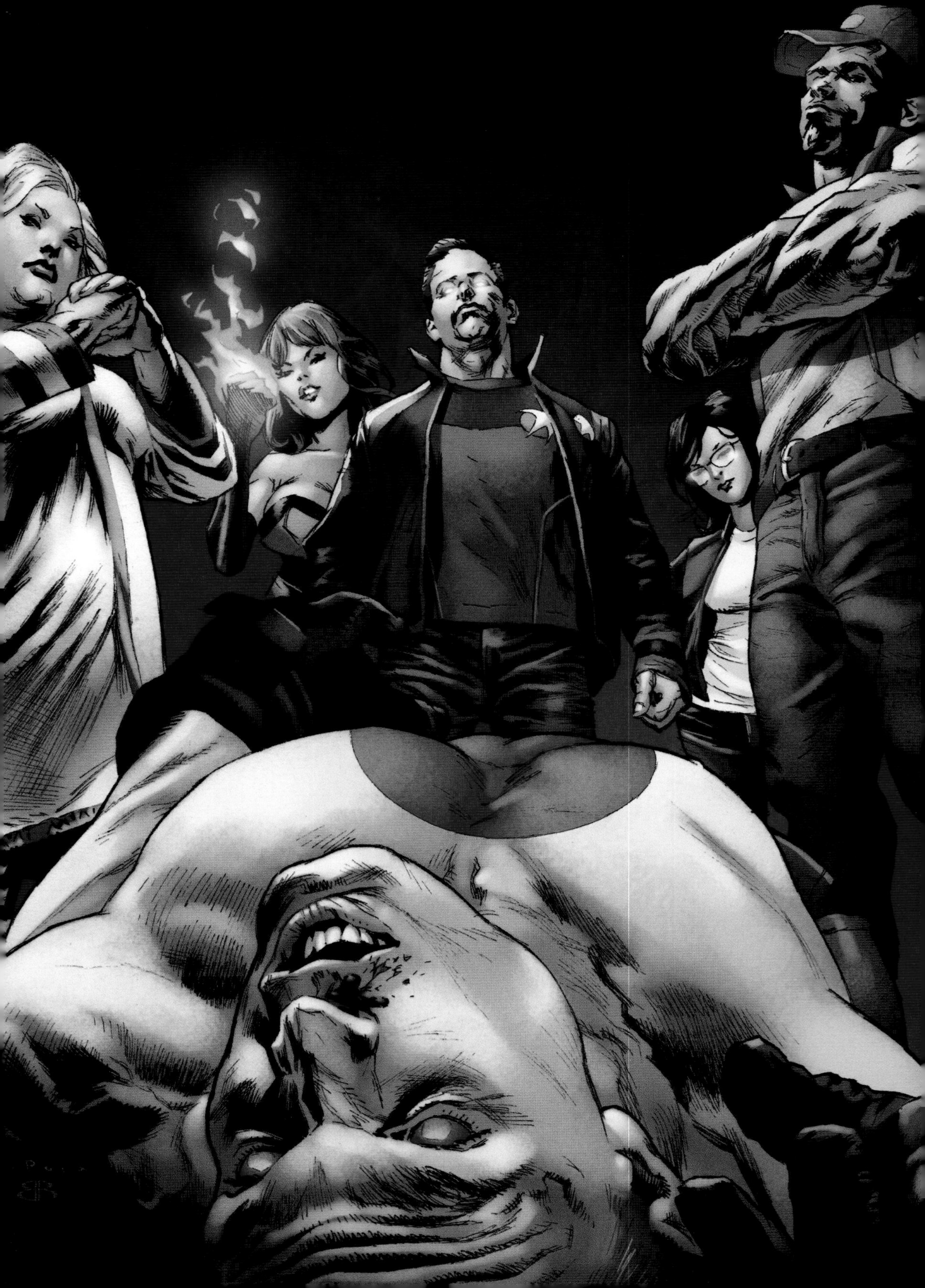

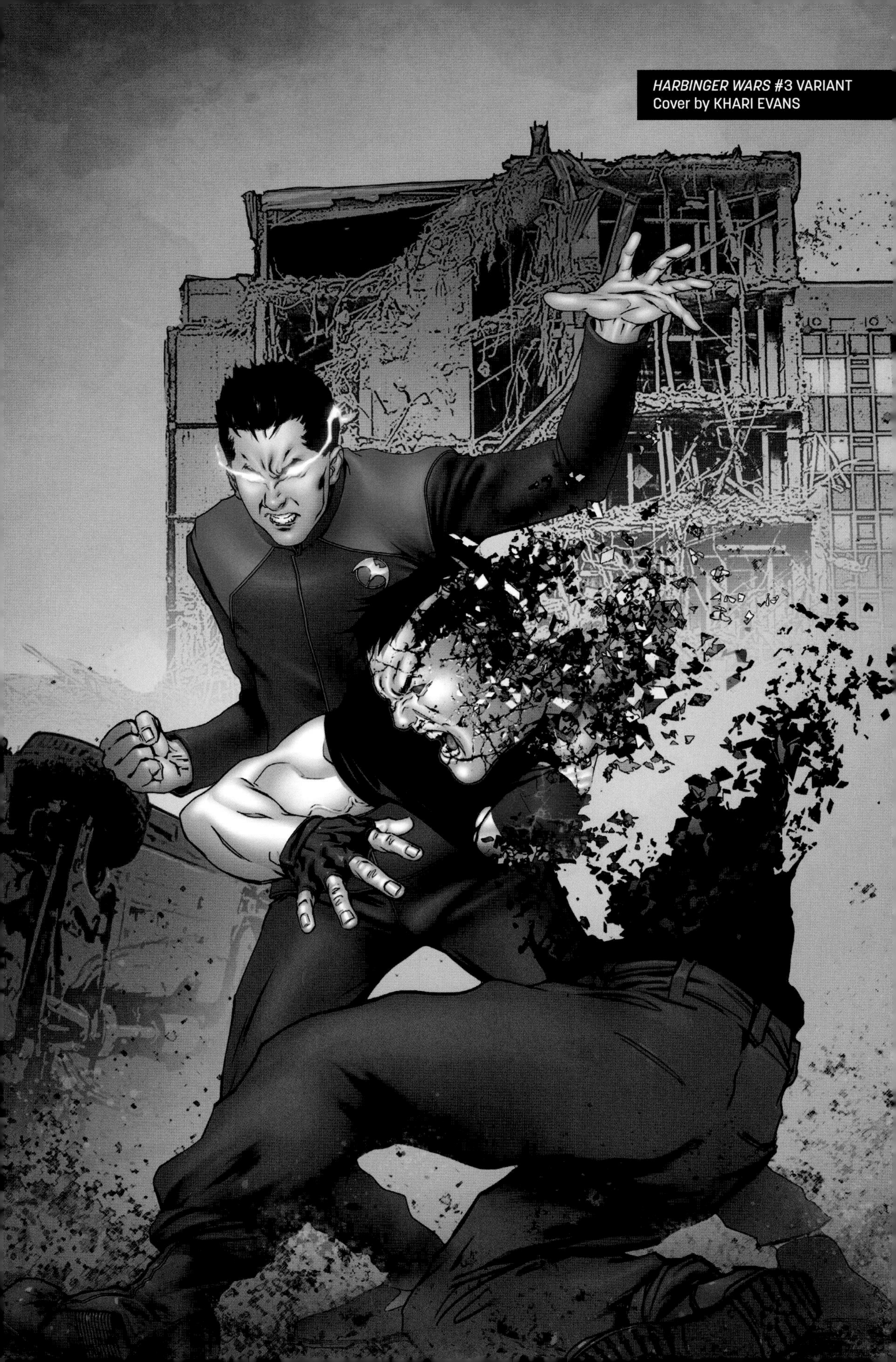

HARBINGER WARS #3 VARIANT
Cover by KHARI EVANS

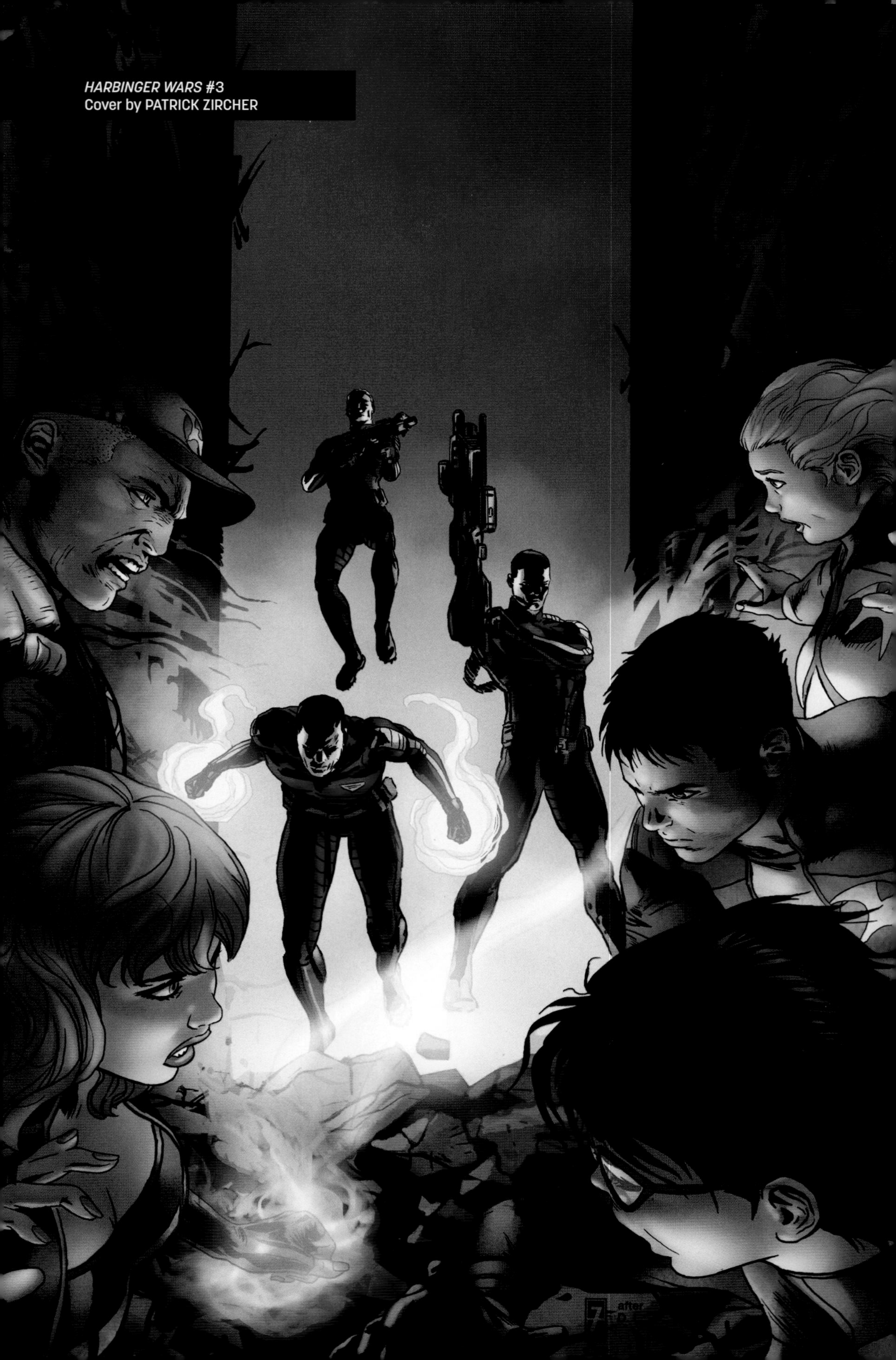

HARBINGER WARS #3
Cover by PATRICK ZIRCHER

HARBINGER WARS #3 VARIANT
Cover by PATRICK ZIRCHER

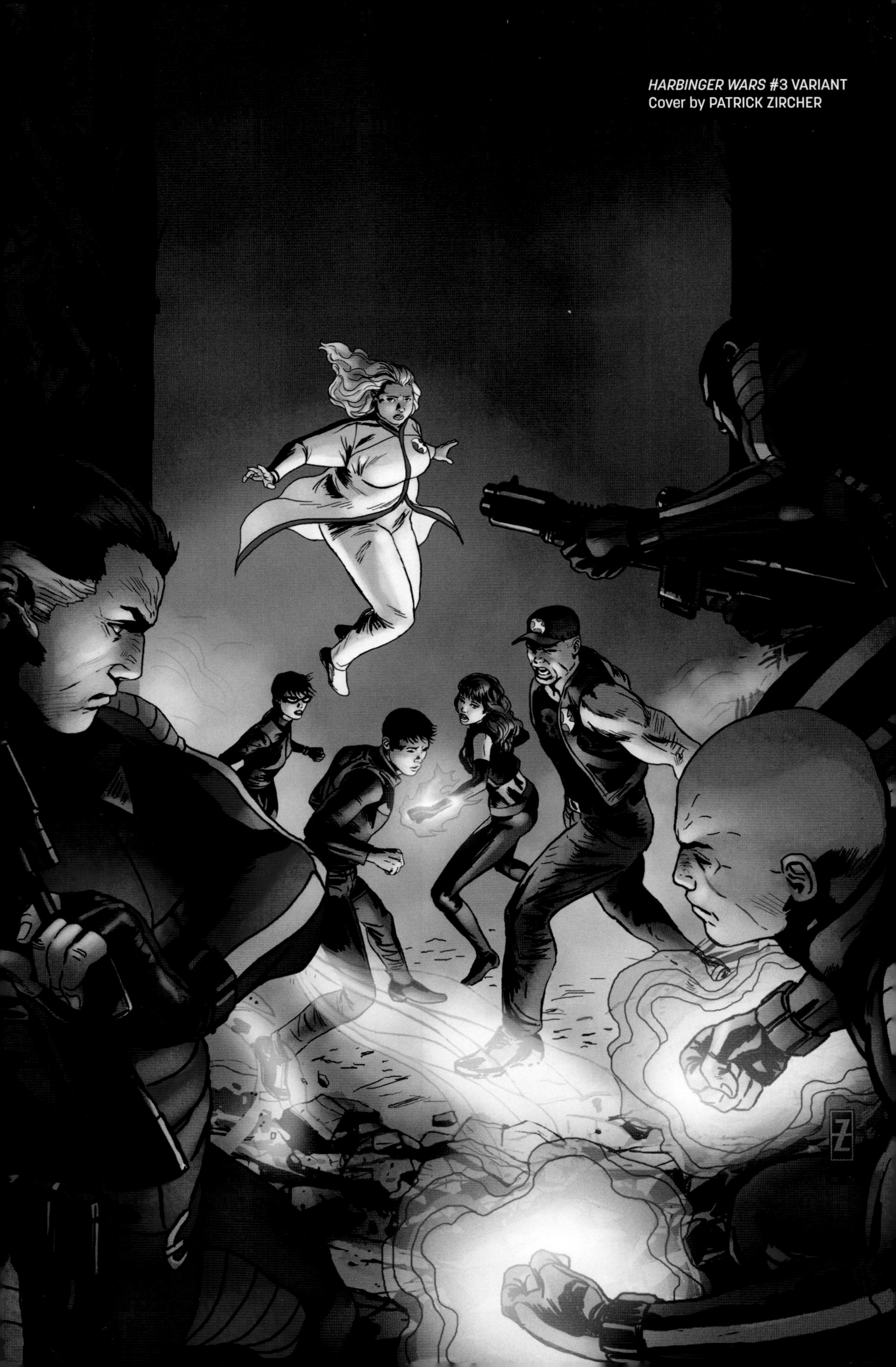

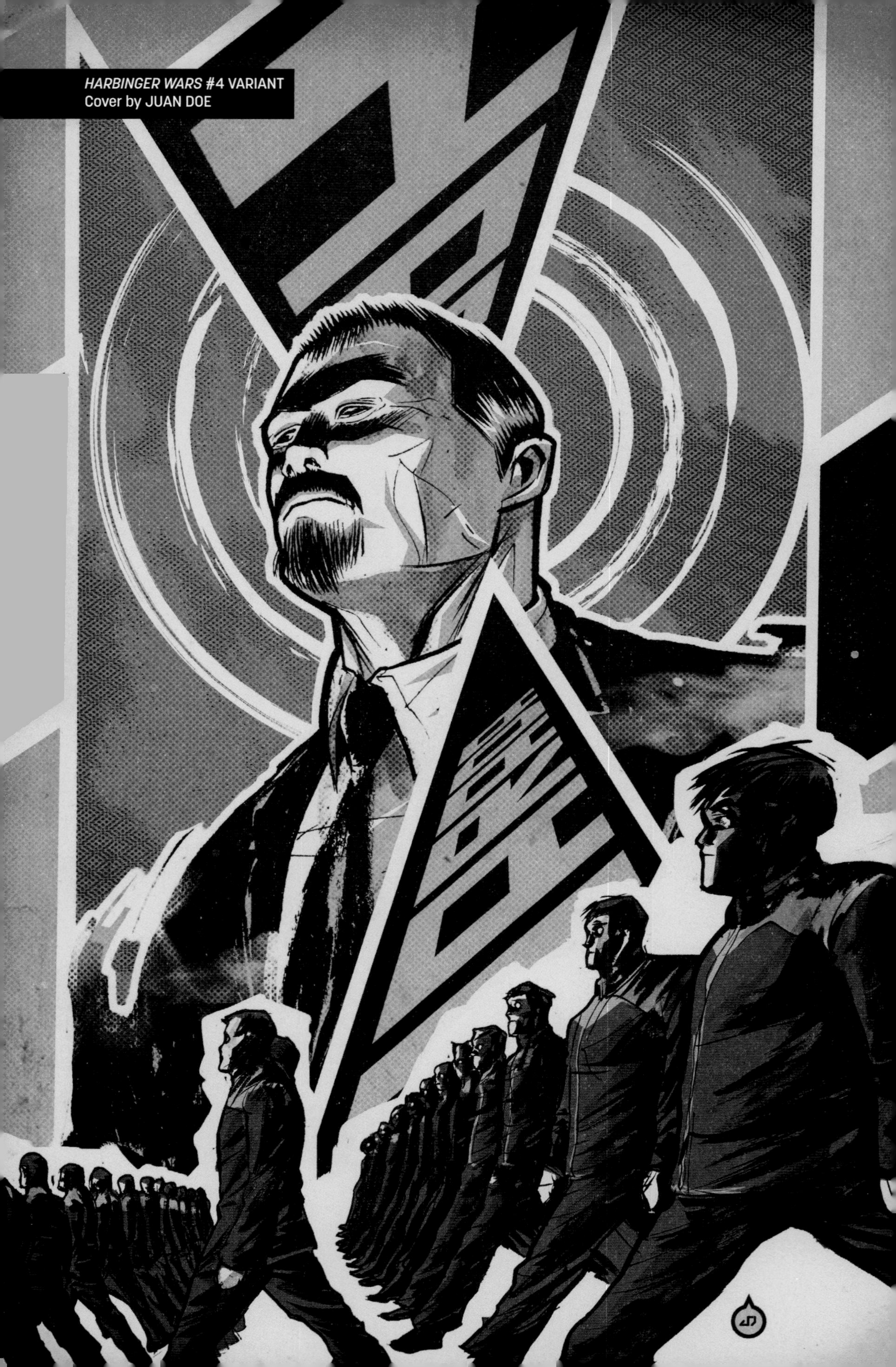

HARBINGER WARS #4 VARIANT
Cover by JUAN DOE

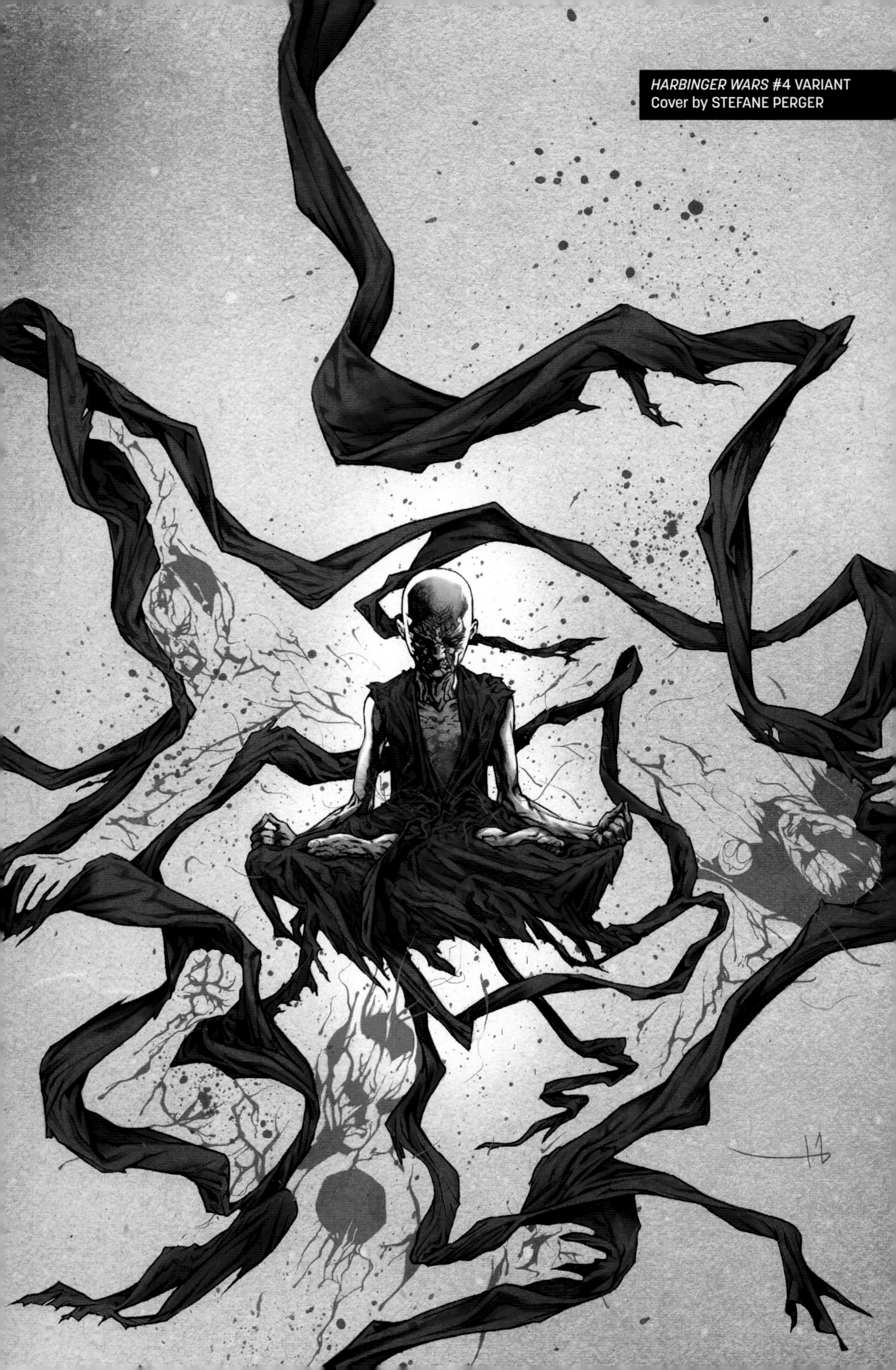

HARBINGER WARS #4 VARIANT
Cover by STEFANE PERGER

HARBINGER WARS #4
WRAPAROUND PULLBOX VARIANT
Cover by TREVOR HAIRSINE

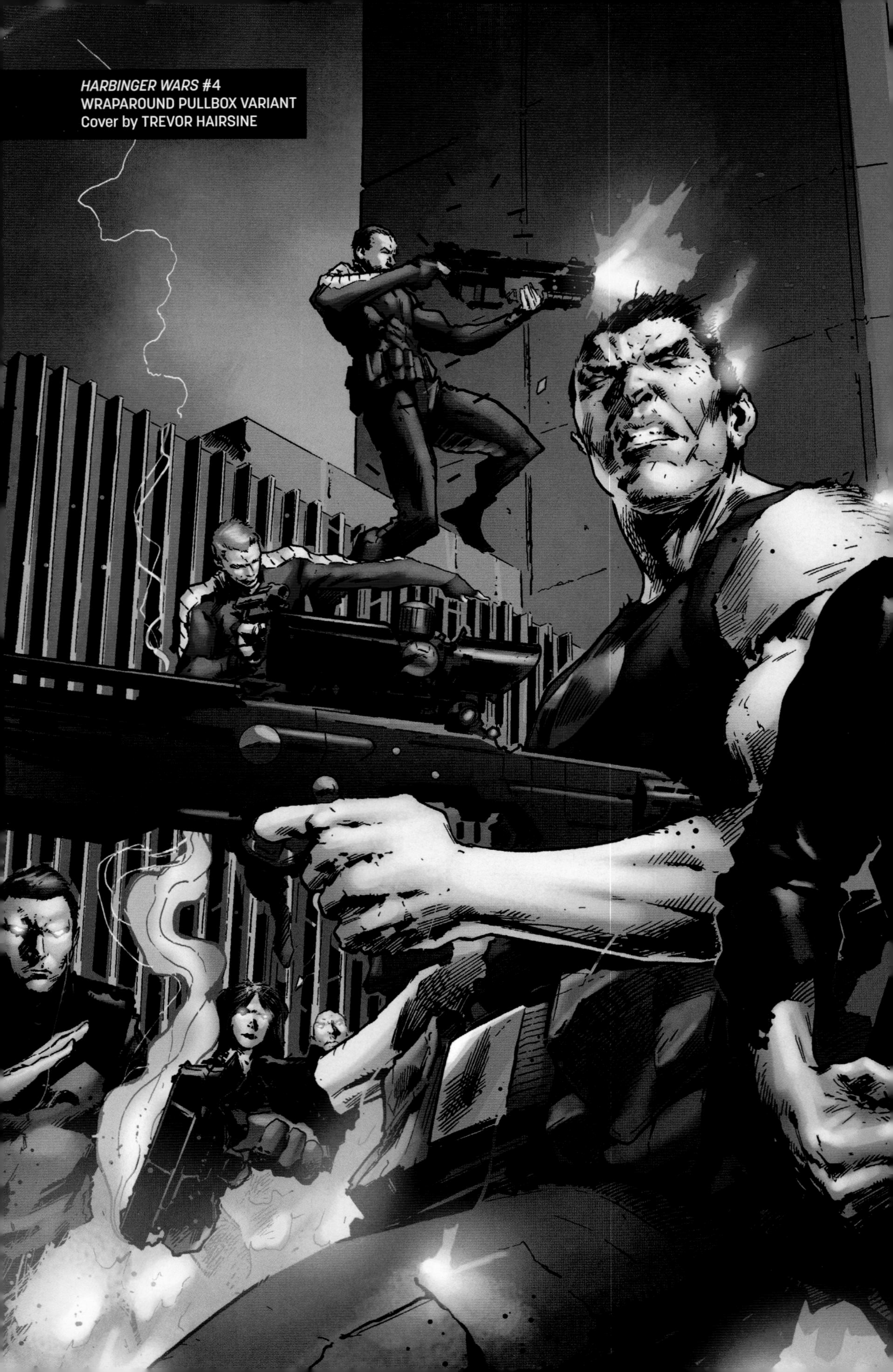

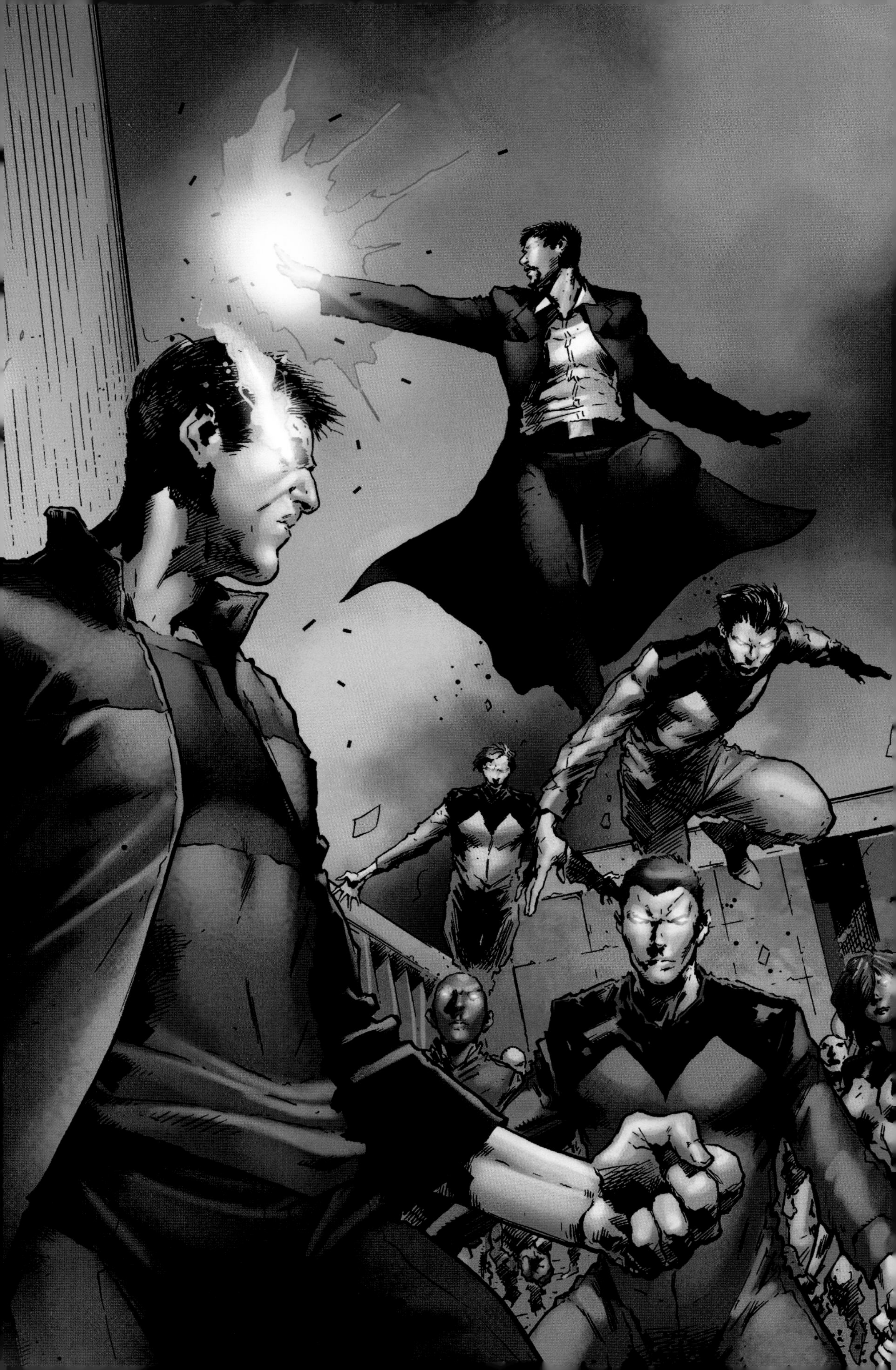

VALIANT MASTERS

A NEW LINE OF DELUXE HARDCOVERS COLLECTING THE ORIGINAL ADVENTURES OF VALIANT'S GREATEST HEROES FOR THE FIRST TIME ANYWHERE! FEATURING CLASSIC WORK BY SOME OF COMICS' MOST ACCLAIMED TALENTS.

VALIANT
KEVIN VANHOOK | DON PERLIN
BLOOD OF THE MACHINE
BLOODSHOT
VALIANT MASTERS
"Bloodshot reigns supreme as one of the best characters ever created."
- Ain't It Cool News

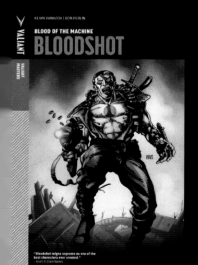

VALIANT MASTERS: BLOODSHOT VOL. 1:
BLOOD OF THE MACHINE

Written by KEVIN VANHOOK
Art by DON PERLIN
Cover by BARRY WINDSOR-SMITH

- Collecting **BLOODSHOT #1-8 (1993)** and an all-new, in-continuity story from the original **BLOODSHOT** creative team of **Kevin VanHook**, **Don Perlin**, and **Bob Wiacek** available only in this volume
- Featuring Bloodshot's first solo mission in the Valiant Universe and appearances by **Ninjak**, the **Eternal Warrior** and **Rai**

HARDCOVER
ISBN: 978-0-9796409-3-3

VALIANT
MARK A. MORETTI JOE QUESADA JIMMY PALMIOTTI
BLACK WATER
NINJAK
VALIANT MASTERS
"Groundbreaking art and epic characters... [Valiant] set comics on its ears..."
- Ain't It Cool News

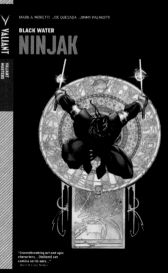

VALIANT MASTERS: NINJAK VOL. 1:
BLACK WATER

Written by MARK MORETTI
Art by JOE QUESADA & MARK MORETTI
Cover by JOE QUESADA

- Collecting **NINJAK #1-6 and #0-00 (1994)** with covers, interiors, and rarely seen process art by best-selling artist and creator **Joe Quesada**
- Featuring the complete origin of Valiant's original stealth operative and appearances by **X-O Manowar** and **Bloodshot**

HARDCOVER
ISBN: 978-0-9796409-7-1

VALIANT
JIM SHOOTER STEVE ENGLEHART BOB HALL DAVID LAPHAM STEVE DITKO
SPIRITS WITHIN
SHADOWMAN
VALIANT MASTERS

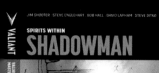

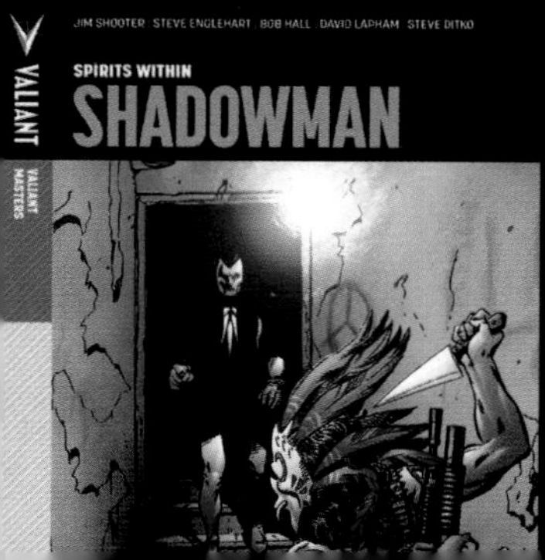

VALIANT MASTERS: SHADOWMAN VOL. 1:
SPIRITS WITHIN

Written by STEVE ENGLEHART, BOB HALL, BOB LAYTON, JIM SHOOTER and MORE
Art by STEVE DITKO, BOB HALL, DAVID LAPHAM, DON PERLIN and MORE
Cover by DAVID LAPHAM

- Collecting **SHADOWMAN #0-7 (1992)** and material from **DARQUE PASSAGES #1 (1994)** with an all-new new introduction by visionary Shadowman writer/artist **Bob Hall**
- The first-ever deluxe hardcover collection to feature the origin and debut solo adventures of Shadowman in the original

XPLORE THE VALIANT UNIVERSE

VALIANT®

VALIANT
BY THE SWORD
X-O MANOWAR

-O MANOWAR VOL. 1:
Y THE SWORD
Vritten by ROBERT VENDITTI
rt by CARY NORD
ollecting X-O MANOWAR #1-4
RADE PAPERBACK

VALIANT
ENTER: NINJAK
X-O MANOWAR

X-O MANOWAR VOL. 2:
ENTER NINJAK
Written by ROBERT VENDITTI
Art by LEE GARBETT
Collecting X-O MANOWAR #5-8
TRADE PAPERBACK

VALIANT
OMEGA RISING
HARBINGER

HARBINGER VOL. 1: OMEGA RISING
Written by JOSHUA DYSART
Art by KHARI EVANS &
LEWIS LAROSA
Collecting HARBINGER #1-5
TRADE PAPERBACK

VALIANT
RENEGADES
HARBINGER

IARBINGER VOL. 2: RENEGADES
Vritten by JOSHUA DYSART
Art by PHIL BRIONES, MATTHEW CLARK,
KHARI EVANS, LEE GARBETT, BARRY KITSON
nd PERE PÉREZ
Collecting HARBINGER #6-10
TRADE PAPERBACK

VALIANT
SETTING THE WORLD ON FIRE
BLOODSHOT

BLOODSHOT VOL. 1:
SETTING THE WORLD ON FIRE
Written by DUANE SWIERCZYNSKI
Art by MANUEL GARCIA & ARTURO LOZZI
Collecting BLOODSHOT #1-4
TRADE PAPERBACK

VALIANT
THE RISE AND THE FALL
BLOODSHOT

BLOODSHOT VOL. 2:
THE RISE & THE FALL
Written by DUANE SWIERCZYNSKI
Art by MANUEL GARCIA & ARTURO LOZZI
Collecting BLOODSHOT #5-9
TRADE PAPERBACK

VALIANT
THE MICHELANGELO CODE
ARCHER & ARMSTRONG

ARCHER & ARMSTRONG VOL. 1:
THE MICHELANGELO CODE
Written by FRED VAN LENTE
Art by CLAYTON HENRY
Collecting ARCHER &
ARMSTRONG #1-4
TRADE PAPERBACK

VALIANT
WRATH OF THE ETERNAL WARRIOR
ARCHER & ARMSTRONG
GOOD LUCK WITH THAT!

ARCHER & ARMSTRONG VOL. 2:
WRATH OF THE ETERNAL WARRIOR
Written by FRED VAN LENTE
Art by EMANUELA LUPACCHINO
Collecting ARCHER &
ARMSTRONG #5-9
TRADE PAPERBACK

VALIANT
BIRTH RITES
SHADOWMAN

SHADOWMAN VOL. 1: BIRTH RITES
Written by JUSTIN JORDAN &
PATRICK ZIRCHER
Art by PATRICK ZIRCHER
Collecting SHADOWMAN #1-4
TRADE PAPERBACK

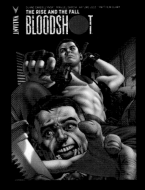

HARBINGER

VOLUME THREE: **HARBINGER WARS**

JOSHUA DYSART | KHARI EVANS | TREVOR HAIRSINE | MICO SUAYAN
HARBINGER WARS
HARBINGER
VALIANT

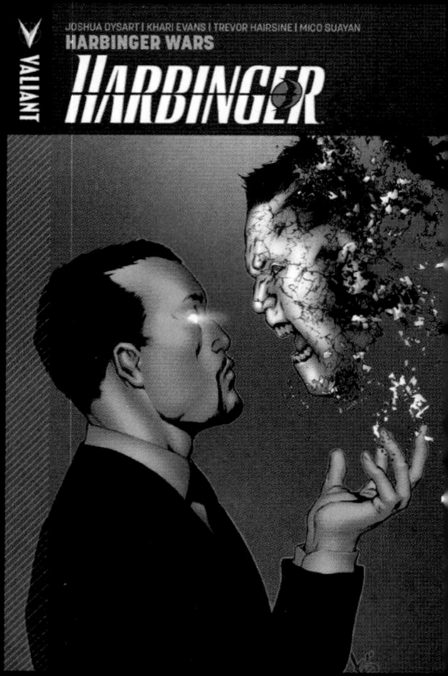

Before the Harbinger Foundation, before Project Rising Spirit, Toyo Jarada spent decades circling the globe, recruiting empowered ndividuals to his cause through coercion, intimidation, and influence. But how is a deal brokered in secret between Harada and Rising Sprit Securities forty years ago wreaking havoc in the modern day? And when the past comes roaring back, how will Peter Stanchek and the est of Harada's most wanted react to the revelation of Rising Spirit's secret mission and the Harbinger hunter known as Bloodshot?

Collecting **HARBINGER #11-14** and **HARBINGER #0**, join New York Times best-selling writer Joshua Dysart (*Unknown Soldier*) and acclaimed artists Khari Evans (*Carbon Grey*), Trevor Hairsine *X-Men: Deadly Genesis*), and Mico Suayan (*The Punisher*) for a complete standalone tale of the dark foundations behind Valiant's irst crossover event.

RADE PAPERBACK
978-1-939346-11-7

BLOODSHOT®

VOLUME THREE: **HARBINGER WARS**

DUANE SWIERCZYNSKI | BARRY KITSON | STEFANO GAUDIANO
HARBINGER WARS
BLOODSHOT
VALIANT

n the deserts outside Las Vegas, Bloodshot has banded together with Project Rising Spirit's most dangerous escapees. But when the Harbinger Wars erupt all around them, can he shape these super-powered children into a force for good - or are they too far gone? He'll find out the hard way as the opposing forces of PRS and the Harbinger Foundation descend on all sides, bringing about a crucible the likes of which the Valiant Universe has never seen...

Collecting **BLOODSHOT #10-13** by acclaimed writer Duane Swierczynski (*Birds of Prey*) and legendary artist Barry Kitson *Amazing Spider-Man*), jump headlong into the uncompromising action of Valiant's first crossover event right here with an all-new standalone story arc that will redefine the weapon—no, the soldier—no, the hero known only as Bloodshot.

RADE PAPERBACK
SBN: 978-1-939346-12-4

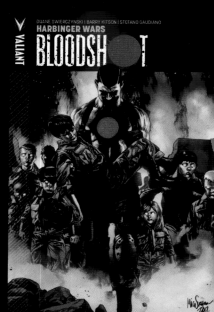